AN ABC FOR THE PCC

AN ABC FOR THE PCC

A HANDBOOK FOR CHURCH COUNCIL MEMBERS

John Pitchford

continuum
NEW YORK · LONDON

Continuum

The Tower Building	370 Lexington Avenue
11 York Road	New York
London SE1 7NX	NY 10017–6503

www.continuumbooks.com

First published 1979 by Wyche Publications
Second edition published 1985 by A. R. Mowbray & Co. Ltd
Third edition first published 1993
This edition published 2003

British Library Cataloguing-in-Publication Data
A catalogue record for this book is available from the British Library.

ISBN 0–8264–6599–4

Typeset by RefineCatch Ltd, Bungay, Suffolk
Printed and bound by Biddles Ltd, Guildford & King's Lynn

For my wife Valerie

Foreword

By Dr Brian Hanson CBE

During my time as Legal Adviser to the General Synod, I was privileged to be asked by John Pitchford to comment on the text of the three earlier editions of this valuable book. Now that I have retired from office, I have had time to read the Fourth Edition, and I have every confidence in commending the handbook to new and old readers alike.

The law is forever changing as a result of both Parliamentary and General Synod 'good ideas'. This means that churchwardens and members of parochial church councils (and parish priests) dare not perform their tasks relying on yesterday's law. Father Pitchtford is to be congratulated that he manages to keep his readers up-to-date with the new legislation and does so in a readable form. His many years as a parish priest, in both rural and urban ministries, and the fact that he was a proctor in Convocation for a number of years, all add up to giving authority to the text.

However, this work is much more than a legal treatise. It is full of good practice which can, with profit, be adopted and there are thought-provoking points in the text on which both clergy and laity need to ponder. In short, a handbook which facilitates the spread of the Gospel.

Brian Hanson
Feast of All Saints, 2002

Commendations of former editions

I warmly commend Mr Pitchford's *ABC* to all priests and Parochial Church Councils. The book fills a long-felt need, and I hope it will be widely read.

The Late Right Reverend John Eastaugh,
Bishop of Hereford (1979)

Mr Pitchford's *ABC* is a magnificent compendium of basic factual information, a host of practical hints and suggestions, and questions for discussion, all of them intended to help Parochial Church Council members and, indeed, everyone in the parish, to work together more efficiently – above all, to be more effective in mission. Mr Pitchford's book should take its place side by side with the *Handbook for Churchwardens and Parochial Church Councillors* as a constant reference point and as a welcome source of fresh ideas. Here indeed is a book full of 'wise saws and modern instances'.

The Reverend Sir Derek Pattinson,
Secretary General of General Synod (1979)

This is not a book for the complacent and it is not only the clergy and PCC members who will find much to interest them. Mr Pitchford quotes the saying 'if you fail to plan, then you plan to fail'. He wants every parish to have a clear and definite policy worked out by the clergy and the PCC, and the congregation.

Canon Michael Hocking in the Church Times *(1985)*

I am very happy indeed to commend *An ABC for the PCC*. Fr Pitchford is an experienced parish priest who has served both in the country and in London, as well as being a member of the General Synod for the Hereford diocese.

The advent of synodical government has brought new opportunities for the Church and clearly demonstrates the need for real partnership between clergy and laity.

I hope this most helpful guide for clergy and people alike will be very widely read.

The Right Reverend and the Right Honourable
Graham Leonard, Bishop of London (1985)

John Pitchford's *An ABC for the PCC* has been valued since its publication in 1979 by churchwardens and Parochial Church Council members up and down the country. A mine of factual information and practical suggestions, it has sold over 14,000 copies and, alongside the *Handbook for Churchwardens and Parochial Church Councillors*, it has informed a generation of PCC members. The current revision has taken account of recent changes in General Synod legislation, bringing it up to date with current church practice. I commend the *ABC* to churchwardens and PCC members and congratulate Mr Pitchford on an excellent revision of a really useful compendium.

The Right Reverend Mark Santer, Bishop of Birmingham (1993)

Acknowledgements

The author thanks and acknowledges the courtesy of the following for their kind permission to use copyright material:

The Bible Reading Fellowship for *The People of the Book*.
General Synod of the Church of England for Canon Law material; The Central Board of Finance for the quotation from *The Christian Stewardship of Money*; Her Majesty's Stationery Office for the Synodical Government Measure (No. 2); The University Presses of Oxford and Cambridge for quotations from the New English Bible; extracts from the Authorized Version of the Bible, which is Crown copyright, are used with permission; SCM Press Ltd for the quotation from *Ministry and Sacrament* (1937); Dr Donald Coggan (formerly Archbishop of Canterbury) for quotations from his Enthronement Sermon at Canterbury Cathedral, and also his Christmas Sermon 1977; Hodder and Stoughton, for the quotation from *Convictions* (1975) by Dr Donald Coggan; SPCK for the quotation from *Ministry and Ordination – an Agreed Statement of the Anglican–Roman Catholic International Commission* (1973) and the Lambeth Conference Encyclical Letter (1958).

The author also wishes to thank the following for their kind help – Mr Derek Pattinson, Secretary-General of General Synod; Mr Brian Hanson, Legal Adviser to General Synod; Barbara England, formerly Publishing Manager of the Church Information Office, and the members of the CIO Publishing Committee.

The following read the manuscript, and the author also wishes to thank them for their kind help and comments – The Right Reverend B. J. Masters, Lord Bishop of Edmonton; The

Reverend Canon George Smith, Rector of Leckhampton, Cheltenham; The Reverend Malcolm Grey, Vicar of Holy Trinity, Winchmore Hill, London.

The author is very grateful to the following for their helpful comments on the typescript: Mr Brian Hanson, Legal Adviser to General Synod; Mr Tim Robinson, Secretary of the Central Board of Finance; Miss Alice Wilkinson, Secretariat of the Church Commissioners; Mr Robin Stevens, Central Stewardship Officer of the Church of England; Mr Martin Howe, Commissioner of the Royal School of Church Music; Mr Jonathan Goodchild, of the Council for the Care of Churches.

Last, but not least, is to acknowledge the considerable help from Mrs Ruth McCurry and Miss Fiona McKenzie of Mowbray, and also Ms Ann Grindrod and Mr Stephen Ryan, and to record the author's thanks to them too.

In respect of the new legislation in the Fourth Edition, Crown Copyright material is reproduced with the permission of the Controller of HMSO and the Queen's printer for Scotland.

The author is very grateful to the following: Mr Brian Hanson, former Legal Adviser of General Synod for the Foreword; Miss J. A. Briscoe, who read the proofs; Mr Malcom Taylor, of the Synod Support Unit; and Mr Jonathan Goodchild, of the Council for the Care of Churches, for their helpful comments. Special mention must be made of Mr Robin Stevens, National Stewardship Officer, for all his suggestions and help, and for permission to quote from the 'Working as One Body' report (1995) and 'The First to the Lord' report (1999).

A

ABOUT THIS ABC   This book gives, in easy-to-read language, the legal duties and responsibilities of PCC members and the priest (*see* pages 132–6). It offers practical and spiritual suggestions, and a variety of ways in which PCC members can help with the work of the church.

Can you improve any of the things you are doing already? Are there any new ideas and challenges for your parish? Every parish is unique in its own needs and expectations and membership. What will work in one parish will not work in the next.

Every parish differs in size, churchmanship, and in the stage of development it has reached. Practical suggestions are given to help 'ordinary' parishes with the life and work of the local church.

Serving on a PCC ideally requires a high degree of commitment, and also a willingness to learn about the work. It involves trying to work out what God wants for his church. Above all, it involves acting and speaking in a Christian way at all times, and particularly at PCC meetings.

The *ABC* is not a perfect blueprint for every circumstance, but it offers a starting point from which to consider the situation in your parish. When contemplating action or change, the starting point should always be prayer.

The *ABC* contains ideas for what has been called 'pastoral evangelism' to build up the life and work of the church.

Question for discussion
What is the Spirit saying to the church in your parish?

ACTIONS – NOT JUST WORDS   Many churches attract a small number of people who like to do a lot of talking. Perhaps a church is one of the few places where people are willing to listen to them. Some will 'talk the hind leg off a donkey' if given half a chance. Christians must be kind and loving to them, as they are often very lonely. The church does need people who are good listeners, but we also need to be good 'stewards of our time', and to make sure that we use our time in the best way.

The church needs people who are willing to get on with the job. Some quotations come to mind: 'Only be sure that you act on the message, and do not merely listen' (James 1.22). Also 'A man may think he is religious, but if he has no control over his tongue, he is deceiving himself' (James 1.26 NEB). 'Not everyone who says, Lord, Lord, shall enter the Kingdom of God, but only he who does the will of my Father, who is in Heaven.'

'Empty vessels make the most sound,' and 'actions speak louder than words'. When discussing who we should invite to join the catering committee, one lady said: 'We want a mover, not a talker.' It is important that the appropriate person or people are chosen to do the work.

Food for thought
When someone is very talkative, two questions might be asked: (1) How important is this? (2) Is it urgent?

ADDITIONAL CURATES SOCIETY ACS is an important agent for mission and evangelism in England and Wales, in a number of ways. ACS pays and prays for curates in parishes which are not able to provide the money for this purpose. 'Almighty God, give us priests.' ACS encourages and fosters vocations to the sacred ministry, and organizes conferences for those who believe they may have a vocation.

ACS arranges 'parish placements' in various parishes around the country, where those who feel they might have a vocation can spend time in a parish, usually for three months to a year. This enables them to explore their call to the priesthood, and it helps the parish concerned. The students also receive whatever academic or other help they might need.

Although of Tractarian (High Church) foundation, ACS has always supported parishes of all shades of churchmanship. There are only two conditions for placing a curate in a parish: (1) There is a financial need in the parish. (2) The curate must be licensed by the bishop. Most dioceses in England and Wales have an honorary diocesan ACS secretary. However, the backbone of the work is done by ACS parish secretaries. Many PCCs give regular financial support for the important work of ACS. Individual Christians give money through ACS Lent boxes, cheque or standing order, and also make bequests, which are invested and continue to support the work of the church for many years to come. Donations made under 'Gift Aid' increase the Society's income substantially.

Supporters are kept in touch twice a year with the ACS Magazine, called the 'Good News'. There is an annual 'Festival Service' and buffet lunch in London, and festivals in other cities from time to time. ACS publishes a wide variety of liturgical and devotional material, and it also undertakes printing for individuals and PCCs. The ACS also produces an eight page magazine insert called 'Christian Life'. This is supplied to PCCs to supplement parish magazines with Christian material. It is printed in A5 size, and can be supplied flat, folded or stapled. Further details about this, and the work of ACS can be obtained from: The General Secretary, The Additional Curates Society, Gordon Browning House, 8 Spitfire Road, Birmingham, B24 9PB. Tel: 0121–382 5533. Email: acsb24@aol.com

ADDRESSES – USEFUL   *See* pages 220–2.

ADMINISTRATION   Every parish is a highly complex community, which has to be administered. Unfortunately, not everyone is a born organizer. The church, the church hall, possibly a school, and numerous church organizations, all have to be looked after regularly. Volunteers with appropriate skills have to be found and guided to the right place. Efficient administration is important in every aspect of parish life, and this will save much time and money, and also prevent chaos and possible aggravation. It is always helpful when lay people can help with the administration of the parish, under the guidance of, and in cooperation with the priest. Surely, the main part of the priest's work should be the spiritual work of the parish. Administration is not the main job of the priest, and it can take up time which can be used in better ways. The church exists to worship God, and to extend his kingdom into the hearts of those who do not know his love. Administration is not an end in itself, but only a means to achieve these ends. But administration has to be done by someone, so that the mission and pastoral work of the Church are not surrounded by muddle. (*See* **DELEGATION** on page 61, and **SECRETARY FOR THE PRIEST** on page 179.)

Questions for discussion
Some parishes now have a paid or volunteer 'parish administrator.' This frees the priest for the work for which he or she is ordained. Would it be possible for your church? How can the PCC or the standing committee help to share more of the workload of the priest?

ADOPTING A BABY *See* **THANKSGIVING FOR THE BIRTH OF A CHILD** on page 204.

AGENDA for the Annual Parochial Church Meeting is given on pages 5–6. The agenda for the PCC is given on pages 144–5.

ANNUAL MEETINGS Two annual meetings have to be held each year. Some parishes have them one following the other, while other parishes have them on separate days.

The meeting of parishioners This was formerly called the Vestry Meeting and it is to elect the churchwardens. It is a joint meeting of those whose names are on the church electoral roll, together with 'persons resident in the parish whose names are entered on a Register of Local Government Electors.' (Churchwardens Measure 2001 paragraph 5(1)). *See* **CHURCHWARDENS** on page 41.

The Annual Parochial Church Meeting This is for those who have their names on the church electoral roll, and it reviews the work of the PCC during the past twelve months. To have two separate meetings, one after the other, could lead to problems, such as having to ask those who are not on the church electoral roll to leave the meeting after the churchwardens had been chosen. There is usually much work to be done at the Annual Meeting, and having two separate meetings can give more time for both of them.

ANNUAL PAROCHIAL CHURCH MEETING – (The Annual Meeting) The main points from the Church Representation Rules (as amended up to 1999) part II, paragraphs 6–13 are summarized below.

The Annual Meeting shall be held not later than 30 April every year.

Who may attend? All lay people whose names are entered on the electoral roll are entitled to attend the Annual Meeting and to take part in its proceedings. No other lay person is entitled to do so. (For clergy entitled to attend, see Church Representation Rules para 6(3) to (5), or any Pastoral Scheme, which affects the parish e.g. for a team or group ministry).

Convening the Annual Meeting   The meeting is convened by the minister with a notice on the main notice board for a period including the last two Sundays before the day of the meeting. (The date is usually, but not necessarily, arranged at a PCC meeting.) The Vice-Chairman of the PCC arranges the meeting in an Interregnum.

The agenda for the Annual Meeting

(1) Opening prayers (during an **INTERREGNUM**, *see* pages 106–9).
(2) Apologies for absence.
(3) Any Other Business. It is helpful if the chairman asks the meeting if anyone wishes to raise any matters under 'Any Other Business'. Time can then be allocated for this later in the agenda.
(4) Minutes of last year's Annual Meeting. (Some parishes duplicate them and send them out with the agenda.)
(5) Matters arising from the minutes.
(6) The Vicar's Report. There is no legal requirement for a report from the vicar, but it is a good opportunity, which priests usually use to good advantage for three purposes: (a) to review the past year; (b) to thank those who have served the church in various ways, and (c) to present a plan or vision for the coming year. It may include review of attendance at worship, compared with numbers of the electoral roll. One of the churchwardens usually proposes a vote of thanks to the vicar.
(7) The electoral roll – The electoral roll officer reports on changes since the last Annual Meeting, or the new roll (every sixth year): (a) the number of names on the Roll; (b) the number of names added; (c) the number of names removed from the roll. The meeting can discuss the roll, and make recommendations to the PCC, but the APCM cannot add or remove a name from the roll. A copy of the roll shall be available for inspection at the Annual Meeting, if required. (*See* **ELECTORAL ROLL** on page 65.)

(8) Annual Report on the proceedings of the PCC and the activities of the parish generally. This is normally given by the PCC secretary.

(9) The financial statements of the PCC for the year ending 31 December, including any 'statement of funds and property'. The meeting can discuss the accounts, ask questions and make recommendations to the PCC, but the Annual Meeting cannot alter the accounts. When adopted by the meeting, the independently examined or audited accounts and statements of funds and property (if any) are displayed on the notice board for a further fourteen days. The treasurer sends a copy of the independently examined or audited accounts to the secretary of the Diocesan Board of Finance (for retention) within twenty-eight days of the Annual Meeting.

(10) Annual Fabric Report. This is presented by the Churchwardens, (together with any amendments to the Report made by the PCC). The Churchwardens must also produce a Statement, signed by both wardens, stating that the contents of the Terrier, Inventory and Log Books are accurate. (This is certifying, among other things, that all the work recorded in them has been properly completed). (*See* **CHURCHWARDENS** on page 41)

(11) Report on the proceedings of the Deanery Synod.

(12) Election of representatives to the Deanery Synod. This is done in every third year.

(13) Election of PCC members. *See **What is expected of me if I become a member of the PCC?*** on page 8.

(14) Appoint the Sidesmen. (*See* **SIDESMEN** on page 184.)

(15) Appoint the independent examiner or auditor for a period of one year. This person shall not be a member of the PCC. To decide whether an auditor or independent examiner is required, *see **Auditor or independent examiner*** on page 72.

(16) Any Other Business.

(17) The Blessing (during an **INTERREGNUM** *see* page 106).

Annual meetings   The Vestry Meeting is usually held immediately before the Annual Parochial Church Meeting, but it can be held at another time. (*See* **VESTRY MEETING**, page 206, and **CHURCHWARDENS**, pages 50–1).

Unpleasant meetings   These do happen when one or two unpleasant people use the APCM to cause trouble and stir up strife. This is not good for the Church, and if any new people or fringe members are present, they could well be put off the Church for the rest of their lives! 'How these Christians love one another!'

Three thoughts to help in this situation: (1) A member of the PCC or a warden could say firmly, 'This is rather an un-Christian note to bring into our meeting. I suggest that it should be considered at the next PCC meeting, or by the vicar and wardens'. Then ask the meeting if they agree with this suggestion; (2) Praying about the meeting for two or three weeks before the APCM. Also ask individuals to pray silently during the actual meeting. If the meeting does turn unpleasant, someone might say 'We need to remember that this is a meeting of God's Church, and we are called on by God to act in a Christian way'. The chairman could ask the warden to read 1 Corinthians 13, to be followed by a short silence and prayer; (3) *See* **TROUBLE-MAKER** on page 205.

The first PCC meeting every year

(a) The churchwardens give their Annual Fabric Report, including action taken and what is proposed. They must produce the terrier, inventory and log book, and any records which will assist the PCC in its duties in respect of the fabric of all church property. This must be accompanied by a statement, duly signed by both wardens, certifying that the contents of the books and their report are accurate.

(b) The treasurer presents the accounts and the proposed budget for the coming year, for presentation to the Annual Meeting. (It may be necessary to consider the accounts at the next meeting, but obviously before the Annual Meeting.)

(c) Any other reports for the Annual Meeting which need to be approved by the PCC.

The first PCC meeting after the Annual Meeting

The first items on the agenda must include the appointment or re-appointment of the following:

(a) Vice-chairman of the PCC.
(b) Hon secretary of the PCC.
(c) Hon treasurer of the PCC.
(d) Standing committee.
(e) Electoral roll officer.

(f)   Any other locally-agreed officers (e.g. hall secretary).
(g)   Authorization of any changes in those who sign PCC cheques.
(h)   Consideration of any resolution passed at the Annual Meeting.

What is expected of me if I become a member of the PCC?
Much indeed is expected of each and every PCC member. No one should stand for election unless he or she clearly understands what is required of them. The PCC is unlike any secular committee because it has a mixture of pastoral, missionary, spiritual, financial and legal responsibilities. Membership of the PCC involves:

(a)   Acceptance of the responsibilities laid down in the Synodical Government Measure 1969 relating to PCCs, and the other legal responsibilities involved. *See* pages 133–52.
(b)   Attend all PCC meetings, and make sure that these meetings have first claim on your time before any secular meeting or social function. Most PCCs meet on a set day every month, e.g. the first Tuesday of the month, except August (*see* Hebrews 10.24–25).
(c)   The PCC has a duty to discuss all matters which affect the life of the parish. Take part in the discussions at the actual meeting, rather than in the car-park afterwards. Ask yourself, 'What does God want us (me) to do in this situation?' Then be willing to vote accordingly. Be open to the leading of the Holy Spirit.
(d)   After the vote, action is usually required by PCC members. Be willing to offer your help. If you voted against the resolution which is passed by the majority, where do you stand as a result? Even if you voted against the resolution, are you big enough and thus able to support the views of the majority? Do you join the others for the sake of unity and corporate loyalty, and for the good of the Church? Or do you sit back and take no action? (Or do you resign?) Obviously, much will depend on the circumstances.
(e)   The function of the PCC includes 'co-operation with the incumbent . . .'. The Church is not helped unless there is a genuine desire and commitment for each PCC member to work together with the priest for the good of the Church.
(f)   PCC members are asked to co-operate with the incumbent 'in the whole mission of the Church, pastoral,

evangelistic, social and ecumenical'. This is clearly the responsibility of all who allow their names to be put forward for election to the PCC, and not simply those who like that kind of thing (*see* **MISSION – EVANGELISM – RENEWAL** on pages 114–20).

(g) Courage is sometimes needed to speak the truth boldly at a meeting, but always with love. Loyalty to the Church, to the priest and to the other members of the PCC are all highly desirable qualities in PCC members. Where does your loyalty really lie?

(h) Love is required of every PCC member, both for God and for your neighbour in its widest meaning. This includes learning to love those who have been difficult at PCC meetings.

(i) Take your spiritual life seriously, and adopt a rule of life which is appropriate for one who is to be a lay representative on the PCC. Priority to prayer is vital for every PCC member. No one can act and speak as a member of the Body of Christ unless they take prayer and Bible reading seriously, and receive Holy Communion at least every Sunday. PCC members should regard Sunday worship as a 'day of obligation' and not even unexpected visitors should keep them from coming to worship on Sunday morning (*see* **SPIRITUAL LIFE**, pages 188–200).

(j) The PCC is responsible for the repair, upkeep and insurance of the Church buildings and the people who use them. *See* **INSURANCE**, pages 97–9.

(k) The PCC must ensure that the church has an adequate income. Legally speaking, the debts of the PCC are not the personal responsibility of individual PCC members beyond the funds belonging to the church. They obviously have a responsibility to do what they can to ensure that the morale of the congregation is good, and that the money comes in regularly. *See* **CHRISTIAN STEWARDSHIP** on pages 29–36.

The PCC members are 'jointly responsible' with the incumbent for the expenditure of PCC funds. *See* **FINANCE**, pages 70–82.

(l) Take seriously the words of St Paul, 'Know the reason for the faith within you'. Read a Church newspaper or magazine every week, e.g. the *Church Times* or *Church of England Newspaper*. When did you last read a religious book?

(m) The most important part of every PCC member's job is to follow our Lord's command: 'Seek ye first the kingdom of God'.

In some parishes, the PCC secretary reads out these thirteen recommendations for PCC members before the election each year.

'ANY QUESTIONS?'   An enjoyable evening with three or four carefully selected speakers for the panel, perhaps including an atheist/agnostic/humanist, a trade union official or local government councillor. A good chairman is needed. The event is an ideal opportunity to invite fringe members and people not connected with the Church. All present will no doubt be exposed to some Christian reasoning. Refreshments make a welcome end to the evening.

ARCHDEACON   The archdeacon is appointed to carry out legal and administrative functions in a large area called an arch-deaconary, on behalf of the bishop and the diocese. The duties of an archdeacon include (1) Seeing that each parish looks after its buildings and the parsonage house; (2) The general discipline of the clergy; (3) Inducting a new priest to a parish – to show that the priest legally has control and possession of the church and the parish; (4) Carrying out parish visitations (inspections), which are often delegated to the rural (area) dean; (5) Admitting the churchwardens to their office every year; (6) Organizing the Quinquennial Inspection of Churches to be carried out by the appropriate architect; (7) Carrying out various legal and financial duties, and sitting on the Diocesan Advisory Committee, which deals with faculties.

ARCHIVES   The Church includes those who are alive at this present time and also those who have worshipped and served God in former generations. Every parish has its own story and there is usually a sense of community and continuity with those who have gone before. Thus it is a good idea to keep relevant documents, newspaper cuttings, cassettes and photographs. It is a good reminder to those who see photographs of former priests in the vestry (or wherever they are displayed) to pray for the former shepherds of the parish.

There is all the difference in the world between a systematic collection and a mass of clutter and junk on top of a dusty cupboard in the vestry!

AREA DEAN   *See* **RURAL DEAN** on pages 175–6.

ARRIVE EARLY It is discourteous and distracting to others to arrive late for a meeting or service, and you certainly cannot be properly prepared for worship if you arrive in a hurry. It is good to be early so that you can settle down before the meeting or service begins.

ARROW PRAYERS *See* **SPIRITUAL LIFE OF PCC MEMBERS** on page 192.

ASSOCIATION OF CHURCH FELLOWSHIPS The ACF exists throughout the Anglican Communion, and the Archbishops of Canterbury and York are the patrons. Membership is not confined to church members, and it is open to all who wish to join, men, women and young people.

ACF offers friendship, and its programmes include some teaching of the Christian faith. ACF seeks to make the worshipping community into a fellowship of friends, and through this, to bring others into the family of the Church. ACF seeks to foster Christian fellowship, and to strengthen the lives of its members through prayer and study, and this is designed to lead on to Christian action, witness and service in the community. Each ACF group develops to suit its own needs in the parish. ACF is linked by deanery and diocesan groups. The headquarters of ACF is at Bickenhill House, 154 Lode Lane, Solihull, West Midlands B91 2HP. Tel: 0121–704 9281.

ACF can supply stationery and publicity material, and an attractive range of its goods are available for sale, which help local groups with publicity and finance. There is a link association with a regular newsletter for members who are local, single and isolated. Each year, ACF chooses a 'charitable project' and all ACF branches are asked to support this appeal.

To start an ACF group, consult the General Secretary at the above address.

AUDITOR – *See* page 72.

BAPTISM A request for Baptism presents every church with a wonderful opportunity, which can either be grasped or missed. The family will need the active encouragement of PCC members and of the congregation to draw them into the Church community. A request for Baptism is not an opportunity to raise any barriers, but for the Church to teach the faith, and to show the love of God.

Baptism

Every parish has its own unique method of dealing with a request for Baptism. It is an area where lay people can be of considerable help, both in the preparation and the follow-up after the service. Careful selection and training will be needed for those involved. There is plenty of material available for the preparation. (If your church is of a particular 'tradition' – have you considered looking at preparation material used in other traditions?) Perhaps the PCC could produce its own video and other material for use in preparation. Follow-up letters could be produced by the parish and sent to the family – or better, delivered by the sponsor – at the appropriate intervals.

It is a good investment for the PCC to give Baptism and God-parent cards, a candle and candle-holder at each baptism. The Additional Curates Society (*see* page 217 **USEFUL ADDRESSES**) sell a four-page Baptism card, with prayers and Christian teaching, and also a candle and an attractive copper candle-holder which will not crumble if the baby sits on it. It has a small cross embossed on it (a cross in every home?) and it is a permanent reminder of an important event.

Another suggestion – that the Church provide a sponsor for each child   This could be the person who visits the family, following the request for Baptism. The aim would be to keep the family in contact with the Church over the years to come, and to try to draw them into the worshipping community. Above all, the sponsor would pray regularly for the baby, parents and God-parents. The agreement of the family to have a church sponsor would obviously be needed. 'More things are wrought by prayer than this world dreams of'. (Lord Tennyson)

BELLS   If your church has bells in its tower, it is important that PCC members and the incumbent have some understanding of bells and ringers, and how they fit into the life and work of the Church. It can be helpful to have at least one member of the ringers on the PCC. The captain of the ringers and other officers should be properly elected every year. The bells need to be kept in good order, and provision should be made for them in the annual budget. Remember that the ringers often spend over an hour in the tower before the service, so do not be surprised if they are not in church for the service, although many are. It is good if the wardens and others can take an interest in the team, include them in parish activities whenever possible, and visit them from time to time in the tower (by prior arrangement).

The Central Council of Church Bell Ringers can give information and advice. Details: The Secretary, 50 Cramhurst Lane, Witley, Godalming, Surrey, GU8 5QZ. Tel. & Fax 01483–682790. Web: www.cccbr.org.uk Email: crogers@ukgateway.net

BEREAVEMENT The Church is in a privileged position to help the bereaved, and this is both a heavy responsibility, and also a unique opportunity. Neighbours and family usually rally round for a few weeks, but this type of caring does not continue indefinitely. After a while, people simply do not want to know about their grief. Sadly, there are some who have no relatives and friends who are willing to provide this support in the first place.

Most priests have one or more funeral every week, and it is simply impossible for them to follow up and help every bereaved family. The opportunity for lay-people to help is there in every parish. Members of the congregation can do a great deal of good, not only for the bereaved, but also for the Church. Careful selection of visitors (or carers) is vital, and particularly in not choosing any who have themselves suffered a bereavement in the last two years. The diocese or deanery can usually provide appropriate help with the necessary training (perhaps arranged with other parishes in the area or through Churches Together?).

Lay people are not usually asked difficult theological questions by the bereaved. It is much more a matter of listening to the bereaved talking about the person who has died. It sometimes involves listening to the same thing more than once, and tears are not uncommon. Much patience is needed, but in time the bereaved will work through their grief. Then, trust and friendship can be built up.

There are different stages of grief. These include guilt, anger, fear, resentment and a feeling of hopelessness and deep grief itself. A number of visits may well be needed over the coming weeks. The visitor has a double aim: the first is obviously to help and comfort the bereaved; the second is to try to bring the person into the worshipping family of the Church. Never try to jump in with Christian answers, but wait until the appropriate moment presents itself. A simple approach: 'This is how I started coming to Church . . .'

Those who have died are often remembered in many churches each year on All Souls Day – 2 November. This is an opportunity to invite all who have been bereaved to a special Communion service (Requiem), either by letter or personal visit (or both). Many find this service is helpful, even if they are not (yet) confirmed. (Refreshments afterwards?)

Above all, regular prayer is needed by the visitors over the years. 'Heavenly Father, you sent your Son to be our Redeemer: send your Holy Spirit to comfort the bereaved, especially _____ that s/he may come to know you and your love in your Son, Jesus Christ our Lord. Amen.'

In some parishes, the priest gives a copy of the funeral address to the next of kin, which normally has a Christian message. An alternative: this could be delivered by the visitor to the bereaved two or three days after the funeral. If there is room on the back of the sheet, additional Christian teaching or Scripture verses could be printed out there. E.g. Psalms 23, 121, 130, 27, 42(1–7) or Isaiah 25,8–9, 1 Peter 1,3–9, St John 20,1–9, St John 14,1–6, 1 Corinthians 15,20 to the end, St John 11,25–26. Appropriate prayers may be added (if there is room!). Various booklets and pamphlets have been published which could be given to the bereaved.

BIBLE   The Holy Bible is a vital resource for every church and individual PCC member. It is not a human book, but it was written under the guidance and inspiration of the Holy Spirit. It is the record of God's dealings with His 'chosen people' and it has unique authority. It is a holy book. Sadly, not everyone agrees about the authority of the Bible, and it seems to cause many problems.

Why do Christians read the Bible regularly?   Life and conditions have changed very much since those primitive times when the Bible was written So why is reading the Bible so important for Christians today?

The sacred scriptures provide spiritual nourishment and strengthen the faith of the Church and of individuals. It is the living word of God. It contains help and wisdom for this world, and guidance to reach Heaven. The Bible challenges, corrects and rebukes us. It builds up our faith and love. The Bible has the power to change people's lives. When we read the scriptures regularly, we come close to God. It gives us a deeper knowledge of God's purposes and ways. It gives comfort, hope and encouragement, and it helps us to respond to the love of God. It educates the conscience. To achieve spiritual wholeness, Christians have to read the Bible regularly, and this has to be balanced by receiving Holy Communion regularly. Another answer is given by St Jerome (AD 342–420). He wrote: 'To be ignorant of the Bible is to be ignorant of Christ.'

Help in Bible reading The Bible is not an easy book (or collection of books). It has different levels of meaning. One method is to read through the four Gospels, reading only a small passage each day (or night) and having a postcard as a bookmarker. Perhaps read again what you read yesterday, and then read your new passage. It is good if you do this slowly, and ask yourself – if I were present at that scene, who would I be in it? What is God saying to me through this passage?

The Scripture Union The policy of the SU clearly states 'We believe in the divine inspiration and entire trustworthiness of Holy Scripture, and its supreme authority in all matters of faith and conduct.' The SU provides various daily readings and notes (and also much other very good material). Details about Bible Reading material, and SU work in schools, from: Scripture Union, 207–209 Queensway, Bletchley, Milton Keynes, MK2 2EB. Tel: 01908 85600. Fax: 01908 856111. Email: postmaster@scriptureunion.org.uk Web: www. scripture. org.uk

BRF – The Bible Reading Fellowship 'BRF resources spiritual growth through Bible reading, prayer, fellowship and training events.' It publishes daily bible reading notes. Appropriate booklets are produced for different age groups, as is the case with the SU. Archbishop Donald Coggan wrote a commentary for the BRF film strip, called *The People of the Book*. He said, 'I believe there are few things – if any – of more vital importance to the life and work of the Church than that its members should have an intelligent grasp of their faith, such a grasp as will enable them to pass it on with confidence and joy. This means a steady and careful study of the Bible by clergy and lay people alike. It is for this that our BRF exists, and I would like to think that every parish had a branch actively at work.'

Details about Bible reading material and the other work of the BRF, from: The Bible Reading Fellowship, First Floor, Elsfield Hall, 15–17 Elsfield Way, Oxford, OX2 8AP. Tel: 01865 319700. Fax: 01865 319701. Email: enquiries@brf.org.uk Web: www.brf.org.uk

The Bible reading secretary   Whether for SU or BRF, the job includes:

(a)   Order the booklets and deliver them to the individuals concerned (usually three or four times per year)
(b)   Order a few spare copies for the bookstall or table at the back of the church.
(c)   Encourage new people to use the daily notes.
(d)   Pray for all who use them.

Which Bible to use?   There are many different translations of the Bible available in bookshops. One new translation is *The Bible – English Standard Version* – published in various versions by Harper Collins. This may do for future generations what the Authorized Version of 1611 (King James version) did for former generations.

Questions for discussion
Instead of having a normal business meeting, could the PCC have a meeting entirely devoted to Bible study?

BISHOP   What are the functions of a bishop? (1) 'The bishop is the guardian of the Faith, first committed by Christ to the Apostles. (2) He is a sign of unity of the world-wide (catholic) Church. (3) The bishop has a "teaching office" (or task) to proclaim the Gospel, and to teach the faith to priests and lay people. (4) The bishop has a "pastoral office" and he is shepherd and pastor of the people of his diocese. (5) The bishop has a "priestly office" and he can celebrate all seven Sacraments of the Church' (from *Discovering the Faith* by the author).

Every bishop is consecrated by the Metropolitan Bishop of the province (i.e. an archbishop) together with at least two other bishops, who have themselves been duly consecrated in the same way by other bishops before them.

A bishop is consecrated either to take charge of a diocese, or to be an area bishop, assistant bishop or suffragan bishop.

Food for thought
Do you pray every day for your bishop and your priest?

BLESSING A HOUSE   Some people ask the priest to come and bless their home, and there are special prayers for this purpose. (Occasionally, a house may need to be 'exorcized' and blessed by a priest. There is a priest appointed in every diocese for this purpose.)

BODY OF CHRIST IN THE PARISH   The whole question of learning how to work together is being forced more and more on people in the secular world and in the Church. The crisis facing the Church has partly led to the rediscovery of the New Testament concept of the body of Christ. The Church – the whole people of God – forms the body of Christ, and it is a continuation and extension of the work of Christ himself, who said 'As the Father has sent me, even so send I you.' He also said 'Receive the Holy Spirit.' (St John 20,21–22)

Every Christian is made a member of the mystical body of Christ by Baptism, but membership is not a reward for services rendered, nor for virtue. Christ took this kind of body because he has work for it to do. He had finished his part of God's work of salvation, perfectly completed in itself, and then he was taken into heaven. Salvation still has to be applied to the world in each succeeding generation. That is why Jesus needed another body to continue his work.

When a limb or organ stops working, the whole body then only limps through life, and other parts of the body have to work harder to compensate for dead areas which no longer function properly. The human body has many parts which function in different ways, and likewise in the body of Christ there is a diversity of function and ministry. Men and women are called within the total work of Christ, according to their abilities and temperaments, to serve in different ways in the mission of the Church and in the situation in which they work and pursue their leisure activities. Christians are always a part of the body of Christ, and the Holy Spirit equips the members with different gifts for the life and work of the whole body.

No single Christian has all the gifts, and no gift can function without the other gifts. God's work is carried on only by the harmonious co-operation of all members working together, with love (the greatest gift) binding all together in one body.

Read St Paul's words on the body of Christ in his letter to the Ephesians – 4,11–16.

Question for discussion
Is the body of Christ discernible in the parish?

BOOKSTALL   Some parishes run their own bookstall or church bookshop. Some are small, situated on a table at the back of church or in the church hall and open only on Sundays. Others have a larger bookstall or shop. It used to be complicated to set up a bookstall, now it is simply a matter of approaching a Christian bookshop and asking them to supply you with books at a discount. The usual discount is ten percent. This is not another way to raise funds for the church, but simply a way to help the bookstall to cover its costs.

For the larger parish bookshop, consult the Cathedral and Church Shops Association, which provides a forum for exchange of information, and arranges an annual conference and trade fair for members in November. It also gives advice and assistance in setting up and running a Church Bookshop. Membership is open to anyone who runs a church shop which is under the control of a PCC, or run for the benefit of the PCC. Details: Hon Sec CCSA, Mappa Mundi Ltd, 5 College Cloisters, The Close, Hereford, HR1 2NG. Tel: 01432 374208.

Food for thought
What about an occasional Book Party?

BUILDINGS   Vast sums of money are spent each year to repair and maintain church buildings. No PCC wants to be faced with an enormous repair bill.

Prevention is better than cure
Unfortunately, many problems with buildings usually creep up on the PCC unnoticed until the costly damage has been done. Constant vigilance is required. The PCC has been entrusted with the care of these buildings which former generations of Christians worked hard to provide and maintain. The careful stewardship of buildings belongs to each successive generation of PCC members.

The best way to avoid costly repair bills is to inspect the buildings regularly. If this is done carefully and thoroughly by the churchwardens – or by someone formally acting on their behalf (as is required by the Care of Churches and Ecclesiastical Jurisdiction Measure 1991) – it can save the PCC a great deal of work and money. *See* **CHURCHWARDENS** on pages 45–6.

The fabric committee   Some parishes appoint a small fabric or building committee. If there is a surveyor or architect in the parish, it can be helpful to have their informal advice. A second and free opinion is always useful. But it is always important to work through the PCC's own architect, under a proper professional relationship.

Whether it is the churchwardens or the fabric committee who look after the building, the key words are vigilance and prompt action (via the due legal channels).

Regular inspections and work   Much needs to be done to look after a large building, especially if the church is an old one. A full, careful and detailed inspection of the entire church is required 'at least once every year'. The wording of the 1991 Measure implies that one inspection is the legal minimum. Much more than one inspection is needed, if proper care is to be taken of the building. The people responsible for finding the money would no doubt be much happier if regular inspections were carried out. The following suggestions are offered:

Early in the year
> Check the outside of the roof and make sure that no slates or tiles have slipped. Check on the inside of the roof to see that no water has been seeping through, particularly in the tower/spire.
> Check *all* gutters, valleys, hopper heads, down-spouts and drains. The best time to do this is during a heavy rainstorm! In this way, you can see where the problems exist. Dripping gutters can cause much damage.

Spring
> Carry out a full inspection of the whole church and prepare a report for the Annual Parochial Church Meeting.
> Check that the gutters, valleys, hopper heads, down-spouts and drains are all right after the frost. Check the roofs for any form of damage, whether from wind, frost, snow or other cause. Check the stonework and brickwork for damage after frost.
> Arrange for someone to clean out the gutters, hopper heads, down-spouts and drains. Also all ventilation holes. Cut down all vegetation on the walls of the church, and apply weed-killer as required until it is completely dead. Clean out the tower/spire, and check the birdproofing mesh. Arrange for a thorough spring clean of the church, and wash the windows.
> Carefully inspect all woodwork, and particularly on the inside of the organ, and the roof timbers, to see if something has been having a nibble! All exposed timber, both inside and outside, should be painted with a wood preservative

every fifth year, including the eaves and the woodwork in the tower/spire. Death-watch beetle, woodworm, wet and dry rot, all need professional advice and prompt action through the church architect.

Summer

Arrange for annual service of central heating system and fire extinguishers. Check for leaks and bleed the radiators.

Check for any signs of dry rot, fungus, or signs of damp on the walls or ceilings, and particularly for any swelling in the plaster.

Make sure that there is good lagging to protect all pipes and tanks from the frost.

Autumn

Leaves will need removing from the gutters, drains, etc. in the late autumn.

Check all gutters and the entire rainwater system. A few buckets of water and some ladders is one way of finding the problems – but an easier way is to inspect during a storm!

Clear out and check all drains, and rod them if necessary.

Check that the froststat is working properly.

Check all snowboards and creosote them.

Check for roof damage after heavy storms.

Winter

Inspect the log book to see that the details of alterations carried out during the last twelve months were all fully recorded.

When there is a fall of snow, check in the tower/spire and any roof space to see if the snow has blown into the church. Remove all snow as soon as possible before it melts and causes damage. Only use a wood or plastic snow scraper – this avoids causing damage to the roof etc.

The lightning conductor needs a visual checking every year.

All ventilators must be carefully checked.

Check and look after all boundary walls, fences and gates. Oil hinges and clean all locks each year.

Leaves, branches and roots from trees can cause problems. Extra vigilance is needed if there is a tree near the church. Should it be removed?

All electrical wiring and the lightning conductor should be professionally tested every fifth year, and each written report should be kept in the church log book. Fires are sometimes caused by faulty wiring, particularly in the organ.

The above is a basic outline of the jobs which need to be done. Some can be done by volunteers from the parish, but it is important (and saves money in the long run) to ensure that specialist jobs are done by people with the necessary expertise. Further information and help can be found on the website: www.churchcare.co.uk

It is good to keep the PCC informed with a very brief fabric committee report at each meeting, and a fuller report when necessary. When detailed consideration is needed, the standing committee could be involved.

The fabric committee can work out how much money will be required for repairs and maintenance for the coming year, and provide an estimate for those who are preparing the annual budget in the late autumn each year.

The duty of the churchwardens to record information   Under the Care of Churches and Ecclesiastical Jurisdiction Measure 1991, it is the duty of the churchwardens, in consultation with the minister, to maintain a terrier, an inventory and a log book in accordance with the recommendations of the Council for the Care of Churches.

The terrier and inventory   A terrier is a list of lands belonging to the church. An inventory is a record of all the goods and possessions of the parish church and any chapels.

The churchwardens must send a copy of the inventory to the person chosen by the bishop as soon as practicable after it is compiled. They must notify this person of any alterations.

The log book   All alterations, additions and repairs to the church, the lands, and articles belonging to them, must be recorded in the log book, and also 'any other events' affecting them. The location of documents must be given, which relate to the alterations, additions, repairs and events – if they are not kept with the log book.

The annual fabric report   The wardens must give the annual fabric report to the PCC at the first meeting each year. This should include an account of all action taken, and what is proposed. They must produce the terrier, the inventory and the log book, and any records which will assist the PCC in its duties in respect of the fabric of church property. They must be accompanied by a statement duly signed by the churchwardens, certifying that the contents are accurate.

The duty of the churchwardens to inspect the buildings each year A serious duty falls on the wardens in respect of the buildings. It is important that they do their job properly. They must inspect all the buildings and all articles belonging to the church. (Alternatively, they must ensure that someone else does this properly on their behalf.) The Measure states that they shall inspect the buildings 'at least' once in every year. It is always wise to keep a careful watch on the state of the buildings, in case something has to be done before the annual inspection.

The wardens 'shall act in consultation with the minister' Hopefully this takes place in all areas of parish life, but it is particularly important in regards to the inspection and maintenance of buildings and the recording of information in the log book. Action should be taken when repair work is required. There should be no unreasonable delay in getting the work done properly.

Maintenance and mission Looking after the church buildings can take up much of the PCC's time, unless the work is delegated to an effective and hard-working fabric committee. Maintaining the building properly is vital, but the question needs asking – Does maintenance hinder the mission of the local church? Maintenance could certainly hinder mission, unless it is delegated. But, on the other hand, the building is a symbol of worship and mission to those who do not belong. For church members, it is the place where they worship and receive inspiration for mission. For outsiders, the building is a silent spiritual witness to the living faith which has endured through the centuries. The building can be a powerful tool in evangelism in various ways, and it can be a focus and symbol for the local community. It is a shrine or sacred place which many seem to want or need, even though they may never come to worship there. Many feel that 'something' is enshrined in the building that is 'life' and which has a sense of eternal changelessness. Security, of course, comes not from the building, but from what it contains – ultimately the benefits of our Lord's death and resurrection. Much goodwill often exists towards the building, and the PCC has to try to channel this interest towards our Creator.

There is a saying: people matter more than buildings. There is truth in this, but buildings are also important, particularly for mission. What really matters is to have the correct relationship between buildings and people, and to encourage enough people to worship and to maintain the church for the future.

State aid The ancient parish churches are a major part of our national heritage, and many things of artistic or historic interest have been gathered in them through the centuries. Grants from English Heritage and the Heritage Lottery Fund are available for repairs of historic churches. Details are available from the archdeacon.

Can more use be made of your church building? Many churches are only used for a limited time each week – and on one day only in some parishes. Are there other ways in which the building could be used to help the work of the Church? All of this has to be balanced by the fact that the Church is a building which is set apart for the glory of God and the worship of His holy name. We must never lose the sense of holiness, and that the Church is a holy place. Sadly, many people today have lost all sense of holiness, and the 'otherness' of God. Any event which will bring outsiders or fringe members in through the church doors is important. Music and drama, a competition for children speaking well-known passages of the Bible, a singing competition, appropriate films, a debate, exhibitions, a wave of prayer, conducted tours of the church?

The fabric fund Most parishes make provision in the annual budget to put away a realistic sum of money into a fabric fund, over and above what is needed for the current maintenance and repairs. The Church has facilities through the CBF Church of England Funds for investing PCC money. There are attractive vehicles for short term cash and long term investments, and interest/dividends are paid without deduction of income tax. Details from the Central Board of Finance (*see* page 74).

Friends of the Church Many people are willing to contribute towards the cost of preserving and improving the church building, even though they have no wish to be involved in its life and worship. Some parishes have set up a 'body of friends' to attract financial support.

The friends have a separate constitution, bank account,

annual meeting, annual church service, and perhaps a reception, lunch or tea. The constitution usually provides for a majority of church members on the committee. For example, on a committee of seven, three are elected by the AGM of the friends, one is elected by the PCC (or APCM) and three are *ex officio* – the incumbent and churchwardens. Advice can be obtained from the booklet 'A Friends' Scheme', published by Canterbury Diocesan Board of Finance, Stewardship Department, Diocesan House, Lady Wooton's Green, Canterbury, CT1 1NG.

Survey of churches (Canon F18) Every three years, the archdeacon – or the area/rural dean acting on his behalf – inspects the church, the chancel and the churchyard. The archdeacon gives directions for any repair work which is needed on the fabric, ornaments or furniture of the church.

The quinquennial inspection All churches must be inspected every five years by an architect or chartered building surveyor approved by the Diocesan Advisory Committee

The architect/surveyor will inform the parish when the inspection is due, and will state requirements, such as ladders to inspect the roof. The inspection can usefully be timed to coincide with the six-monthly clearing of gutters. Someone from the PCC should meet the architect, and ensure that all parts of the church normally locked (towers, boiler rooms, vestries etc) are open. Any detached hall may not be inspected as part of the scheme; if so, the PCC should arrange for the hall to be covered.

The fees of the inspection and report will be paid either by the PCC or by the diocese, under the terms of the diocesan scheme.

The report following the inspection is sent to the PCC secretary, the incumbent, archdeacon and DAC. The report will recommend professional tests of the electrical system and the lightning conductor, if not already carried out in the last 5 years.

The report will contain recommendations, which will vary in terms of urgency and cost. Some recommendations, such as blocked gutters, should be tackled straight away. Other recommendations will be categorised in terms of urgency. Some repairs will have major cost implications, and advice should be sought on grants. In due course, the architect/surveyor should be contracted (for which separate fees are payable) to prepare specifications and seek tenders. A faculty will be required, and the archdeacon and DAC will be ready to give advice.

Faculties Churches and churchyards are subject to the jurisdiction of the diocesan bishop, which means that no alterations, additions, removals or repairs affecting the church and churchyard may lawfully be carried out without approval, which is given by way of a faculty from the diocesan consistory court. It is the duty of the minister and churchwardens to obtain such permission. Some very minor work may not require a faculty, and guidance on this will be available from the diocesan office.

PCCs are sometimes irritated by this strict faculty procedure. The reason for having a faculty procedure is to keep the control of church buildings in the hands of church members. The alternative would be for people who are not members of the church (e.g. the local planning authority) to make decisions about what we can or cannot do in our church buildings. The faculty system protects the churches and their contents for future generations. It protects PCC members and the incumbent from criticism and legal action, as well as protecting the rights of individuals and parishioners.

How to apply for a faculty Depending on the scale and complexity of the work involved, it may take some time to obtain a faculty. Here is the standard way of proceeding:

(a) The minister and churchwardens should discuss the matter informally.

(b) Where alterations or new work is involved, the advice of the Diocesan Advisory Committee should be sought at an early stage. The DAC will usually be willing to send a delegation to discuss the work, and will advise on any other consultations and paperwork necessary, and other necessary approvals such as planning permission. Where major changes to a listed church building are proposed, it is good practice (and saves time in the long run) to include amenity societies and English Heritage in the consultation at an early stage, as well as the local planning authority.

(c) Advice should be sought from the architect/surveyor, who should be instructed to prepare drawings and specifications.

(d) The PCC considers the matter and passes a resolution to petition for a faculty.

(e) The matter is considered formally by the DAC, which issues a certificate.

(f) Notices are displayed inside and outside the church for 28 days giving the opportunity for objections.

(g) The faculty petition, signed by the minister and church-wardens, is sent to the Diocesan Registrar with all the relevant paperwork.

(h) Where the work is minor and there are no objections, a faculty is issued on the authority of the archdeacon. With more major work, or where there are objections, or the DAC has not recommended the work, the matter is considered by the Chancellor, the judge of the consistory court. Where major work is involved, he/she may require further consultations with outside bodies. When this has been done, the Chancellor determines the petition judicially, either on the papers submitted, or (in a very few cases) at a hearing of the consistory court.

(i) Where a faculty is issued, it may be subject to conditions, and therefore a copy should be passed to the architect/ surveyor and any contractor.

When work is undertaken without a faculty, then the PCC has to apply for a confirmatory faculty. Full statutory fees are payable by the PCC, and also a written explanation is required about the circumstances. If any work is done without legal authority and a faculty would have been turned down if an application had been made, then the chancellor can give an order for the work to be undone. In this case, the cost of the work, and all legal expenses and fees, have to be paid for by those who were responsible for the illegal work being done in the first place.

Council for the Care of Churches   *See* page 59.

Visitation   The archdeacon's visitation is an annual event, held in the first part of each year. Churchwardens are sent Articles of Enquiry, which deal with matters such as parish life, faculties, insurance etc. These are completed and returned to the archdeacon. The churchwardens are then summoned to a visitation, usually held at a central place in the archdeaconry. At the visitation, there is usually a service, the archdeacon delivers a charge, and the churchwardens are admitted to their office. There may be an opportunity for a short interview with the archdeacon at the visitation.

Food for thought

1. Does the PCC have a contract with a builder to clean out the gutters and drains for the church and the church hall (and the vicarage?) each spring and autumn?
2. Have the church buildings deteriorated – or improved – during the period for which you were a member of the PCC?

CATERING (*See* **HOSPITALITY** on page 97.) Providing refreshments is a very important part of parish life. Occasional events include harvest supper or harvest lunch, Shrove Tuesday Party, Christmas Lunch, monthly Sunday Lunch, Lent or hunger lunch, buffet lunch after a lunchtime lecture. Sherry or Wine plus nibbles is easy to provide.

Perhaps the parish needs a hospitality group (whatever name is used). Imagination and variety are desirable when planning menus, while at the same time keeping the costs within sensible limits. Attractive presentation is helpful, and need not cost extra money.

A large hard-backed note book is desirable to record date and occasion, numbers served, quantities and cost of all food and wine, profit or loss, and the names of those who did the work. Comments for the next time the menu is used may be helpful.

Most churches have a long-term interest in providing food for large parish functions. It is wise initially to use profits from catering events to buy modern catering equipment, including a proper catering oven, refrigerator, and microwave.

Another idea for a monthly Sunday lunch. Ask people to offer to bring food to share (say, for six or eight people). A list requesting help in this way should be displayed for two Sundays before the lunch. A charge is made, and those who brought food are repaid in full for costs incurred.

Food for thought
If one does not already exist, would it be a good idea to form a catering team for the parish?

CHANGES IN THE PARISH God created the Church to bring the gospel to the world. In some ways, the Church has to change, but in other ways the gospel and the cross, the discipline of prayer, and many other things, are just the same as always.

Changes in the parish

The PCC is usually dealing with the things which can and do change, without affecting those things which are eternal and unchanging.

To change or not to change is often a problem in a parish. It is natural to try to preserve those things which were successful in the past, but some things can outlive their usefulness, and now serve only to hinder the work of the Church. A job may have been done in the same way for many years, because no one has worked out a better way. The PCC – or the priest – may be in a rut with parochial blinkers. People often see changes from their own point of view, rather than ask the question 'What is best for God's Church? What would our Lord want in this situation?' No one in their right mind would want to change for change's sake. However, it is very desirable to change if that change will help God's work in the parish.

Some PCC members can cope quite well with change, and see changes as an opportunity for growth. PCC members are elected 'to co-operate with the incumbent in the whole mission of the Church' and this requires them to be forward-looking, and sometimes to take calculated risks. Did not God take an enormous risk by entrusting the gospel of eternal salvation into the hands of the local church?

How often do people say, 'But we have never done it that way before!'? Why not give it a try, upheld by prayer and careful planning?

Christianity is a process of listening to what God has done for us in Jesus Christ, and what he is doing today. We need to listen carefully, and then to respond. The PCC has to work out how to apply Christian beliefs and insights to each item on the agenda at the PCC meeting. It involves sharing thoughts, reflecting on them, making decisions and then acting on them. Sometimes, the first thing that the PCC has to do is to become aware of the need for change. For example, if the PCC is satisfied with the number of people in the parish who belong to the Church, then there will be no need for change. Every PCC needs a vision, and this gives us a sense of purpose and encouragement.

Changes sometimes lead to discontent and problems, but change can also lead to growth. How much better when changes and new ideas are welcomed and encouraged with helpful and constructive comments. In all the changes in the Church, remember that the toughest and most precious commodity is love. Cardinal Newman said 'To live is to change'.

Whatever the situation in the parish, it is helpful to remember that we all belong to the same Body of Christ, even though some will want to move on, and others will prefer to remain where they are at present. Tension and hurt are often involved when decisions have to be made, but PCC members are elected to make decisions. Careful communication and explanations by PCC members can do much to help forward God's work in the parish.

Food for thought

1. Are any changes needed in your own life? Should any of your priorities be changed?
2. Should any of the weekly activities of the church be changed?

CHILDREN – PROTECTION FROM ABUSE *See* pages 160–5.

CHOIR *See* **MUSIC IN WORSHIP** on pages 124–30.

CHORAL SPEAKING Join in all parts of the service which are spoken by the congregation with a clear and firm voice. Do not get ahead or behind the others, as this can be most distracting. Listen carefully to the rhythm of the congregation and especially to the priest taking the service.

A thought – Do some people try to rush quickly through the Lord's Prayer because they are spiritually uncomfortable with it?

CHRISTIAN STEWARDSHIP Parishes differ enormously, but most PCCs have been involved in Christian stewardship, either to find the money to pay the diocesan quota, or as part of a deliberate policy about stewardship. The principles of Christian stewardship are firmly based on the Bible, and they are a sound basis for the life of every parish. They can also help to identify a vision about the needs and opportunities of the Church.

What is meant by stewardship? The definition given by the Lambeth Conference (1958) is as follows:

There can be no forward steps without a full acceptance of Christian Stewardship. By Stewardship, we mean the regarding of ourselves, our time, our talents, and our money – as a trust from God to be utilized in his service. This teaching is an urgent need in every congregation; a parish without a sense of Steward-ship has within it the seeds of decay.

The Church needs both this traditional view of Christian stewardship and also a vision for the parish, which is based on the Gospel.

The fundamental principle of Christianity is 'giving'. God created us, and he gave us life. His gift of life is under our own control, and we can do what we like with our lives. Sadly, most people ignore God and forget his ways. Because of this rebellion against God, he gave his only Son, so that we may not perish but have life. Thus, there are two parts of God's giving (creation and redemption). First of all, he gives us the gift of our lives. Sec-ondly, he gave us himself in his Son on the Cross at Calvary. It takes time for most of us to realize the full extent of God's love and total self-giving to us.

How can a Christian give thanks to God in practical ways for what he has done for us on the Cross? We can respond to God's love for us by giving back to God a proportion of our money, our time and our talents. Self-giving is perhaps one of the main aspects of the Christian life, both God's total giving to us, and our learning to give back to God what he has first given to us. It involves a certain amount of self-surrender to God. Christian stewardship invites us – and perhaps challenges us – to think about the following three areas: (1) our time, (2) our skills and talents, and (3) our money, and to make a definite decision about each of them. Stewardship is about our personal response and commitment. We ourselves are stewards (not owners) of our time, our money and our skills, and we are responsible for how we use them at each stage of our lives.

Stewardship of time People today have much more spare time than in former generations. Modern technology makes our daily work-load easier. We are stewards of the time which God has given to us here on earth, and we alone are respon-sible to God for how we use our time. Our time is a gift from God, and it really belongs to God. We can acknowledge this by offering back a proportion of our time to God each week. How do you work out what is a responsible amount of time to give for God's work each week? It is important to work out some-thing specific – rather than waiting for a job to turn up in the parish.

Stewardship of skills and abilities (talents)   Perhaps no one in your parish is a true genius, but virtually everyone has been given some natural skill or ability by God, and this can be offered back to God. We are expected to make something of the different skills, resources and energies which we've been given, and to develop them to the best of our abilities. It is so easy for our abilities to be unused or eroded by laziness, selfishness, lack of thought and courage. In a similar way, we have received a rich spiritual heritage, and it is easy to be self-satisfied simply by being a part of this spiritual heritage today. But are not all these blessings from God given to us on trust, which we can use for the work of his Church?

One approach is to produce a list of jobs which need doing in the parish. Perhaps a better approach is to identify the various talents and skills which exist among members of the congregation. Then try to work out how these talents and skills could be used. (Which comes first – the vacancy, or the individual with the talent?) For example, you may discover three musicians in the congregation – how could their musical skills be used?

Stewardship of money   Stewardship is not a new idea to solve the financial problems of the Church. It goes right back to the Old and New Testaments. It is interesting to note that the Bible has more references to money than to any other subject. The standard of giving set for the people of God in the Old Testament is one tenth (the 'tithe'). Genesis 14,20: 'Abraham gave him a tithe of all the booty.' Deuteronomy 14,22: 'Year by year, you shall set aside a tithe of all the produce of your seed, of everything that grows on the land.' Deuteronomy 16,16–17: 'No one shall come into the presence of the Lord empty-handed. Each of you shall bring such a gift as he can in proportion to the blessing which the Lord your God has given you' (NEB). The tithe is not put forward in the New Testament, but emphasis is given to sacrificial and thankful giving. It also stresses the blessings which will come to the giver as well as to the recipient. St Luke 6,38: 'Give, and gifts will be given you. Good measure, pressed down, shaken together, and running over, will be poured into your lap; for whatever measure you deal out to others will be dealt to you in return.' 2 Corinthians 9,6–8: 'Remember, sparse sowing, sparse reaping; sow bountifully, and you will reap bountifully. Each person should give as he has decided for himself; there should be no reluctance, no sense of compulsion; God loves a cheerful giver. And it is in God's power to provide you richly with every good gift; thus you will have ample means in yourselves to meet each and every situation, with enough and to spare for every good cause' (NEB).

Not everyone can give a tenth of their income, but a tithe is perhaps a good standard to have before us, and one which some people use to work out their giving to the Church today. Other people aim to work towards giving 5 per cent of their net income – which was the standard which General Synod recommended for giving to and through the Church.

Christian stewardship invites us to be responsible stewards of our money. What, then, is a realistic and responsible proportion of your income to give back to God through his Church? You cannot make a responsible decision without taking the trouble to work out the facts about your income. One way (after deduction of income tax) is to calculate what is 2 per cent, 3 per cent, 4 per cent, 5 per cent and 10 per cent of your weekly income. Then work out what is the right 'proportion' of your income to give back to God through the Church. It is a good idea to think about it for at least 24 hours after you have worked out the figures. Then pray about it. What does God want you to do about it?

Some people try to strike a balance between the amount which they spend on themselves and the amount they give back to God.

Stewardship of money is learning how to give according to your means. Whatever method you decide to use, it should be realistic and responsible. Pray about it, and make a deliberate decision (each year).

A vision for the pilgrim people of God   It is so easy to think of Christian stewardship mainly in terms of money. But the Church is much more than money. In the PCC annual accounts, it is better to have a heading 'stewardship of money' rather than 'stewardship income'. The Church of God is a pilgrim people, and we need a Christian approach not just for our money, but for the whole of our lives. Our Christian commitment should pervade all aspects of our daily lives.

The stewardship committee and the annual renewal   A Christian stewardship programme is a defined opportunity. But it is only the beginning. The important part of stewardship is the challenge to maintain the teaching and impetus about giving, and stewardship principles, year after year. An efficient stewardship committee is needed to maintain and raise the level of giving, and to bring new people into the scheme when it is appropriate to do so. In this way, there should be no need to have separate, one-off campaigns, providing the stewardship committee does its job properly throughout the year. It is wise to keep in contact with the diocesan stewardship adviser each year, to see what new programmes are available for the parishes.

A job specification for the stewardship committee

1. To maintain and increase regular giving and to bring new members into the scheme when appropriate.
2. To communicate regularly with those in the scheme, and also to thank them.
3. To organize the annual renewal, and to recommend to the PCC when the committee would like to have another diocesan directed programme.
4. To organize the time and talents side of stewardship in the parish.
5. To develop the teaching of Christian stewardship principles, and to create a vision for the growth of the Church and its service to the community.
6. When no other group is responsible for mission audit, perhaps the stewardship committee could include this in its work?
7. To keep the stewardship records (and electoral roll) up to date, and to remove the names of those who have died.

A definition of christian stewardship
by Robert Williamson (former Bishop of Southwark)

> It is a personal conviction of mine that money is congealed life. It is my work, my talents, my personality, reduced to negotiable form. In so far as I give money to God, or anyone else, I give that which represents me. Whether my model for stewardship reflects the Creator-creature or the Redeemer-redeemed relationship or a proper combination of the two, I am faced with responding to the tremendous generosity of God. If I claim to be his child, and if, by his Spirit, I am being changed into his likeness, then I must surely expect some of his generosity to rub off on me and to see my Christian giving move from the level of obligation through the level of generosity to the level of sacrifice.

Christian stewardship

A recommendation and a challenge from general synod:

(1) This Synod encourages the parishes to seek out and to own the vision which God has for them in their communities, in order to inspire and to unite them in purpose.

(2) Thankful to God for His generosity to us, and noting the continued pressure on the finances of the Church, and the call to growth, challenge Church people to give in proportion to their income, and recommend 5% of take-home pay as an initial target to aim for giving to the Church.

A vision of the church in the parish:
'We continue to seek and to develop our vision of what God has been doing, and longs to do through us. As we catch the vision for a confident, outward-looking Church, seeking to grow, to spread the Gospel, and to serve this country better, we also need to see how we will resource that vision. A part of that vision is that I give my money, so that others can minister where I cannot be.'

'Working for growth is a mark of a faithful Church. Now is the time to affirm this, as we seek to resource the Church from that which God has already given us.' ('First to the Lord' Report).

The report – 'working as one body'
Three points to consider:

1. It is important to see money as one of the many gifts of God, and not simply as an unfortunate necessity.

2. The 'theology' of Stewardship is not simply a way of getting people to give, but it is essential to the Church's teaching about grace and generosity.

3. Without a dynamic and positive attitude to money, the Church will fail to provide enough to make proper use of this essential resource.

The love of god
'The first question to ask is not: "What do I need to give?" – but – "How can giving reflect something of God's love for me?"' (Archbishop George Carey)

'Action points'
– recommended to every PCC by the Finance Committee of the Archbishop's Council.

1. How has your total parish voluntary giving changed over the last five years?

2. How has your average giving per donor changed in the same time?
3. Is all possible giving made by Gift Aid? If not, why not?
4. When were money and stewardship last preached about on a Sunday – and what happened?
5. Has your parish used the services of your Diocesan Stewardship Adviser?
6. How often does your PCC consider finance and giving, rather than just the Budget?
7. Does your Parish Priest teach about money?
8. Who is responsible for following up those who default on their planned giving?
9. How do you help those in the Church community to make or to renew their financial commitment?

PCC Agenda The Finance Committee also recommends the following questions are put as the 'first item' on your PCC Agenda for each of the next five meetings:–
1. 'Each person gives according to their means' (St Paul writing to the Corinthians). Discuss how this applies in today's world.
2. 'If we love God half as much as we love our grandchildren, money would be coming out of the Church's ears!' Discuss.
3. 'The level of giving is a reasonable barometer of the spiritual health of the parish.' Discuss.
4. 'Our giving as Christians should be in response to the love of God rather than the demands of the parish budget.' Discuss.
5. 'Every Church should give away 10 per cent of its general fund income to other missionary or charitable purposes before anything else.' Discuss.

Questions for discussion
1. What vision does the PCC (and the parish) have for the growth of the Church and its service to the local community in the coming years? Will the financial commitment of the PCC match this vision?
2. What policy does the PCC have to develop its teaching about Christian stewardship? Is this policy regularly reviewed?
3. Does the PCC have a system for reviewing the levels of giving each year? Is this policy clear to the PCC members and to the congregation?

4. Does the parish have a policy for teaching Christian stewardship as part of Christian formation, e.g. in preparation for Confirmation?

5. How can people be inspired with a vision of the Church's mission and ministry? How can they be inspired to make the work of the Church a high priority for their giving?

6. Does your PCC work out the cost of its mission to the parish each year, review progress, and initiate new plans?

7. How does Christian stewardship measure the extent of your trust in Christ?

8. To what extent is stewardship a barometer of the spiritual health of the parish?

9. In what direction should the stewardship committee now be concentrating its efforts?

10. Do the PCC and the stewardship committee know what help and support is available from the diocese? Does the parish make use of these resources?

CHURCH ARMY   The Church Army covers a whole range of 'churchmanship' and the officers are all united by service and evangelism. There are over 350 full time Evangelists, who share the Christian faith through words and actions. They also help by training others to do the same. There are 200 Church Army staff who are devoted to a wide range of service in Anglican Churches.

Parish missions   The CA conducts missions in a parish, and careful preparation by the parish and follow-up is always needed. The CA also provides Evangelists to work in parishes. It has also organised 'church planting'.

Social evangelism   The CA is involved in helping single homeless young people, and the elderly. They operate eighteen hostels for this work. In addition, much work is done with HM Forces, holiday camps and seaside resorts. There is a farm adventure station at Sheldon in Devon run by the Church Army.

Church Army resource centre   The CA undertakes teaching and training sessions in parishes, including the Christian Advance Training Scheme, which helps people to be involved in the work of the local church. The Resource Centre has a large stock of audio-visual material and literature, and a good book centre. Details: The Church Army Headquarters, Independence

Road, Blackheath, London, SE3 9LG. Tel: 020–8318 1226. Fax: 020–8318 5258. Email: information@churcharmy.org.uk Web: www.churcharmy.org.uk

CHURCH HALL Together with the church and vicarage, the hall is one of the main assets of the parish. A basic question: What is the purpose of having a church hall? To build up the fellowship of the congregation? To provide a meeting place for studying the faith, recreation and entertainment? To serve as a meeting place for community organizations, wedding and baptism receptions, and dances? The hall can be a powerful element in mission, and also generate income which can help to balance the PCC's budget in some parishes.

In order to attract people, the appearance of the hall must be appealing. It has to compete with high standards and facilities which are available elsewhere. It is a great disadvantage to have draughts, bare floor-boards with knots, dull brown or green paint which was put there sixty years ago.

Imagination and bold long-term planning can achieve a remarkable transformation, carried out in stages when the money becomes available.

Questions for discussion

1. Is the hall fulfilling the purposes which the PCC intends it to fulfil?
2. Are improvements desirable in the kitchen, lavatories, cloakrooms, stage, notice boards, entrance area, committee rooms? Would a new front door or extended entrance improve the facilities and appearance? Would carpets be appropriate in certain places? More comfortable chairs?
3. Is the hall adequate for the needs of the parish? Should the PCC be thinking in terms of building a new one?
4. The church has a thorough inspection every five years, and a written report is sent to the PCC. Should the PCC also ask the architect to inspect the hall? Is a report made every year to the Annual Parochial Church Meeting about the condition of the hall, the work done in the past year, and plans for the future?
5. Is a log book kept for the hall, where details are recorded of all repairs, alterations and improvements?
6. Is there room in the hall to make a parish office? If not, could one be built adjacent to the hall or church?

CHURCH HOUSING TRUST *See* **HOUSING ASSOCI-ATIONS** on page 97. This is a fund-raising charity which works for the needs of the homeless. It provides hostel accommodation for the single homeless, where they can stay for a maximum period of six months. During this period, CHT tries to find a place to re-settle them in the community. Some elderly residents become permanent, as it would be unkind to turn them out. CHT also owns a small number of houses which are used for homeless families.

Church Housing Trust deals with drug and alcohol addicts, ex-offenders and ex-psychiatric patients.

Church Housing Trust was originally the Church Housing Association and the Church Army Hostels (both Anglican) but it became ecumenical in 1991 when it was merged with the Baptist Housing Association. Much of the income comes from donations from PCCs, and perhaps your PCC might consider supporting CHT. Further details from: Church Housing Trust, Sutherland House, 70–78 West Hendon Broadway, London NW9 7BT. Tel: 020–8202 3458. Fax: 020–8208 1440. Email: info@cht.dircon.co.uk Web: www.charitynet.org/~cht

CHURCH NEWSPAPERS Many Christians read a church newspaper each week to be well informed about their faith and to see what is going on in the wider Church family. It is good for PCC members to know what is happening in the Church outside the parish boundaries. Could the PCC sell or provide a newspaper every week?

The *Church Times* is available from the Subscriptions Department – Tel: 01502 711171 or write to the Subscriptions Manager, *Church Times*, 16 Blyburgate, Beccles, Suffolk, NR34 9BT. Web: www.churchtimes.co.uk

The *Church of England Newspaper* – phone 020–7878 1510 for details, or write to the *Church of England Newspaper*, 20–26 Brunswick Place, London, N1 6DZ. Tel: 020 7417 5843. Web: churchnewspaper.com. You can ask for a free sample from both publishers.

CHURCH PASTORAL AID SOCIETY Founded in 1836, the object of the society is 'the salvation of souls, with a single eye to the glory of God, and in humble dependence on his blessings'. CPAS provides grants for curates and lay workers to help the clergy in parishes of both the Church of England and the Church of Wales. CPAS has a distinct protestant and evangelical position in doctrine and principles.

The society is involved in youth work and youth camps, women's action, and the administration of patronage of 'evangelical' livings. CPAS also produces leaflets, adult Christian education material, teaching aids, videos and film strips, and mission resources. Details from: The General Secretary, CPAS, Athena Drive, Tachbrook Park, Warwick, CV34 6NG. Tel: 01926 458458. Fax: 01926 458459. Email: info@ cpas.org.uk   Web: www.cpas.org.uk

CHURCH SCHOOLS Every school, whether Christian or secular, is a community full of energy, opportunity and hope. Every PCC is encouraged to look at ways in which it can serve and support all schools (and colleges) in or near the parish.

The Church of England has a magnificent record in creating and supporting Church Schools and Colleges. In our post-Christian and multi-cultural society, the work of church schools is of vital importance. Every PCC is encouraged to take its responsibilities seriously regarding a church school. This should involve all PCC members and the congregation, as well as those serving as school governors or managers.

Every church school is called upon to be a distinctively Christian institution, which is fully integrated into the life of the local parish church. There should be a growing unity of purpose in the parish to support the church school. The PCC is called upon to give time at regular intervals in order to achieve these aims.

The National Society for the Promoting of Religious Education

The Society exists 'for promotion, encouragement and support of religious education in accordance with the principles of the Church of England.' It works closely with the Board of Education, but as a voluntary body it is free to initiate any form of new work. It supports Christian education and Christians in education.

The Society was founded in 1811, and it was largely responsible, in co-operation with local clergy and others, for setting up the network of church schools in England and Wales. It was also a pioneer in the education of teachers, through church colleges.

The Society gives legal advice to schools and publishes a wide range of literature. It helps and supports those who are responsible for RE and worship in any school or college, as well as the clergy and lay people in parishes. The Society works closely with Diocesan Boards of Education. The NS has an excellent resources centre, and publishes an annual 'Schools Catalogue'.

Details: The National Society for Promoting Religious Education, Church House, Great Smith Street, London SW1P 3NZ. Tel: 020–7898 1518. Fax: 020–7898 1493. Email: info@natsoc. c-of-e.org.uk

Management of church schools   All involved in governing bodies now have considerable legal and moral responsibilities – for both the staff whom they employ, and the children. It is recommended that carefully worked out procedures are adopted. The following documents are invaluable:

> *Selecting, Appointing and Developing Staff in Church Schools*
> *Redundancy Procedures*
> *Managing Staff Sickness Absence*
> *Grievance and Discipline Procedures*
> *Contracts* (it has six different versions)
> *Capability Procedures*
> *Church Schools and Charity Law*
> *Resources for School Assemblies and Teaching Material*

CHURCH UNION   Founded in 1859 as a result of the great catholic renewal in the Church of England which began in Oxford in 1833, the purpose of the Church Union remains 'to uphold the catholic doctrine, worship, order and discipline of the Church of England, and to renew and extend catholic faith and practice within that Church both at home and abroad'. The main areas of work include renewal and mission, theology, literature and publishing, children and young people, social concern, liturgy and unity. Membership is open to both individual members and parishes who support the work of the Church Union by their subscriptions and by donations. They receive a journal, the *Church Observer*, three times a year; this contains general articles and news of Union activities, and details of coming events. *Living Stones* is published twice a year, and contains articles concerned with renewal in schools, colleges and parishes. It carries both theological and practical articles on liturgy and catechesis. There is a large, world-famous bookshop at the headquarters in London, supplying, in addition to books, sacristy supplies, objects of devotion and recorded music, and preparation material for Confirmation and Sunday School. Details from: The General Secretary, The Church Union, Faith House, 7 Tufton Street, Westminster, London SW1P 3QN. Tel: 020–7222 6952. Fax: 020–7976 7180. Email: churchunion@ care4free.net

CHURCHWARDENS   Status and dignity are attached to the ancient office of churchwarden, but much more is expected of those who accept office today. The warden has a strong mixture of legal, spiritual and pastoral responsibilities, as well as looking after the church and its contents. It is a role of leadership, and it sometimes needs courage, insight, and the ability to stand up and speak up, when necessary.

It is vital to have the right people as churchwardens, because so much depends on their loyalty, leadership and hard work. Anyone who is asked to be a warden should carefully consider the responsibilities involved, long before allowing his or her name to go forward for the election. If you have just been asked to consider becoming a churchwarden, do not be put off by these thoughts. Every warden grows into the job in the course of time, and God gives us all the necessary grace to do his work. Is this what God wants you to do?

Canon Law and the churchwardens   The duties and responsibilities are clearly set out in Canon E1, para. 4, and they are quite a tall order to fulfil properly! Presumably no one would accept office without truly intending to do his or her very best for God's work in the parish, and each warden signs a formal declaration about faithfully and diligently performing these duties. The Canon Law has been subdivided to make it easier to comment on each section:

'The churchwardens when admitted are officers of the ordinary'
The ordinary is the bishop. The wardens carry their wands of office in front of the bishop when he visits the parish, because they are the representatives of the bishop in the parish. What does this mean? 'Once in a blue moon' a situation may arise where the priest persistently and wilfully neglects to carry out his duties, or commits a serious moral or criminal act. Fortunately, a major problem of this nature does not happen very often. Most clergy work hard and pray and do their utmost to fulfil the high calling of the sacred ministry.

As a lay officer of the bishop, a churchwarden has the responsibility to report to the bishop if there is a major 'neglect or default' by the priest in carrying out his duties. It is, of course, a very serious step indeed to report the priest to the bishop, and it should only be done as a very last resort, and after serious consideration and much prayer. A question to ask is – 'What would our Lord want in this situation?' The warden has to weigh the good which might result from talking to the bishop, with the harm which would come to the priest's future ministry, to the parish, and perhaps to the Church as a whole. If the action leads to a court action, or a libel case, who will pay the costs? What harm would be done to the relationships of those concerned? The warden might also ask – 'Have I neglected any of my duties as a warden?' Remember the words of our Lord, 'Let him that is without sin throw the first stone'. The priest may also appoint another churchwarden at the next vestry meeting. The bishop will probably send a photocopy of correspondence to the priest. If a difficult situation does arise, the first step is for the wardens to talk to the priest about it. After all, the wardens have a loyalty to the priest and to the parish who elected them as wardens, as well as a loyalty to the bishop. This is not a pleasant subject, especially as the first item in the Canon Law, and fortunately most churchwardens will never be called upon to act in such circumstances.

'They shall discharge such duties as are by law and custom assigned to them' Customs vary from parish to parish, but the law is the same everywhere. We look at law and custom separately:

Duties assigned to the wardens 'by custom' What does this mean?

(a) *Routine work* It is a well established custom that the Churchwardens have a prominent role in the Church in every parish. Much work has to be done behind the scenes, as well as in the limelight. It is a question of how much time and effort each warden is able and willing to give for God's work. There are many routine jobs to be done. Ideally, the Churchwardens should not simply be there to lend a hand, but rather to shoulder the responsibility for organizing routine events. In this way the priest can be free to get on with the work of a priest.

(b) *Job Master* The wardens can help a great deal if they become Job Masters. This involves helping to find the right person as a replacement for a specific job, as and when necessary. Obviously, this should be done in consultation with the priest. When the Church arranges a special event, much thought and planning is needed, as well as finding people to do the extra work which is usually involved.

Each year, leaders are needed for the Lent Course; someone to organize door-to-door collections for Christian Aid and the Children's Society, and asking individuals to do the actual collecting; someone to look after the grass cutting rota (when the PCC does not pay for someone to do this). Other duties are finding a new Hall/Church Cleaner or Verger; arranging an annual spring clean and polish, including a window wash; arranging sidesmen for Festivals, weddings and funerals; recruiting new sidesmen; finding someone to deal with the heating system and any breakdowns as and when they happen, arranging for it to be serviced regularly; routine maintenance jobs; replacing light bulbs, oiling hinges and locks. The appearance of the Church and the hall are important (grass, hedges, litter).

(c) *Getting to know people by name* It is customary for the wardens to have an unofficial pastoral role for the congregation (and for parishioners too). Thus it is important for the wardens to get to know members of the congregation by name. To greet someone by name shows that the Church is a caring Church. To visit and get to know the various groups and organizations who use the hall is an added bonus, including uniformed organizations, youth club, servers guild, choir and the bell-ringers.

(d) *Worship* It is desirable for both wardens to be at the main service every Sunday morning, and if possible at the Sunday evening service too. This is also true for the major festivals (Ascension Day, Ash Wednesday, Holy Week services, Patronal Festival, Christmas services etc). There is a spiritual aspect in being an official of the Church, and it is desirable for the wardens to be people of prayer who regularly pray for the priest and the Church.

(e) *PCC and Annual Meetings* It is customary in many parishes for the Wardens to sit on one side of the priest, and the Secretary to sit on the other side at meetings. This is not just a place of honour, but to show that they are a united team who work together throughout the year, as well as at meetings. This aspect of working together with the priest is of the greatest importance to the work and worship of the Church.

(f) *Summary* To sum up, it is customary and desirable for the wardens to be actively involved in the whole life, work and mission of the Church. This is aiming very high, and not every churchwarden will be able to give time for all these things! However, each will know how much time he or she is able to give for God's work. It is desirable to talk these things over with the priest (and perhaps the other warden) – and also to pray about it – long before allowing your name to go forward for the election. (In most parishes there are usually only two candidates standing for election as wardens.)

Duties assigned to the wardens 'by law'

1. *Terrier and Inventory and Log Book* (Care of Churches and Ecclesiastical Jurisdiction Measure 1991, para. 4) The wardens, in consultation with the minister, must maintain

    (a) a terrier of all Church lands,
    (b) a full inventory of all articles which belong to the Church
    (c) a Log Book. The wardens must record all alterations, additions and repairs to the Church, and anything belonging to the Church, in the Log Book.

        The terrier, Inventory and Log books must be in the form recommended by the Council for the Care of Churches.

        The wardens must record all alterations, additions and repairs to the Church, and anything belonging to the Church, in the Log Book.

        A copy of the inventory must be sent to the person nominated by the bishop at the appropriate time and this person must be notified of all alterations.

2. *The Archdeacon's visitation* The archdeacon sends Articles of Enquiry every year to the Churchwardens, about such matters as parish life, insurance, gutters and facilities etc. The wardens are formally admitted to their office at the visitation – usually at a central place in the deanery or archdeaconry.

3. *Annual Inspection of the Church by the Churchwardens* (para. 5 of the 1991 Measure) The wardens must inspect the Church

buildings and all articles belonging to the Church at least once every year. Alternatively, they must arrange for someone else to carry out this inspection for them. The wardens must act in consultation with the minister.

What is involved in the Annual Inspection? What are the main things to look for in the inspection?

(a) Fire Risk. Sadly, many churches are destroyed by fire – some are caused by arsonists. The other cause is usually old or faulty wiring, or dampness. The wiring should be checked by someone with appropriate qualifications to check the whole system (and give a written report about it every five years ?).

(b) Water and Damp. Look out for any patches of dampness or fungus. Check the roof visually. The gutters should be cleared in the late autumn. (Some recommend clearing them also in the Spring.) Dampness can be caused by soil above the damp course. The cost of dealing with the damage caused by wet or dry rot can be considerable, especially if it is not discovered in the early stages.

(c) Movement in old buildings. Check for cracks and any signs of weakness.

(d) Shrubs and Trees. Roots under the Church and leaves in gutters cause many unnecessary problems.

(e) Death watch beetle. Keep a careful watch for any sings of infestation.

4. *The Annual Fabric Report and 'Statement'* The Report must be presented to the PCC meeting immediately before the Annual Parochial Church Meeting. This PCC meeting has to be held early each year to approve the Accounts and Fabric Report and other reports for presentation to the Annual Parochial Church Meeting (AGM). The wardens present the Fabric Report, together with any amendments made by the PCC, to the Annual Meeting. The Wardens must also produce a Statement, signed by both Churchwardens, stating that the contents of the Terrier, Inventory and Log Books are accurate. This is certifying, among other things, that all the work recorded in them has been properly completed.

5. *The wardens are the legal owners of the moveable contents of the Church during their period of office* This includes moveable

furniture, ornaments and plate. It is in the interests of the wardens to see that the PCC fulfils its responsibilities in regard to insurance cover, and proper repairs and maintenance as and when necessary. (The priest has, of course, the right to use all these items as and when he or she feels appropriate). Neither the wardens, nor anyone else, can remove anything, nor introduce anything new, without a Faculty.

6. *Allocation of seats in the nave of the church* (Canon F7 (2))   The wardens are responsible for allocating all seats in the nave of the Church. (The priest allocates seats in the Chancel.) To ask someone to move to another seat can cause great offence, even if there is good reason to ask them to move. It should only be done when absolutely necessary, and done in as tactful a way as possible.

7. *Alms for charitable and pious purposes*   The wardens are no longer involved in the allocation of alms. The 'Rubric' (rule) in the Book of Common Prayer 1662 has been overruled by Canon B17A and all Alms and other collections are allocated by the Incumbent and PCC.

8. *Sidesmen and sideswomen*   It is the responsibility of the wardens to organize a rota of sidesmen and women to take the collection during the service. In some parishes, members of the congregation put money and envelopes on a large plate near to where the hymn books are handed out, and in this case no collection is needed. (Some parishes feel that a collection disturbs the worship, while others think they get more money if a collection is taken – as opposed to having a plate near the entrance. In some parishes, the organist plays quiet music during the collection.)

   It is the responsibility of the wardens, assisted by the sidesmen, to organize the counting of the money and to open and record the contents of the stewardship envelopes. It is a wise custom to have at least two people present when the money is counted, in order to protect those concerned and the finances of the Church. Those who count the money should always record the amounts and then sign the Register of Services.

9. *An interregnum*   When a priest retires, dies in office, or moves to another parish, then the benefice becomes vacant. The wardens have an even greater job to do when there is no priest. One or both wardens are usually (but not always)

appointed as Sequestrators (usually with the Diocesan Secretary) See **INTERREGNUM** on pages 99–109.

10. *When the PCC fails to appoint a treasurer*   In this circumstance, it is the legal duty of the wardens to take over the duties and responsibilities of the Treasurer of the PCC (until an appropriate person is found who will take over the job). (Church Representation Rules 2001 appx. 2 (e)(1)). Under normal circumstances, it is definitely not a good idea for a churchwarden to hold the additional office of PCC Treasurer. This is because the work of warden, if done properly, is in itself very demanding. Under new legislation, the work of Treasurer is also demanding!

11. The wardens should try to ensure that the PCC pays the Common Fund in full each year. This could be seen as their duty as 'Officers of the Ordinary'. In the same Way, they should also ensure that all the working expenses of the priest and curate are paid in full.

'They shall be foremost in representing the laity and in co-operating with the incumbent'   At first glance, this seems to be difficult, but in practice there should be no conflict of loyalty. The wardens have been called the 'go-between' through whom parishioners can make known their views to the priest. At the same time, the wardens must also be 'foremost in co-operating with the priest'. It is desirable to have a parish policy written down. The wardens certainly have an important leadership role at PCC meetings, particularly in the whole matter of co-operation with the incumbent. The church will only succeed if there is this co-operation, together with mutual support, loyalty and good teamwork with 'united endeavours'. It is interesting to note that the Synodical Government Measure and Canon Law both use the same phrase of 'co-operating with the incumbent'.

'They shall use their best endeavours by example and by precept to encourage the parishioners in the practice of true religion'   This sentence has many implications for churchwardens and for the parish. Canon Law gives a clear and definite leadership role to every warden to encourage parishioners in the practice of true religion. 'Parishioners' includes church members and also those who live within the parish boundaries. Canon Law gives to the wardens a task which is similar to that given to every PCC member in the Synodical Government Measure – 'to co-operate with the incumbent in the whole mission of the Church, pastoral, evangelistic, social and ecumenical'.

The wardens are asked not only to set an example for other people to follow, but actively to encourage people in the practice of true religion. Not an easy task for any leader, whether lay or ordained, but a word of praise and encouragement from the warden can often do a great deal of good for the Church. Just because this is a difficult task assigned to the wardens by the makers of Canon Law, it does not mean that the warden can quietly forget about it. How the wardens fulfil their responsibilities in this matter will, to a large extent, influence and govern how the rest of the PCC carry out their responsibilities in this matter. To 'use their best endeavours' will surely require much thought and prayer, which hopefully will lead on to action.

'And to promote peace and unity among them' This clearly assumes that there will be problems in every parish from time to time. Even the apostles had their quarrels, and on one occasion Paul and Barnabas quarrelled so much that they parted company and went on separate missionary journeys.

What causes problems to arise? Does the answer include tactless remarks, jealousy, fears, personality clashes, people putting their own interests before God's wishes, changes in the parish, and resistance as church membership grows (the devil getting worried by the success of the Church so he makes a counter-attack)? It is also helpful for people to know and to respect the boundaries and areas of responsibility (*see Rights and responsibilities of the incumbent,* and *of the PCC* under **PAROCHIAL CHURCH COUNCIL**, on pages 135–9). PCCs do on occasions have an extraordinary capacity for causing division in the parish. As God's kingdom advances, so there is resistance. Unresolved tensions between individuals or groups might surface from time to time. Some people may pull in one direction while others are striving to go in the opposite direction, like a tug of war.

What a difficult job is given to the wardens to promote peace and unity among the parishioners! 'Blessed are the peace-makers.' But peace must never be appeasement, by giving in to wrong. When faced with a difficult situation, every warden would do well to consider two questions carefully: (a) What are all the facts in the matter? (b) What would our Lord want us to do in this situation? The wardens may on occasions need courage to speak out at a meeting, and perhaps to visit people in their homes to try to resolve the problem. Usually a problem will not go away on its own, and it is the responsibility of the wardens to take the appropriate action. It is, in most cases, not helpful to allow a problem to simmer, unresolved, just below the surface of parish life. Unless the PCC is able to heal its own divisions, no one outside the Church will take seriously its gospel of reconciliation and love and peace. Planning ahead and anticipating problems is an important part of the warden's work.

'They shall maintain order and decency in the church and churchyard, especially during times of divine services' The enemies of the Church usually ignore public worship, and it is unlikely that the vicar's sermon will cause a riot! Even so, the doors may well have to be guarded if a crowd of noisy drunks tries to invade the church for a midnight service. People sometimes use the churchyard in unfortunate ways, and children will climb on to the church or hall roof if at all possible. All these and similar matters are clearly the responsibility of the churchwardens, but it is unlikely that they will have to exercise the power of arrest which is vested in them under the Ecclesiastical Jurisdiction Act 1860.

Choosing a new churchwarden The Churchwardens (Appointment and Resignation) Measure 1964 has now been replaced by the Churchwardens Measure 2001. When a churchwarden is not standing for re-election, it is helpful to inform the priest as soon as possible. This gives the priest and others time to consult and make discreet enquiries about a successor, who in their turn can have time to consider the duties and responsibilities involved. This avoids making a quick decision at the Annual Meeting, without due thought and prayer.

Qualifications of the wardens The two wardens must be (a) baptized, (b) have their names on the Church Electoral Roll, (c) be actual communicants, (d) aged twenty-one years and upwards, (e) not be disqualified under section 72(1) of the Charities Act 1993 (c.10), nor convicted for any offence in Schedule I of the Children and Young Persons Act 1933 (c.12), nor disqualified under Section 10(6) of the Incumbents (Vacation of the

Benefices) Measure 1977. (The Diocesan Bishop may make exceptions regarding (b), (c) and (d) in special circumstances.)

No person shall be chosen as churchwarden unless he or she has actually signified their consent to serve in writing. The person concerned must not have consented to serve as warden in any other parish for the same period of office. No person shall be chosen as warden who has been rejected as warden of another parish.

How long can one serve as a warden? The answer is six successive periods of office. (A meeting of the parishioners may decide by resolution that this does not apply in the parish. Any such resolution may be revoked by a subsequent meeting.) An important question needs to be considered carefully when thinking about this matter – 'What is best for God's work in the parish?'

Time and manner of choosing the wardens Two wardens shall be chosen annually by a Meeting of the Parishioners, and not later than 30 April each year.

Nominations for election Candidates for election must be nominated and seconded in writing by people who are entitled to attend the meeting. Each nomination must include a statement signed by the candidate that he or she is willing to serve, and is not disqualified (see above). A nomination is not valid unless it is received by the Minister before the beginning of the meeting.

> If it appears to the Minister that the election of any particular person nominated may give rise to serious difficulties between the Minister and that person in carrying out of their respective functions, the Minister may, before the election is conducted, make a statement to the effect that only one churchwarden is to be elected by the meeting. In that event, one churchwarden shall be appointed by the Minister from among the persons nominated, the name of the person so appointed being announced before the election is conducted, and the other shall then be elected by the meeting. (Churchwardens Measure 2001, 4 (5))

The meeting of the parishioners (This used to be the Vestry Meeting.) The meeting is convened by a notice signed by the Minister (or by the Churchwarden when there is no Minister, or the Minister is unwilling to call a Meeting). A Notice must be fixed on a notice board on or near the principal door of the Church (and on every other building licensed for worship in the parish) – for a period which includes the last two Sundays before the meeting. The Notice must state the place, day and hour at which the meeting is to be held.

Who is entitled to attend? (1) Those whose names are on the Church Electoral Roll. (2) Those who are resident in the parish and whose names are entered in the Register of Local Government Electors.

The Minister is Chairman, or, if he/she is not present, a chairman is chosen by the meeting. When voting is equally divided on any motion, the Chairman does not have a second or casting vote. The motion is thus lost. This does not apply in the election of Churchwardens.

Clerk to the meeting The meeting may elect someone to serve as Clerk. (Usually the PCC Secretary is the 'Clerk').

Should the meeting of parishioners be separate from the Annual Parochial Church Meeting? The Vestry Meeting was normally held immediately before the Annual Meeting (APCM). Some parishes believe it is helpful to have the meetings on two separate days, while others have the one following the other. The Meeting of Parishioners may transact business other than simply electing the two wardens, if it so determines.

Churchwardens officially admitted to their office The two people chosen as wardens must appear before the bishop (or his substitute, usually the Archdeacon) annually not later than 31 July each year. They make a declaration that they will 'faithfully and diligently perform the duties of their office'. They also sign a declaration that they are not disqualified (see above). The wardens are then formally admitted, and their period of office begins from that time. The wardens continue in office until their successors are formally admitted in this way.

Emergencies Not a legal but a very practical matter. Every warden (and members of the Fabric Committee) should know the location of the stopcocks for the water mains, the electrical fuse boxes or switches and the mains gas tap for the Church, Church Hall and Vicarage.

Resignation of a churchwarden   A churchwarden may resign by writing a letter to the Diocesan Bishop, to be sent by post. The resignation shall normally have effect at the end of two months (or earlier, as may be determined by the Bishop, in consultation with the Minister and the other churchwarden).

A deputy churchwarden   There is officially no such office or title. It can be very helpful to have a deputy warden, both as a good way to introduce someone to the job, and also to help the two official wardens with their workload. It is the task of the Sidesmen to act as assistants to the Churchwardens.

Further thoughts to consider when you have been asked to be a churchwarden   It is a very important job in every parish. The ability to work with the priest, and loyalty to the Church and its priest(s), is essential. The job quite often involves putting God first, and social functions second. A warden surely cannot do a good job for the Church if he or she has too many commitments in the community.

A good warden needs to have his or her feet firmly on the ground, but it is also necessary to see the work from a spiritual point of view. Prayer is not mentioned in any of the legal documents which deal with churchwardens, but praying about people and things in the Church is an important part of the job.

CHURCHYARD   First impressions are lasting, and a well kept churchyard can create a good impression. An untidy churchyard shows no respect for the departed, and gives the impression that the Church is uncaring and ineffective.

Mounds and kerbs make it difficult and costly to cut the grass – but a strimmer will work where a mower is useless. Where graves are over fifty years old, and it is obvious that no one attends them, the answer is to apply for a faculty to remove kerbs and mounds. Careful research should be undertaken to be certain that there are no living relatives. A notice could be placed in the local paper long before any work begins, asking for information about relatives. This is far better than an article after the deed has been done, attacking an 'uncaring' church for removing the kerbs. Obviously, it is not good to allow any new kerbs into the churchyard: particular consideration should be given to the needs of the disabled.

Burial space is scarce, and it is costly to purchase new ground (if available). One solution may be to re-use the churchyard, which is possible fifty years after the last burial has taken place. Always consult the archdeacon about this at an early stage: a faculty will be needed for the exhumation and/or removal of memorials.

When a churchyard is full, the PCC can apply to the Home Office for it to be officially closed by Order in Council. Then the responsibility for maintenance can be transferred to the local government (while the ownership remains with the Church). Alternatively, the local authority can make an annual contribution towards the upkeep of an open or a closed churchyard. It is possible to close part of a churchyard, while using the remainder for burials.

Garden of Rest   A faculty is required 'to set apart a portion of the churchyard for the burial of cremated ashes'. It is desirable to make at least two rules: (1) Ashes to be buried without any casket. This is the practice followed at many crematoriums, and it prevents disturbing or cutting into the casket with a spade when further ashes are buried. It eliminates the problem of people digging up and stealing caskets, for they are usually buried fairly near the surface. (2) No cremation tablets or memorials. To sink a small stone slab into the grass can cause many problems in the future. An alternative is to have a book of remembrance inside the church – with suitable prayers nearby.

CLERGY – HOW TO ADDRESS THEM   Not a vital matter, but it can be useful to know the correct procedure. Simple styles were introduced by the Lambeth Conference 1968 for letters, as follows:

Archbishop	The Most Revd & The Right Hon. the Archbishop of . . . (In speech – Your Grace, or Archbishop)
Diocesan bishop	The Right Revd The Lord Bishop of . . . (In speech – My Lord, or Bishop)
Assistant and retired bishops	The Right Revd J. Smith (In speech – Bishop)
Dean	The Very Revd The Dean of . . . (In speech – Dean)
Archdeacon	The Venerable The Archdeacon of . . . (In speech – Archdeacon)
Canon	The Revd Canon J. Smith (In speech – Canon)

Clergy – how to address them

Prebendary	The Revd Prebendary J. Smith (In speech – Prebendary)
Other clergy	The Revd J. Smith – or the Revd Mary Smith
Ordained husband and wife	The Revd J. and the Revd M. Smith
Clergyman and wife	The Revd J. and Mrs Smith

In speech, the parish clergy are addressed in different ways, partly depending on the traditions of the parish: vicar, rector, Father Smith, Mr Smith, Mrs Smith, Father John. Some clergy encourage the use of christian names, while others feel some formality is more appropriate.

CLOCKS   A useful snippet of information. Local government authorities have power to pay the cost of repairing, maintaining and lighting public clocks, including clocks on church towers, even though the local authority does not own the clock.

COFFEE AFTER THE SERVICE   The Church is more than a collection of isolated individuals and interest groups. It is a family – the family of God where different groups are built into a community by sharing and partaking in the Eucharist. But fellowship needs to be built up in other ways to express the unity of the church family. One well-tried method is to have coffee and biscuits after the service every Sunday. This is also a good opportunity to welcome and introduce new people to the congregation.

Where there is no church hall, and no possibility of building one, one answer is to serve coffee at the back of the church (obtaining permission to remove a pew or two). A rota of helpers is needed, and a practical job like this is one way of bringing in fringe members.

Having said all of this, we must recognize that not everyone is of an extrovert nature, keen to meet other people. The very idea of being introduced to a group of unknown strangers can be a very frightening prospect to some people. A thought comes to mind – how many people actually stay away from church because they are afraid of the social gatherings after the service?

COMMITMENT   In days gone by, the church was the centre of life for most people, but today there are many other attractions and demands on our time. How, then, should PCC members think about their commitment to their church?

The answer will vary for each individual. Surely, no PCC member thinks of the church in terms of just another social club, to which they give their time so long as it does not interrupt anything else? Many think of commitment in terms of one hour's worship on Sunday, the responsible giving of money and attending PCC meetings. Some regard PCC meetings as a priority, which they put before any other social function. Others think also of commitment and loyalty to other PCC members, to their priest and to God.

There is a simple story about commitment. A hen and a pig were looking at a poster on a church notice board. It was inviting donations for 'Feed the Minds'. The hen said to the pig, 'You and I could help with this problem. We could supply them with bacon and eggs.' The pig thought for a moment, and then said, 'For you, that is only a token offering. For me, it is complete commitment.'

It raises the question – does the level of commitment vary among PCC members? What prevents firmer commitment in some people? What encourages commitment in others? Is there any connection between commitment and Christian steward-ship? *See* **MOTIVATION AND MORALE** on pages 120–1.

COMMUNITY ACTION *See* **SOCIAL RESPONSIBILITY AND CONCERN** on pages 184–5.

COMMUNITY CARE *See* **PASTORAL CARE** on pages 149–51.

COMMUNITY LUNCH *See* **HOSPITALITY AND PARISH CATERING** on pages 94 and 27–8.

COMMUNITY VOICE The Christian point of view is some-times not put forward on issues of local importance. When the occasion demands, how many are ready to speak out clearly and firmly to put the Christian point of view? It must be done with humility, and not in an arrogant manner. It will not always be popular. Likewise, the PCC can send a letter to the local gov-ernment council, or to the press, when the occasion demands it.

CONFIRMATION 'Confirmation means to make firm, strengthen or complete. Confirmation strengthens the grace already given in Baptism. A special mark or "character" is made on the soul in Confirmation, which can never be removed. In Baptism, we are united with Christ. We become children of God, and inheritors with Christ of the Kingdom of Heaven. In

Confirmation

Confirmation, the Spirit gives special skills to each of us. These gifts can be used (or not used) to share in the work of the Church' (quoted from *Discovering the Faith* by the author).

Finding candidates for Confirmation   In many parishes, candidates just seem to appear each year, when the preparation course begins. In other parishes, perhaps a letter could be sent to appropriate individuals, with an invitation to an informal meeting (with refreshments?) to think about Jesus Christ and what the Church has to offer to people. (It may be appropriate to follow this up by a visit from a PCC member.) This could be supplemented by an article in the Magazine or weekly newsletter.

Another idea – print the following on the Confirmation order of service: 'Anyone who has not been confirmed (or baptized) and would like to think about it, please have a word with the vicar.'

Asking the congregation to find candidates for Confirmation
Ask each member of the church tactfully to approach someone, and ask them to think about what the Church has to offer. This needs to be started soon after the Confirmation service, in preparation for the service in the following year.

The age of the candidates   Young people mature at a much earlier age than in former generations. Teenage years can be difficult for teenagers, parents and the Church, as they go through emotional and physical change and growth (and even emotional contradictions). They examine their beliefs and some reject the faith, partly because it makes demands on their newly acquired freedom.

In former years, young people were confirmed at about 11 years of age. There is a practice in some parishes for young people to be formally admitted by the parish priest to receive Holy Communion, but only after careful preparation. This usually takes place at 7 or 8 years of age. Confirmation follows later on, and it is administered by the bishop as a sacrament of Christian maturity and commitment. In many dioceses, the bishop's formal approval in writing is required for this approach to take place.

Preparation of candidates   There is a considerable amount of material, booklets, prayer material and videos available to help in the preparation of the candidates. Each parish will no doubt choose what is most appropriate and helpful for the traditions of the parish, and the benefit of the candidates.

Adult help in preparing young people (and adults)   One area where the PCC and members of the congregation can help is to be willing to share their faith with the candidates. Perhaps the candidates could meet with three or four adults. It might start with each adult saying why the Church is important to them, speaking about how they pray, the difficulties they have, and the peace and joy it brings, and why they started to come to Church in the first place.

Why do some candidates lapse after Confirmation?   Jesus said in a parable, 'A sower went out to sow his seeds. Some fell along the path, and were trodden underfoot, and the birds of the air devoured them. Some fell on the rock, and as it grew up, it withered away, because it had no moisture. And some fell among thorns, and the thorns grew with it and choked it.' His disciples asked him what this parable meant. Jesus said, 'The parable is this: The seed is the Word of God. The ones along the path are those who have heard, then the devil comes and takes away the Word from their hearts, that they may not believe and be saved. And the ones on the rock are those who, when they hear the Word, receive it with joy; but these have no root, they believe for a while and in time of temptation fall away. And as for what fell among the thorns, they are those who hear, but as they go on their way they are choked by the cares and riches and pleasures of life, and their fruit does not mature. And as for those in good soil . . .' (Luke 8 RSV)

How can members of the congregation and the PCC help the candidates to remain faithful to Christ and his Church?
(a)   The most important thing that each individual member of the church can do is to pray regularly during the period of preparation, during the confirmation service, and in the years ahead. One suggestion: 'O Lord, strengthen in the faith all who have been baptised and confirmed in this parish, and their families.' Take prayer seriously.
(b)   Try to get to know the candidates and their families. Get to know their names, and take an interest in them, their families and friends, school/college and hobbies. (A word

of encouragement from time to time may do wonders. Perhaps you might even consider giving a small confirmation present to one of the candidates).

CONGREGATION AND CONVERSION You may feel this is a strange heading for, after all, a congregation is a group of people who come and worship God week by week. So why does a congregation need to be 'converted'? One answer may be found in our Lord's words, 'Not everyone who says to me Lord, Lord, shall enter the kingdom of heaven, but only those who do the will of my Father who is in heaven.' Another answer – the members of the congregation will no doubt all be at different stages of spiritual growth. Some will have a deep love and knowledge of God, and others will be near the beginning of their spiritual pilgrimage.

Some people are 'converted' suddenly, as happened to St Paul, while for most people the process seems to be slow and gradual. However, no one is free from sin during this earthly life, and everyone needs God's forgiveness each day. Jesus said at the beginning of his ministry, 'Repent and believe the gospel'. The word conversion means a turning to God, and every Christian needs to turn to God again and again and again.

What prevents spiritual growth? Is it sin? Apathy? The doors of heart and soul firmly closed to the influence of the Holy Spirit?

What helps and encourages spiritual growth? A combination of the Eucharist, personal Bible reading, and private prayer (similar to the Benedictine triangle?).

The gospel makes us revise and change our thinking, and it frequently contains the unexpected. It keeps us from becoming self-centred and puts God back in the centre again. It gives us a new awareness of his presence, and it helps to change the hearts of both the congregation and the priest.

Questions for discussion

1. To what extent is the church 'a school for sinners'?
2. When new people join the congregation, is it just left to chance whether they come again or not? Does it depend on the priest? Or the friendship of the congregation? Or is there a Nurture and Welcome group?
3. Is it possible that some people come to church regularly, but are virtually untouched by the word of God?

CONSISTORY COURT   Ecclesiastical law is administered in each diocese through a Consistory Court, and the judge of the court is called the Chancellor. PCC applications for faculties are dealt with in the Consistory Court, and when there is a dispute it is possible to appeal to the Court of Arches. Appeals are always costly.

COUNCIL FOR THE CARE OF CHURCHES   The PCC is responsible for the care and maintenance of the church buildings, but it cannot make alterations without proper authority to do so. Each diocese has a Diocesan Advisory Committee for the care of churches which gives formal advice to the diocesan chancellor about any proposed change in a church. The DAC will also give informal advice to the PCC to help them in their difficult task of caring for ancient buildings.

The Council for the Care of Churches (CCC), which forms part of the Cathedral and Church Buildings Division, is a permanent commission of the Archbishops' Council of the Church of England. It has a range of statutory responsibilities and also assists parishes in their task of maintaining church buildings. One of the CCC's main tasks is to co-ordinate and guide the work of all the diocesan advisory committees.

The CCC offers advice to parishers on all aspects of the care and conversation of church buildings, their furnishings and fittings and administers grants for their conservation. It produces a wide range of publications of interest to all those concerned with the care of churches, their contents and churchyards. The CCC has an extensive library and holds a register of artists who undertake work for churches. Address: Council for the Care of Churches, Church House, Great Smith Street, London, SW1P 3NZ. Tel: 020–7898 1866, email: enquiries@ccc.c-of-e.org.uk

CURATE   The rector or vicar has 'the cure of souls' in the parish, so the curate is really the Assistant Curate. However, the assistant priest is known as the curate, who assists the vicar or rector in the parish.

The ministry of the Church is a corporate ministry, in which bishops, priests, deacons and members of the congregation all have a distinct role. A curate, whether deacon or priest, has a share in the corporate ministry of the Church, but it is important to remember that a curacy is also a time of training, and growing in confidence, spirituality and maturity. The basis for the future pattern of ministry is firmly established during the curacy years, and there is much to learn, particularly from the vicar.

DAILY OFFICES OF MORNING AND EVENING PRAYER Canon Law states: 'Every bishop, priest and deacon is under obligation, not being let by sickness or some other urgent cause, to say daily the Morning and Evening Prayer, either privately or openly. . . . He is also to be diligent in daily prayer and intercession.' (Canon C26/1)

PCC members and the daily offices Many priests go into the church for Morning and Evening Prayer at a set time each day, and advertise it in the parish magazine and notice board. It is good when members of the congregation are willing and able to join the priest in church for these daily offices, whether occasionally or on a regular basis. Some PCC members might use either Morning or Evening Prayer – or both – at home on a regular basis. They form a solid foundation for personal prayer and intercession, and provide for the regular and systematic reading of the Bible, with appropriate readings for each day and season of the year. An individual using Morning and Evening Prayer by himself at home is not praying alone. He or she is part of the worshipping community of the whole Church of God, in Heaven and on earth.

Food for thought

1. Could those who use Morning and Evening Prayer in their homes form a community of prayer, praying for each other every day, and for their bishop, priest and church?
2. Would Morning and/or Evening Prayer be a helpful way for husband and wife to pray together?

DANCING IN CHURCH Not 'slow, slow, quick quick, slow'. The very thought of dancing in an act of worship will horrify some people, even if they are only spectators. Early hostility by more traditionally minded people can be modified, or even disappear, after they have experienced liturgical dance.

There are different types of dance. In some churches, the congregation regularly sways from side to side, and people raise their hands as they sing. This is part of charismatic worship, and the author has no experience of this type of dance.

A more cautious approach is to have a group of people performing for the rest of the congregation. This type of liturgical dance can be used with powerful effect during the Eucharist at the Gloria, Sanctus, Benedictus and Agnus Dei. Biblical passages and themes can also be portrayed in a powerful way through dance.

Christianity is about the whole of life and not just worship and spiritual matters. 'Here we offer and present our souls and bodies to be a living sacrifice.'

Young people or adults can be involved, but proper training is required. The training itself is useful, as those involved have to think carefully about the meaning of the words they will express in actions with their bodies.

A service with liturgical dance can only be done very occasionally, and even so, it will not appeal to everyone.

DATES FOR THE COMING YEAR   It is helpful if the Standing Committee does some forward planning and works out dates of the main events for the coming year. These can be discussed by the PCC and published at the New Year, with a request that everyone enters them in their new diary. (Patronal Festival, Harvest, the fête, carol services, barbecue, outings, PCC meetings, social evenings, parish conference, retreat.)

DEANERY SYNOD   *See* **SYNODS OF THE CHURCH** on pages 202–4.

DELEGATION   The priest is not a one-man band, and a great deal of delegation takes place in every church. We are all called by God to share in Christ's ministry and work. Everyone, if willing, has something to offer, no matter how small. Talent spotting is a very important part of the work of the priest and the churchwardens. Acorns must be given the chance to grow into oak trees.

The initial explanation of the work is important. You need to give a clear statement of what is involved before you ask someone to take on the responsibility. Perhaps for some jobs, it may be wise to write down a job specification – (for your own use, and not to be given to the person concerned). The following need consideration:

1. How much authority is being given?
2. How much time is needed to do the job?
3. Will anyone else be involved in this work?
4. Who is available to help when a problem arises?
5. What are the arrangements for a progress report?
6. Is any preparation or training needed to do this work properly?

It may be appropriate to discuss how long the person will do the job: one year, five, or . . . ?

DIARY A large parish diary is useful in planning future events for the parish. It is helpful to keep it in a place where it is accessible to all who need to consult it (e.g. the bell ringers, hall secretary, choir, PCC secretary, etc.). It needs to be kept up to date!

DIOCESAN BOARD OF FINANCE *See* **FINANCE** on pages 70–82.

DIOCESAN SYNOD *See* **SYNODS OF THE CHURCH** on pages 202–4.

DISABILITY DISCRIMINATION ACT 1995 Every church should be a loving and a caring community, and this Act of Parliament puts into the law of the land what every church should already be doing. The Act requires that 'providers of goods, facilities and services' should take reasonable measures to ensure that they do not discriminate against disabled people. The Act covers all churches, church halls and churchyards.

Action is needed in the following areas:

1. Access for wheelchairs.   The Church must be accessible to everyone, whether or not they are in a wheelchair. Everyone has a right to access.
2. Mounds and kerbs in churchyards.   Someone attending a funeral must be able to come close to the grave. People in wheelchairs need to be able to visit graves at any time, particularly at the anniversary of death. (This is surely a powerful reason for not having kerbs and mounds.)
3. Hard of hearing.   A loop system will enormously benefit those who are hard of hearing.
4. Disabled toilet.   When toilets are provided in a church or hall, then one must be provided for the disabled.
5. Car parking.   One (or more) space(s) should be provided for parking cars for the disabled, which should be as near as possible to the entrance to the church or hall (or both).

This is an important matter, both in terms of the law of the land and in Christian action. Unless action has already been taken, advice should be sought from the archdeacon and the church architect.

DONATIONS BOOK   A well-bound 'gifts and donations' book placed on display on a table at the back of the church is useful to record recent donations (e.g. a new Bible) to the parish church.

DRAMA IN CHURCH   Life was hard and often violent in the Middle Ages. The Church used religious drama to brighten up the lives of ordinary people when there was virtually no other entertainment. Religious drama was also a very effective way of teaching people about the life of Jesus. Religious drama began with the mystery (miracle) plays, and later on came the morality plays.

All religious drama was forbidden during the Reformation. But since the end of the nineteenth century, there has been a revival of the use of drama in churches and cathedrals, presented by both professional and amateur companies.

Religious drama is still a very effective and also an enjoyable way of furthering the Christian cause. It provides an opportunity for young and old to work together and to use their skills and talents on a project which can be spiritually enriching. Non-believers will sometimes come to a play in church, while they would not come to a religious service.

There is a wide range of religious plays which are suitable for use in church. A short dramatic sketch might occasionally be used instead of a sermon! A longer drama could be quite a challenge for the parish, e.g. a church dedicated with the name of St Thomas a Becket might consider performing *Murder in the Cathedral*.

RADIUS (The Religious Drama Society of Great Britain) was founded in 1929 to assist and bring together those who create drama as a means of Christian understanding. Radius maintains an extensive lending library, publishes a quarterly magazine and organizes summer schools, workshops and play writing competitions. Details: The Secretary, Radius Office, Christ Church and Upton Chapel, 1a Kennington Rd, London SE1 7QP. Tel: 020–7401 2422. Web: www.radius.org.uk

DRAWING PINS   A small point which needs stressing – drawing pins and nails leave a nasty hole in church furniture and doors. No member of the congregation would put a drawing pin in a valuable piece of antique furniture in his own home. One solution, apart from buying or making a notice board, is to use

Blu-Tac (similar to putty) which does not leave any woodworm-like holes in the furniture.

EASTER OFFERING   *See* **FINANCE** on page 78.

ECUMENICAL   A divided Church is a sin, and it is one factor which prevents the spread of the gospel. God wants his Church to be one. In the Creed, we say 'We believe in one holy catholic and apostolic Church.' Different churches should no longer do separately those things which with a good conscience they can do together. Canon Law encourages and makes provision for sharing worship with other Christian Churches. (Canon B43 and B44.) (Sadly, many problems and divisions do still remain.)

Churches Together   This 'unites in pilgrimage those Churches which, acknowledging God's revelation in Christ, confess the Lord Jesus Christ as God and Saviour according to the Scriptures, and, in obedience to God's will and in the power of the Holy Spirit, commit themselves:

− to seek a deepening of their communion with Christ and with one another in the Church, which is His Body;
− to fulfil their mission to proclaim the Gospel by common witness and service in the world to the glory of the one God, Father, Son and Holy Spirit.'

Anglicans, Roman Catholics and the Free Churches are members of Churches Together. The PCC usually appoints one or two representatives to serve on the local Churches Together, along with their priest.

EDUCATION OF CHRISTIANS   *See* **CONFIRMATION** on pages 55–8 and **CHURCH SCHOOLS** on pages 39–40. Christian education is often assumed to be for children only. If this is so, the Church should not be surprised when children discard their faith when they grow up.

Questions for discussion

1. Is the weekly sermon the only form of ongoing adult Christian education in the parish? If so, what is needed to provide additional educational facilities for the congregation and interested fringe members?

2. The question needs to be considered briefly – Education for what?
3. Is the PCC aware of the training opportunities provided by the diocesan education team for adults, for those who work with adults as group leaders, and for those who work with young people?
4. How can the PCC help to link the work done by the Sunday School with the adult worship of the congregation?
5. Does the PCC have a copy of 'Roots', the magazine for Church teachers and Sunday School leaders (published ecumenically)?
6. Is there any project, or holiday scheme, which the PCC could organize for children *and* parents together?
7. Has the PCC discussed and written down a parish education policy for people of all ages in the parish? And with the help of the diocesan education team?
8. Do PCC members as individuals take responsibility for their own Christian growth and learning?
9. Is the PCC's ministry to children weak or strong?
10. Is the PCC aware of the needs of the children of one-parent families, broken homes, and those who are mentally and physically handicapped?

ELECTORAL ROLL   This is not to be confused with the register of local and parliamentary voters. The (Church) electoral roll is the foundation of the whole structure of synodical government in the Church. The legislation is found in the Church Representation Rules, as amended in 1999.

Who is eligible to be on the electoral roll?   To qualify to be on the roll, a person must be:

(a)   baptized,
(b)   16 years of age or over before the date of the Annual Meeting.
(c)   A member of the Church of England, or of a Church in communion therewith and resident in the parish;
       OR, not being a resident in the parish, to have habitually attended public worship in the parish for six months prior to enrolment;
(d)   OR a member in good standing of a church which subscribes to the doctrine of the Holy Trinity (not being a church in communion with the Church of England)

and who is also prepared to declare himself a member of the Church of England, having habitually attended public worship in the parish for six months prior to enrolment.

A person may have their name on the electoral roll of more than one parish, providing they are entitled to do so under the above qualifications, but must choose one parish to be qualified for election to a Deanery, Diocesan or General Synod.

Name and address The electoral roll shall, where practicable, contain the address of every person whose name is on the roll. (Failure to comply shall not prejudice the validity of any entry.)

The duties of the electoral roll officer The appointment is normally made by the PCC each year, at the first meeting after the Annual Parochial Church Meeting. The duties of the electoral roll officer (subject to any directions made by the PCC) are as follows:

(a) Keep the roll up to date by adding or removing names as necessary.

(b) Report any additions or removals at the next PCC meeting.

(c) Publish a list of all amendments to the roll for 14 days on the main notice board before the Annual Meeting. This notice must always contain the statement that any appeals about the electoral roll must be made within 14 days of the date of the notice to the lay chairman of the Deanery Synod (give name and address). Appeals about the register of lay or clerical elections must be sent in writing to the Chairman of the House of Laity, or the Chairman of the House of Clergy, of the Diocesan Synod (give their names and addresses).

(d) Notify the secretary of the Diocesan Synod of the number of names on the electoral roll at the time of the Annual Parochial Church Meeting. This has to be done by 1 June every year.

(e) Put a copy of the certificate (letter sent to the secretary of the Diocesan Synod as in (d) above) on the Church notice board for at least 14 days.

Removal of names from the roll A person's name shall be removed from the roll if

(a) They have died

(b) They have been ordained.

(c)   They ask in writing for their name to be removed from the roll.

(d)   They cease to live in the parish, except when they continue, 'habitually to attend public worship for six months, unless prevented from doing so by illness or other sufficient cause.'

(e)   They are not a resident, and have not habitually attended public worship during the last six months.

(f)   It is discovered that the person was not entitled to have their name on the roll in the first place.

The circumstances for removing a person's name from the roll may change. If they acquire the right by fulfilling the appropriate qualifications, their name may be entered on the roll again.

The annual revision of the electoral roll   'The minister, or [someone] under his direction' shall display a notice for not less than 14 days before the commencement of the revision. (This normally means the electoral roll officer, who asks the minister about the appropriate dates).

The revision shall be completed not less that 15 days – or more than 28 days – before the Annual Meeting. All additions and removals since the last annual revision shall be reviewed by the PCC. New additions and removals shall be made as required.

When the revision is completed, a copy of the revised roll – together with a list of the names which have been removed – shall be published for viewing on the notice board for not less than 14 days before the Annual Meeting. During this period, any errors or omissions may be corrected, but no names shall be added or removed during the period between the completion of the revision and the close of the Annual Meeting.

Preparation of a new electoral roll every sixth year   A completely new roll was prepared in the year 1990, and a new roll has to be made every succeeding sixth year from this date. The timetable is as follows.

Not less than two months before the Annual Meeting, a notice 'shall be affixed by the Minister or under his direction' for not less than 14 days. The person conducting the services shall inform the congregation of the preparation of the new roll at every service on each of the two Sundays in the period of the 14 days. (Where there is no service on either or both Sundays within the 14 days, notice shall be given at the first Sunday when there is a service after that date).

The PCC shall 'take reasonable steps' to inform every person whose name is on the roll that a new roll is being prepared. If a person wishes to have their name on the new roll, they must apply for enrolment on the application form (copy enclosed with the letter). There is no need to notify anyone whose name could be removed from the roll (see above). A new application form is required for every person whose name is on the previous roll.

The new roll shall be completed not less than 15 days – or more than 28 days – before the Annual Meeting. A copy of the new roll must be displayed on the notice board for not less than 14 days before the Annual Meeting. During that period, errors and omissions may be corrected, but no names may be added or removed between the completion of the new roll and the close of the Annual Meeting. When the new roll is published, the old roll ceases to have effect.

Procedure for adding and removing names   When a person applies for enrolment on the roll and signifies their desire that their name should be removed from the roll of another parish, notice must be sent about this to the former parish. When a person's name is removed from the roll because they have moved to another parish, notice of this should be sent from the original parish to the new one. (This is because people often lose contact with the Church when they move to another parish.)

Certificate of numbers of names on the roll   The number of names on the electoral roll at the time of the Annual Parochial Church Meeting must be sent to the secretary of the Diocesan Synod not later than 1 June every year. (This is usually done by the electoral roll officer.) A copy of this certificate must be fixed on the notice board when it is sent to the secretary of the Diocesan Synod, and it must remain on the notice board for a period of not less that 14 days.

Guild churches   Special provisions are made for members of Guild churches. (Church Representation Rules 1999, para. 5.)

An active electoral roll officer   The electoral roll officer has certain legal tasks to perform every year. In addition, he or she can do a great deal for the church by approaching people and asking them if they would like to be included on the church electoral roll (perhaps having a word with the priest before approaching the person concerned). This raises a question: how many people in the church know the names of all the members of the congregation? It is helpful if the electoral roll officer can put a face to a name and address.

EMPLOYING PEOPLE PCCs often employ paid staff. There is a great deal of legislation which affects the employer-employee relationship. The PCC must make regular PAYE payments. The PCC has wide statutory responsibilities and obligations which should not be taken lightly. Some dioceses have a Lay Employee Agency which will give advice and encourage 'good employment practice'. Otherwise, consult your archdeacon for advice, particularly when problems arise.

ENQUIRY CENTRE OF THE CHURCH OF ENGLAND This provides answers to a wide range of questions from people in England and all over the world. It is possible to find the answer to many questions on the web site, but some people prefer to speak in person to the enquiries officer. Details: Mr Stephen Empson, The Enquiry Centre, Church House, Great Smith Street, Westminster, London SW1P 3NZ. Tel: 020–7898 1445. Fax: 020–7222 6672. Email: steve.empson@c-of-e.org.uk Web: www.cofe.anglican.org

EUCHARIST *See* **HOLY COMMUNION** on pages 90–5.

EVANGELIZATION *See* **MISSION – EVANGELISM – RENEWAL** on pages 114–20.

EXPENSES OF CLERGY *See* **FINANCE** on pages 78–9.

FACULTIES *See* page 25.

FÊTE Many parishes organize an annual church fête, some to make money for their own funds, and others to support the Church overseas or some specifically Christian charity. Many people will support a charity, but it is usually only Christians who support the Church overseas and specifically Christian charities.

A fête can generate much interest and goodwill towards the Church, and many fringe and non-church members are willing to lend a hand at the fête. Who knows – perhaps even a church fête may lead someone into the kingdom of God!

Fête

The date of the fête should be arranged at the beginning of the year when the other church events are planned for the coming year. The fête committee could well include non-church and fringe members, and it is wise to start planning for the fête about six months before the event.

It is useful to keep brief records in a notebook for the following year. Careful planning, good publicity, imagination, and new attractions every year, are a good recipe for success – if you are lucky with the main uncertain factor in arranging a fête – the British weather!

FINANCE   The finances of the Church have been considerably altered by the passing of the Charities Act 1993. It is helpful if every PCC member does have some understanding of Church finance.

The Hon PCC Treasurer will obviously need much more information than is provided here. Most Dioceses and/or Deaneries now arrange a meeting for PCC Treasurers and Churchwardens each year. The purpose is to explain the Diocesan Budget, and how the PCC share, called Common Fund or Parish Share, is worked out. The Treasurer can obtain information by contacting the Diocesan Treasurer (or Diocesan Secretary in the first place). Amongst other pamphlets, an up-to-date edition of the 'Charities Act 1993 and the PCC' (published by Church House Publishing for the Finance Division of the Archbishop's Council) and 'Church Accounting Regulations 1997–2001' is useful for the PCC Treasurer (the second edition was published in 2001). Here is a very brief summary of some of the main parts of the Charities Act, which affect the finances of the PCC:

Two different types of PCC accounts   By law, only two types of accounts are acceptable. This is a complicated matter, and it is important for the PCC to make the right choice between the two types of accounts:
(a)   Receipts and Payments Account – with an associated statement of assets and liabilities.
(b)   Accrual Accounts with a SOFA (statement of financial activities) and an associated balance sheet and notes. (A halfway house, such as an Income and Expenditure account and balance sheet, is no longer acceptable by law).

Different types of PCC funds   PCC finance has to meet the requirements of the Charities Act 1993, and this lays down that there are three different types of funds:

(a) 'Unrestricted Funds' This is the General Fund of the PCC, and the majority of the parish income is placed in this account. It is used to pay all the everyday expenses of the Church. The fund is 'unrestricted' because the income of the Church is given on the understanding that the PCC will use it at its discretion to further the mission and work of the Church.

(b) 'Restricted Funds' The restriction is made by the donor (not the PCC) in responding to a particular appeal, or by stating to what use a donation must be put.

(c) 'Endowment Funds' This is either for money given with the specific instruction that only income gained from it can be spent, or an asset that has to be retained for use by the Church. Endowment Funds should be broken down into 'Permanent Endowment' (which must be held permanently), or 'Expendable Endowment' (which, in certain circumstances, may be spent).

The PCC is required by law to account for all its funds. When a PCC holds Restricted and Endowment Funds, these must be shown separately from the Unrestricted Fund in the Annual Accounts. Clear records should be kept of restricted money so that it can easily be identified.

Timetable for preparing the annual accounts and annual report The PCC Treasurer has much work to do in order to prepare the annual accounts for the Annual Parochial Church Meeting:

1. Early in January, prepare the annual accounts in the prescribed manner for the year ending 31st December.

2. The (written) Annual Report is a separate legal document. The Report is usually drawn up by the Secretary and Treasurer – and others may be involved in its drafting. Like the PCC accounts, the Report is the responsibility of the whole PCC. This Annual Report is quite separate from any address which the priest may wish to give to the annual meeting. It must review the past year, and link financial plans to the vision for the future.

3. Arrange for the accounts to be 'audited' or 'independently examined', together with all books, documents, vouchers and receipts (see below).

4. Arrange the timetable with the priest, or Standing Committee or PCC. Present the accounts and report to the PCC. After discussion (and possible amendment), the resolution is

proposed 'that the PCC accepts the Annual Accounts and Annual Report for presentation to the Annual Parochial Church Meeting'. The Chairman presiding at the PCC meeting then signs the audited or examined Accounts and the Report at the PCC meeting.

5. A copy of the Accounts and the Report has to be fixed on the Church notice board for a continuous period of at least seven days before the Annual Parochial Church Meeting (including one Sunday when the Church is used for worship).

6. At the annual meeting, the resolution is proposed 'that the Annual Accounts and Annual Report be adopted.' The Annual Meeting cannot alter or amend the accounts – it can only accept or reject them (the latter only in very extreme circumstances).

7. After the Annual Meeting, the Accounts and the Report must be on the Notice Board for a further 14 days.

8. A copy of the Accounts and the Report has to be sent to the Secretary of the Diocesan Board of Finance within 28 days of the annual meeting (for retention by the diocese).

Once the PCC accounts and report have been accepted by the PCC, they become the PCC's accounts, and the Treasurer should thus be able to expect the full support of PCC members over all aspects of the accounts.

Auditor or independent examiner? The accounts must be audited or independently examined every year. The person concerned should not be a member of the PCC, or in any way connected with a PCC member, which could prevent them from carrying out an audit or examination in an impartial manner.

When the gross annual income of the PCC exceeds £250,000, then a registered auditor must be appointed (Charities Act 1993 section 43(2)). It is wise to approach this appointment carefully, perhaps asking whether the person concerned would be able to act under the terms of the Charities Act 1993.

When the gross annual income of the PCC is below £250,000, then an independent examiner can be appointed. An independent examiner is 'an independent person who is reasonably believed by the trustees (PCC) to have the requisite ability and practical experience to carry out a competent examination of the accounts.' (When the PCC income is below £10,000, PCC accounts must still be examined by an independent examiner, even though they do not need to be so examined under the Charities Act). Parishes whose gross income exceeds £100,000 must prepare accounts on an accruals basis (with a statement of financial activities).

Church accounting regulations are a legal requirement for every PCC, and if they are not observed, then the PCC as Trustee will be breaking the law.

Annual budget   A budget is a plan of action using figures. It is wise for the finance committee (or standing committee) to plan ahead for the coming year in November (or earlier) and then to work out the costs of the plans. It should be noted that the treasurer does not make policy decisions, e.g. the treasurer does not say, 'We cannot do this because we do not have the money'. The correct procedure is for the treasurer to say, 'The PCC has £x available, and this means that the PCC will have to raise £y to do this'. But the PCC makes the decision. It is a good idea to get the principle right first, and then to work towards the principle. It is always desirable to involve as many people as possible in formulating the policy and plans of the church. Once the plan has been accepted by the PCC, it is (in many cases) a good idea to present it for discussion at the APCM or a Parish Meeting. The aim is to obtain support and commitment from as many people as possible.

The budget is brought to the PCC at the first meeting in the New Year, usually at the same time as the annual accounts.

What are the most important items in the budget? To put it another way, how should the money be used if there is a short-fall of income? Should the PCC borrow from reserves? Each PCC must work out its own order of priority about making payments from PCC income, after payment of urgent bills. How far would you agree with this suggested order?

1. Payment in full of the Common Fund. This has first claim on parish income. Otherwise the life of the Church in the parish and in the diocese would grind to a halt.
2. Missionary giving for the Church overseas – at 10 per cent of the gross income of the PCC. *See* **Donations made by the PCC** on pages 77–8.
3. Full cover for all aspects of insurance.
4. Parochial expenses (i.e. expenses of the clergy).
5. The church roof (assuming careful stewardship and regular inspections of the buildings).

6. Missionary work in the parish (e.g. a free magazine delivered to every home in the parish).
7. Vicarage improvements and redecorations.

Central Board of Finance of the Church of England (CBF)

These funds provide a ready-made investment service to look after money exclusively for Church of England parishes, dioceses and other charitable trusts. They aim to avoid unnecessary risks, while at the same time give satisfactory returns. There are three CBF Church of England Funds available which are very useful to meet the needs of the PCC. They are exempt from liability to tax on either income or capital gains, and the dividends or interest are paid gross, after recovery of all reclaimable tax. The three funds are as follows:

(a) The CBF Church of England Investment Fund. This fund is for capital which needs to be invested for a long period. It has a widely spread portfolio of shares, mainly in the UK. The aim of this fund is to provide a steady growth of income and capital. Gross dividends can be paid direct into a bank account, or they can be re-invested to purchase further units in the fund. (Weekly share dealings.)

(b) The CBF Church of England Fixed Interest Securities Fund. This fund invests only in fixed interest stocks, and thus it offers a higher income than the Investment Fund. It is intended to supplement the initially lower income yield from the Investment Fund. Gross dividends can be paid each quarter into a bank account, or re-invested to purchase further units in the fund. (Weekly share dealings.)

(c) The CBF Church of England Deposit Fund. This money fund is for cash balances, which should be available at short notice and with minimal risk of capital loss. Deposits in the fund obtain a rate of interest close to money market rates, even on small sums of money. There are facilities for daily deposit and withdrawals.

Church Commissioners

They were created in 1948 when the Ecclesiastical Commissioners (formed in 1836) were united with the Queen Anne's Bounty (formed in 1704).

The main functions of the Commissioners are to look after the ancient endowments, to pay the clergy, to approve redundancy schemes, and to make pastoral orders. The capital assets are held in trust, and legally this means that only the income and not the capital itself can be used. The income is mainly used:

1. To provide support for parish ministry, particularly in areas of need and opportunity.
2. To pay the pensions of retired clergy and clergy widows earned before January 1998.

The income of the Commissioners is large, but not nearly large enough to meet all its demands. Once the Commissioners paid the lion's share of clergy stipends. Now, a greater proportion of the Commissioners' income goes to pay clergy pensions. Thus a larger amount of money from the parishes through the Parish Share makes up a growing proportion of the clergy stipends.

The wealth of the Church Commissioners has been a great blessing. It has enabled the Church to pay the clergy through difficult times, and to keep clergy working in areas which could not otherwise afford a priest. But in some ways, the Commissioners' wealth has been a mixed blessing. Present-day Christians have depended to a considerable extent on the generous giving of Christians in former times. As the resources of the Commissioners are not sufficient to meet the needs of the Church, so PCCs are asked to provide more money. This challenge usually brings new spiritual life and commitment in a parish, and often a response which includes the principles of Christian stewardship. *See* pages 30–5.

Address: The Church Commissioners, Church House, Great Smith Street, London SW1P 3NZ. Tel: 020 7898 1000. Fax: 020 7898 1002. Email.commissioners.enquiry@c-of-e.org.uk

Church hall accounts The rent from the hire of the hall is a significant part of the income in many parishes, and there is certainly great potential there which is not always fully realized. Does the PCC charge a realistic amount per hour for hall lettings? What charge is made by neighbouring churches? Does the PCC charge church organizations for the use of the hall? Does the PCC measure how much electricity and gas are used per hour in the hall for annual calculation purposes?

Churchwardens and the accounts When it is not possible to find a PCC treasurer, then it becomes the legal duty of the wardens to take over the work of the treasurer. *See* **CHURCH-WARDENS** on page 47, para. 10.

Collections and stewardship envelopes Two sidesmen or women should always be present when envelopes are opened and cash collections are counted. The amount contained in each envelope must always be written on the outside by the sidesmen to prove that the money has actually been paid to the Church by the donor (under Inland Revenue Rules). The total cash collections and the stewardship of money totals are entered in the Register of Services, and it is then signed by both sidesmen. All money should be kept in the church safe, and banked on Monday morning by the treasurer, or someone acting for the treasurer. A paying-in book is useful, and the source of the money should always be recorded.

Diocesan Board of Finance (DBF) The DBF recommends to the Diocesan Synod how much money needs to be raised from the parishes each year through the Parish Share (Common Fund). The income of the DBF comes from five main sources:

(a) Quota payments from the parishes. This is the DBF's main source of income.
(b) The Archbishops' Council's allocation, which is only payable to some dioceses, and which is mainly for clergy stipends (salaries).
(c) Income from any investments and trusts held by the DBF.
(d) Bequests from wills, and donations to the DBF. *See* **LAST WILL AND TESTAMENT** on pages 209–10.
(e) Fees from weddings, funerals, and any part-time chaplaincy work done by parish clergy. The vicar's 'fees' are either deducted from the stipend, or alternatively they are 'assigned' and paid to the DBF.

The main diocesan expenditure is the payment of the clergy, which is done through the Church Commissioners. The diocese is also responsible for the upkeep of all vicarages and other diocesan property, and for paying diocesan staff, the education team, Christian stewardship advisers, etc.

Donations – Gift Aid When someone makes a 'one-off' donation to the Church of £400 or more, the Church can reclaim the tax paid on this gift, under a scheme with the Inland Revenue called Gift Aid. This also applies to donations of £400 or more on a Gift Day.

Donations made by the PCC   Individual Christians are asked to give in a realistic and responsible way for God's work through the Church. Individuals expect the PCC in its turn to exercise the same stewardship principles when the PCC is giving money to missionary societies and the Church overseas. What percentage of its income did the PCC give away last year? It is useful to compare this figure each year with the previous years. In this way, the PCC can see how much progress has been made in this area.

Christians give for different reasons. Some give generously because they want to use the church building, and to keep it in good repair. Others give generously because they want to give money away through the Church to help in its worldwide mission.

The PCC should not be 'tight-fisted' when it comes to giving away money: 'Cast your bread on the waters, and it will return to you'. God is very bounteous and generous, and the PCC too should aim to be generous. Some PCCs give as much money to the Church overseas as they spend on themselves. Others give away any surplus balance at the end of each year (after paying the quota, all bills, and giving 10 per cent to the Church overseas).

The need for financial support is still urgent in many overseas churches. Priests will be withdrawn and the gospel will not be heard in some areas, unless money is sent from this country for some years to come. (There is also a need for people – ordained and lay – to work for the Church overseas. This need is particularly urgent in countries where Christians are heavily outnumbered by members of other faiths.)

Many PCCs give 10 per cent of their income to the Church overseas, as recommended by the General Synod. Others give more than 10 per cent. Some PCCs have their own problems, but the call from overseas is urgent. Does your PCC have the Church overseas high on its list of priorities when the annual budget is discussed?

One PCC treasurer was concerned about the production costs of a large and glossy magazine. Thus he wrote to all the missionary societies and asked:

(a)   What percentage of your total income was spent on administration last year?

(b)   How much was spent on publicity and magazines?

Finance

Food for thought

1. Does the PCC have an active overseas mission committee?
2. Does the parish use the diocesan intercessions list regularly?
3. Does the PCC give 10 per cent of its income to the Church overseas?

Easter offering   In former years, all collections on Easter Day were presented to the vicar to thank him for his work and ministry during the past year. Likewise, the collections at Pentecost (Whit-Sunday) were given to the assistant curates.

The Easter offering is no longer presented to the priest (in most parishes), because if it is, it is usually deducted from the stipend by the diocese. Parishioners now normally find other ways of thanking their priest.

Expenses of the clergy   Clergy cannot produce their best work if there is a constant worry about money. *See* **MOTIVATION AND MORALE** on pages 122–3. The more a priest works, the more it costs in 'parochial expenses'. In most parishes, the PCC treasurer repays in full all expenses which the priest incurs in carrying out normal parish work. The following are generally recognized as parochial expenses, accepted as such by the Inland Revenue and reimbursed by PCC treasurers:

(a)   Car road tax, insurance, depreciation, maintenance, repairs and servicing, petrol and oil.
(b)   Public transport expenses.
(c)   Telephone.
(d)   Purchase of modern office equipment.
(e)   Secretarial help, to free the priest for the work for which he was ordained. A secretary can help with typing/word processing, general administration, filing, registers, returns, minutes, weekly notice sheets, answer the phone and doorbell, and carry out routine tasks for which a priest is not needed.
(f)   Postage and stationery.
(g)   Maintenance of robes.
(h)   Payment of fees of locum tenens (visiting clergy) and their travelling expenses.
(i)   'In-service' training.
(j)   Hospitality. This includes meals for visiting preachers, committee meetings, parish party, numerous cups of tea and coffee during the year (and snacks for tramps?).

When a priest looks after more than one parish, it is helpful for the wardens or group council to work out what proportion each parish pays towards the whole (one method is to base this on the diocesan quota).

It is of more help financially to the priest if the PCC treasurer pays certain bills direct, rather than reimbursing the priest afterwards, e.g. the priest's secretary, and the telephone bill. Concerning the use of car and telephone, the proportion for private use is worked out and agreed with the Inland Revenue, e.g. one-fifth for private use.

Fabric fund   It is desirable that the finance or standing committee work out what percentage of the PCC's income should be transferred to the fabric fund each year, and recommend this to the PCC in the budget.

Faculties   All alterations, additions and removals regarding the church require legal authorization. When work is done without a faculty, the PCC may be ordered by a Consistory Court to pay the costs of putting the work back to its original state, and also reimbursing the legal costs. *See Faculties* under **BUILDINGS** on pages 25–6.

Fees   The Official Table of Parochial Fees (weddings, funerals, etc.) is usually displayed on the notice board and a copy kept in the vestry. It shows the current fees payable to the incumbent, to the PCC, (and the clerk or sexton, if there is one). The table does not include payments for 'extras' which are charged in addition to the statutory fees. These extras include charges for the director of music/organist, choir, organ fund, flowers, photographs/video (which sometimes incur double fees for the choir and director of music/organist), sweeping up of confetti, bell ringers and belfry fund, heating. These charges are set by the PCC and incumbent, and are agreed by the incumbent with the people concerned. The incumbent's fee always goes to the incumbent, even when an assistant curate takes the service. Many incumbents pay the fees direct to the Diocesan Board of Finance. If they are retained by the incumbent, they are deducted from his or her stipend. When a family want to bring their own organist to a wedding or funeral, the resident organist is entitled to the fees. (This is because in the organist's contract with the PCC, all 'fees' form part of his or her remuneration as church organist.)

The 'Gift Aid' scheme Every PCC has charitable status, and is thus exempt from paying income tax. Most of the people who give money to the Church will pay tax, and the tax which they pay on their giving can be reclaimed by the Church from the Inland Revenue. There is no advantage of giving under Gift Aid for those who pay insufficient or no tax. The scheme is of considerable help to the Church for basic rate or higher rate taxpayers.

Gift Aid for Regular Donors. Each donor must complete a Declaration, which must include the following: the donor's full name, address and post code; the name of the Church; a description of the donations; a statement that the donor wants the donations to be Gift Aid donations; a note explaining that the donor must pay income tax (or capital gains tax) equal to the tax deducted from his donations; and the date of the declaration.

Gift Aid for occasional worshippers and visitors, who are UK taxpayers. This can include people attending a wedding, baptism or funeral, and tourists. The Declaration used for regular donations could be altered appropriately, and printed on an envelope. The opportunity to receive more money is there, and it is important that every PCC makes full use of this opportunity.

The PCC must appoint a Gift Aid Scheme Officer (whatever title is chosen), and the appointment must be recorded in the PCC minutes. This person may be the Treasurer or Christian Stewardship Recorder etc. This officer must write to the Inland Revenue Charities (Repayments), Room 140, St John's House, Merton Road, Bootle, Merseyside, L69 9BB and ask for an Official Authorisation Form. It needs to be countersigned by another PCC official.

Keeping regular and accurate records is vital, and they should be able to show 'an audit trail, linking each banked donation to an identifiable donor, who has completed a Gift Aid declaration'. Declarations should be kept for as long as they are valid, or for 6 years, whichever is the longer. Other records, including envelopes with a Declaration printed on it, should be kept for 6 years from the date on which a claim is submitted. A Donor Register and Cash Book and Bank Statements should all be kept up to date and in good order.

In some Dioceses, reclaiming tax is done through the Diocesan Board of Finance. In others, it is done by the Gift Aid Scheme Officer. It is now much easier to make a claim for repayment of tax.

The Inland Revenue provide help lines as follows:

Web	www.inlandrevenue.gov.uk
Gift Aid	0151 472 6056 or 6038 or 6055
Payroll Giving	0151 472 6029 or 6053
Giving Shares	0151 472 6043 or 6046
Forms Order line	0151 472 6293 or 6294

The Inland Revenue makes 'audit visits' to parishes to check Gift Aid schemes from time to time. The auditor will write to the Gift Aid Scheme Officer, usually about six weeks before the visit. This is to check all the parish records dealing with Gift Aid, and particularly to check the 'audit trail from receipt to banking'. The auditor may suggest alterations or improvements for the keeping of records, and a report is sent about six weeks after the audit.

Insurance   The PCC is legally responsible for insuring the church buildings, the hall, the contents and those who use them. *See* **INSURANCE** on pages 97–9.

Interregnum   Special financial arrangements have to be made about PCC finances when there is a vacancy in the living (i.e. the priest has moved, died or resigned). *See The sequestration account* under **INTERREGNUM** on pages 102–3.

Shares   It is possible to make a gift to the Church of shares, unit or investment trust units, money, property or land. This can be done as a gift, or under the terms of a will. Neither the donor, nor the Church, has to pay any form of capital gains tax, inheritance tax or any other tax on such a gift.

Stewardship   *See* **Christian stewardship** on pages 29–36.

Treasurer of the PCC   The treasurer is elected by the PCC at the first meeting after the APCM from among its membership. If this is not possible, someone may be co-opted to full membership of the PCC. If no one is willing to take over the treasurer's job, then it is the legal responsibility of the churchwardens jointly to discharge the office of treasurer. No payment can be made for the work done by the treasurer.

Obviously the treasurer is a prime candidate for election to the standing committee each year. The treasurer's job is to look after the money, to report to the PCC on the financial situation, and to advise the PCC on the financial implications of any decision it is about to make. When the treasurer gives advice, not only the liabilities and resources must be taken into account but also the order of priority which the PCC attaches to the expenditure of its money.

It is wise to make as many payments as possible by cheque. This protects the treasurer, and it ensures that a record is kept of all transactions. All petty cash payments should be recorded, and vouchers and receipts kept safely.

Some parishes have a team of treasurers, or an assistant treasurer. Whatever the situation, it is helpful if a new treasurer and the existing treasurer can work together (if possible for a whole year?) before the handover.

The treasurer is responsible for paying the organist, choirmaster, choir, cleaner, verger, hall caretaker, the parish/vicar's secretary, and the expenses of the vicar and assistant curates.

Prompt payment of the Parish Share (Common Fund) via a monthly standing order with the bank is to be highly recommended. Long discussions and grumbles about the quota are not helpful. Most deaneries and dioceses have by now produced a system which is as fair as possible for every parish. The money has to be found – otherwise the Church in the whole diocese would simply grind to a halt. It is wrong (and un-Christian?) to withhold payment of the Parish Share until the very end of the financial year. The diocese then has to borrow money, at commercial rates of interest, and this causes an increase in the quota for every parish in the future. (Some dioceses publish each year a list of parishes which pay late – or do not pay in full – in the diocesan accounts.)

Proper records should be kept of all financial transactions, and the books kept up to date and checked with the monthly bank statement.

Obviously, it is not good stewardship to keep too much money in the current account. *See* entry about CBF deposit and other accounts on page 74.

Bills should always be paid promptly. It gives the church a bad name if they are settled late.

FLAG The proper flag to be flown on a church is the St George's cross, with the arms of the see in the first quarter. (Earl Marshal's regulation 1938.)

FLOWERS IN CHURCH   A church is an ideal place for flower arrangements and in recent years there has been an enormous growth of interest in this subject. Happily the Church has gained from this and the standard of floral decoration in many churches is quite stunning. Often, only the simplest and humblest things are needed. Imagination is cheaper than hothouse flowers.

A flower guild or church flower club can be helpful, even if it meets only once a year to watch a demonstration. Those who belong are, of course, asked to do one flower arrangement in church during the year, and if possible to help at festivals. Outsiders can be asked to help at festivals, and perhaps brought on to the flower rota.

People often like to give flowers on the Sunday nearest to the anniversary of the death of a loved one. They can be invited to do this through a magazine (distributed to every house in the parish?).

If flowers are kept in the church throughout the week the water will need checking, as dead flowers give the impression of an uncaring church. If the church is locked during the week, the flowers can be sent out while still fresh on Monday morning to someone who is ill or housebound. A notebook for names, addresses and dates will be required for this purpose. A rota of four people (one for the first Monday, another for the second, etc.) can prepare and deliver the flowers, together with a card 'With best wishes from St Peter's Church', and signed by the vicar.

There are no flowers in church in Lent and Advent, as these are penitential seasons of preparation for Easter and Christmas. Also flowers are very costly during those periods.

Church buildings are large, and flower arrangements need to be bold and large. Plenty of long stalks and green foliage can be effective. Proportions need to look right from a distance, as well as close at hand. A flower stand at the side of the altar is better than thin vases on the altar. A large flat container is most suitable for the flower stand, with a deep layer of sand, flower arranging 'oasis', or crumpled wire mesh, to keep the flowers in position.

As a general suggestion, deeper and darker coloured flowers are better in the centre with the softer colours around the edges of the arrangement. The most suitable colours are red, orange and yellow, but others can be used with great effect.

Flowers and candles look good together. Two ideas – a paschal candle (in the sanctuary from Easter Eve until Ascension – the

Great Forty Days) can be effectively decorated with flowers, and secondly, the four Advent candles.

The author is not skilled at flower arranging, and recommends more reliable sources, such as *Flowers in Church* by Jean Taylor (Mowbray).

Food for thought

1. Could more fringe people be included on your flower rota (and hence be slowly drawn into your church)?
2. When did your church last have a flower festival?

FRIENDSHIP How often is Christianity accepted or rejected by watching and hearing the behaviour and manner of a professed Christian? '*Oh*, I'm not going to church. I can't stand the vicar.' Or 'How that group of tea makers argue and squabble! I'm keeping out of their way.' This can be an absolute barrier, and many people never look beyond, for Christ. This is our fault and our tragedy.

The friendliness of church members to each other and to outsiders is vital. A friendly contact built up at general times can then be expanded and deepened in a time of need, such as illness, trouble or bereavement.

New friendship is valuable in itself for the people concerned, and a friendly church community has a powerful influence to attract outsiders.

FUNERALS *See* **BEREAVEMENT** on pages 13–14.

GENERAL SYNOD *See* **SYNODS OF THE CHURCH** on pages 202–4.

GROUP COUNCIL A council with lay representatives and clergy from all the PCCs in the group of parishes, who consult together on matters of common concern. Much work can be co-ordinated and things can be done together which in the past have been done separately by the individual parishes.

GROUP AND TEAM MINISTRIES (*See also* **PASTORAL REORGANIZATION** on pages 153–4.) A team ministry is usually more formally defined in legal terms, while a group ministry is more open-ended and informal. What are the differences between groups and teams?

In a team ministry, one or more parishes form a single benefice or unit. It has a team rector, and other clergy who are called team vicars (usually two or more). The team vicars normally have a five- or seven-year leasehold agreement, and they work under the leadership of the team rector.

In a group ministry, each parish has its own incumbent and its own separate legal existence, but the clergy and lay people work together and co-operate in all the parishes of the group. The clergy of the group are entitled to attend PCC meetings and the annual meetings of all parishes within the group.

Whether a team or a group, great benefits can undoubtedly be found when clergy work together. What are these benefits? The clergy worshipping together during the week is helpful to the clergy themselves and to the laity, and it also provides a spiritual base or power-house for the area. (The strength and enthusiasm of the early Church perhaps came partly from their united daily worship, and also some of the ideals of the monasteries come to mind.)

No priest working in isolation can be good at all aspects of parochial ministry. There can be a division of labour and skills when clergy work together, and this is a benefit to the parishes and to the individual concerned. One magazine for all the parishes is another important benefit, particularly if it is delivered free to every home in the area.

Working together provides support and encouragement for the clergy, and an opportunity for studying the Scriptures and theology together. The clergy can find fellowship in this way, and parish problems (and perhaps personal problems?) can be shared and discussed. It is much easier to provide 'cover' for services for holiday periods and illness.

Curates, non-stipendiary priests, readers and licensed lay workers can all share in the corporate ministry, together with the churchwardens and lay people from the different parishes. Roman Catholic clergy often work together, and over the years the results have been a steady advance for the Roman Catholic faith. Perhaps we are learning from their experience?

What then are the problems? Many of the difficulties can be summed up in two words – human nature. Another difficulty can arise if a small number of priests are asked to look after too large (and increasing) a number of churches. In that situation, unless there is an increase in the number of non-stipendiary priests, the question has to be asked – should any of the churches in the area be closed?

It is easier for the clergy if there is only one PCC. However, it is far better if each parish has its own PCC and its own accounts (and perhaps with a lay chairman in some situations?). The reason for retaining PCCs is simple – there is a strong loyalty to the local parish church, but not so strong towards the 'main' church some four or eight miles away. The parish is the bedrock of our pastoral and missionary work, even in a group or team situation. However, policy and major decisions have to be made by the group committee or group council at the centre, with lay representatives from each parish putting forward the views of their own PCC.

Unless there is a considerable increase in the number of ordination candidates for the full-time ministry, it seems probable that there will be an increase in the number of large pastoral units such as teams and groups (and with an increase in non-stipendiary priests helping to work the system?). Whatever the details of the system, exciting possibilities exist for teams and groups, with much lay involvement, and this could well be one of the main areas of growth and advance for the Christian faith.

This *ABC* does not cover all the rules relating to group ministries and team ministries, and the reader is advised to consult the Synodical Government Rules for further details.

GROUPS – DISCUSSION GROUPS AND THE PCC The Church has been involved in groups ever since Jesus called twelve men to follow him. Groups exist to carry out specific tasks and also to meet certain needs. Meeting as a group can create problems and personality clashes but it can also release energy for good, and give support and encouragement.

Those involved in leading groups are well advised to learn fully about the subject. Most diocesan education teams run courses, and may even be able to offer help in the parish. Here are some basic thoughts.

Well in advance of setting up groups, certain questions need to be asked. Will an existing group – or groups – be used? If not, how will the groups be formed, and by whom?

Careful selection and training of leaders is essential. How many leaders will be needed? Who will train them? How much time is needed for training?

If the group is ongoing, what will be required to monitor its progress? At what stage will it have outlived its usefulness?

For the smooth running of any group – including a PCC – there are three subjects which require careful attention.

1. *The task of the group* When people meet together for a

specific purpose, the task is obviously clear. But in some circumstances, it is not clear – such as for a particular item of the PCC agenda. It is vital that people understand the task, and that all agree with it.

2. *The needs of individuals* Some people are anxious, embarrassed or afraid to speak in a group situation, in case they appear foolish. For this reason, they sit and listen, while others have a field day and say far too much! A good leader can help people to feel at ease, and the members of the group can help to do the same. The individuals who make up a group often have questions for which they are subconsciously searching for answers. These questions may include such thoughts as – How safe do I feel in this group? How close will I be able to get to others in it? How important am I? Who is the most important person here? What is actually going on here? Where do I fit into this situation? Who am I?

The individual 'needs' of each person do in fact play a large part in determining how well the meeting will go. Thus it is important that people should feel at ease, and a short time at the beginning for people to relax and have a chat is time well spent.

3. *Maintaining the life of the group* People come together, but what keeps them there? Is it enough to say that they are there to do God's work, and hope that this will keep them together? More than this is needed, and people's efforts need harmonizing, encouraging, correcting and guiding. The situation in a group needs careful and constant observation. The situation reached sometimes needs to be clarified, and a consensus of opinion needs testing from time to time.

The task of the group, the needs of the individuals, and the maintenance of the life of the group are not three separate compartments. Each area overlaps the other two, and a breakdown in any one will affect the working of the group and prevent the task being carried out effectively. *See* **MOTIVATION AND MORALE** on pages 122–3.

GROWTH Some people feel that going to church is what Christianity is all about, while others try to console themselves that if they are actively doing things for the church, this is all that is required of them. But unless each Christian thinks in terms of bringing others to a knowledge and love of Christ, then they are not fulfilling the command of our Lord.

Growth

Growth of the local church starts with the spiritual awakening and renewal of individual PCC members. Renewal is not external but internal. It must be growth in the likeness of our Lord, and this involves individuals (and the PCC as a whole?) having a look at their own prayer life, and their openness to the Holy Spirit. Perhaps there is something in ourselves which needs to be put right first, before growth can take place. But it is not enough to have a deeper spirituality. Knowledge is also needed, because you cannot love a person unless you know that person. There is no growth without spiritual renewal in the lives of individuals, and all growth comes from God.

Our Lord's parables contain many thoughts about growth: the vine, the barren fig tree, the seed growing secretly, the mustard seed, the wheat and the tares, the sower, to name but a few.

Stages of planning for growth   A basic weakness of the Church is that there is too much talking, and not enough praying, leading to action. The PCC can approach the subject of growth in different ways, e.g. a day given to the subject, and involving the whole congregation; or two or three evening sessions, again with the members of the congregation present. Here are some thoughts which may be useful:

1. How is the Holy Spirit working in the parish, and in what ways can the members of the church share in this work?
2. What are two of the main problems which hinder growth in the local church? (Do not include buildings and money problems.)
3. How can a process of growth be set in motion in the parish?
4. How is the PCC organized for growth?
5. How do PCC members relate to each other? And how does this help or hinder the growth of the church?
6. Are the plans for growth being made in a spirit of prayer, and with an openness to the workings of the Holy Spirit, without whom no growth is possible?

Reasons for failure to grow   Would the PCC feel that any of the following things prevent growth in the parish?

1. The attitude that 'nothing changes here – we've always done things this way before'. A failure to move with the Holy Spirit?
2. The PCC is too busy maintaining buildings and organizations.

Discussion about growth is perhaps not welcome by PCC members?

3. 'We have tried many projects before, and they have made little difference.' (Why?)

4. The age-old conflict between good and evil?

GUEST SERVICES   Members of the congregation are asked to invite one family to a special guest service. A verbal invitation and explanation is best, and this can be supplemented with a written invitation. How true is the saying, 'The medium is the message'?

It is a good idea to have something after the service, where the guests can meet the members of the congregation – e.g. coffee, or sherry – or a meal, e.g. harvest lunch, or a Christmas lunch. Perhaps each PCC member could undertake to invite two families to the guest service.

Could these invitations be done in a systematic way? Prayer for the families concerned is important, not simply at the time of the guest service, but on a regular long-term basis over the years.

GUILD OF ST BARNABAS   It was founded in 1876, and it is mainly a 'postal' fellowship of prayer for nurses and members of the caring professions. Its aim is to encourage the development of the spiritual life of members who are trying to witness to their Christian faith in their work.

Details: Mrs Mary Morrow, Organizing Secretary, 16 Copperwood, Ashford, Kent, TN24 8PZ. Tel: 01233 635334.

GUILD OF ST RAPHAEL   The Guild was founded in 1915 to restore the ministry of healing in the Church. Members of the Guild undertake to pray each day as a regular intercession for all who suffer in mind or body. Members are also asked to pray at each Eucharist for God's blessing on the work of the Guild.

To pray for the sick and the dying is an important part of the work of the whole church in every parish. To have a branch of the Guild of St Raphael in the parish can be a great help in this work.

The members usually gather together in church (in the Lady Chapel) once a month. Before the Guild Office (short service), a brief meeting is held to sort out any changes on the sick list. Each member undertakes to pray for certain people who are sick. Then the Guild Office is said and the sick are prayed for by name. Sometimes Evensong is said before the Guild Office. The Guild Office can, of course, be taken by a lay person.

Guild of St Raphael

The Guild publishes a quarterly magazine, available to all members of the Guild.

Details: Ms. Jo Parry, 2 Green Lane, Tuebrook, Liverpool L13 7EA. Tel & Fax: 0151–228 3193. Email: straphael@ enterprise.net

HEALING   There is new interest in the healing ministry of the Church and, of course, all healing comes from God. Sometimes individuals and groups are channels used by God in the healing process, and prayer and the sacraments of the Church can have a powerful effect. Is it possible that human channels can sometimes be blocked through sin, or neglect of daily prayer?

St James 5.13–15 describes anointing the sick with oil. On Maundy Thursday, the bishop blesses three oils used for anointing. The three oils are (1) for Baptism, (2) for Confirmation and (3) for the sick.

HOLIDAY CLUB   Children are often at a loose end during holidays, especially in summer. Here is an opportunity for the church to provide a holiday club each day for a week or fortnight. Parents and others can work together to plan programmes, rotas and menus. Many things are possible, including drama, music, and painting. Also a variety of games, expeditions, picnics, hikes, competitions, concerts and a short daily act of worship.

What about a 'holiday at home for the elderly' – with outings and eating together for a week?

HOLIDAYS   Holidays are part of God's plan for mankind. When you are away from home on a Sunday, try to attend the nearest parish church. We don't need holidays away from God! (You may come home with new ideas.)

HOLY COMMUNION   It is said that the Church of England has 'found religion in its old age' through the spread of the Parish Communion movement in the twentieth century. A vast amount of literature exists on Holy Communion – or whatever name you use for this special service. The Mass comes from the Latin 'Ite missa est', which means 'You are sent out', i.e. to do God's work in the world. The Eucharist means the thanksgiving. The Lord's Supper reminds us of the meal in the upper room. The word Communion means sharing. Christians share together in the life of Christ because of their new birth at Holy Baptism.

The Eucharist is a celebration – not in any rowdy sense – but a celebration of joy and thanksgiving. The Church lives and grows through the celebration of the Eucharist, done in response to our Lord's invitation and command, 'Do this in remembrance of me'.

Participation in the Eucharist   Much more is required of PCC members and the congregation than to be mere spectators of something done for them by the priest and the choir. It involves preparation by everyone before the service. It involves putting a special effort into singing, and concentration during the sermon, prayers and readings. 'You shall love the Lord your God with all your heart, and mind and soul and strength.' When everyone takes part in a full and active way, then the worship is enriched and the congregation grows in worship. People learn to co-operate with the grace of God, and this gives a feeling of life and love, of joy and fellowship, as well as awe and wonder. These things can be noticed and felt by visitors and occasional worshippers, and they have a powerful effect in drawing people into the life of the Church.

Lay involvement in leading the worship   Certain parts of the service can only be taken by a duly ordained priest. However, the priest may invite suitable people to lead other parts of the service. Providing the selection is done carefully, and there is proper preparation, then the worship can be greatly enriched by lay participation. People participate in worship in a number of ways, by praying and singing and by sharing and receiving the precious gift of our Lord himself in the consecrated bread and wine, listening carefully, shared silence, exchanging greetings at the peace, and sometimes by movement. Worship lives in and through the members of the Church, and in their fellowship and relationship with each other and with God.

Reading a lesson   First, some basic thoughts on preparation.

1. Read it until you have a good understanding of its meaning. The congregation can tell very quickly whether or not you have prepared the passage. This is God's work, and you should offer only of your best to God.
2. Work out what is the common theme between the Old Testament and the New Testament readings and the gospel.
3. Work out which words to stress, and where to pause.

Remember that the verb is always an important word in every sentence.

4. Beware of dropping your voice in the middle of the reading, so that people have extreme difficulty in hearing. Try to listen to your own voice, and work out if people can hear you. It is far better to be too loud, than for people to miss much of what you are reading. It would be wrong to ask any reader to bellow, but reading does require much extra effort and volume in a large building. The words have to be pushed out and projected with force and firmness, in order for them to travel.

5. Practise your delivery and make sure that everyone in the church can hear each word you speak. Aim your voice slightly above the congregation, at an imaginary deaf person on the back seat. Never hold your head low when reading, as the words will be lost in the book. Make sure your voice comes out slowly and distinctly, without anything coming between you and the congregation. Sound is easily absorbed by a congregation. Extra effort is always needed in these circumstances. Deep breathing and filling the lungs before reading is helpful. Careful preparation is all wasted unless the people can actually hear what you are saying.

6. When using a microphone, practice is vital. The reader always has to listen to the sound of his or her voice coming through the loudspeakers. Are you too near or too far away from the microphone? Most microphones are good at picking up a voice, but it is always wise to speak towards them.

7. When you have 'competition' from a baby or a road-digger outside, speak more loudly to compensate for it, so that people can still hear each word you say.

8. Do not read in a dull and stodgy way. Make the reading come alive.

9. Come out and be ready to read as soon as the congregation has settled down quietly. Silent pauses are good, but not when waiting for the reader to start reading.

General thoughts about reading a lesson The Eucharist is divided into two main parts – the Ministry of the Word, and the Ministry of the Sacrament. The reading of the Scriptures is the basis of the Ministry of the Word, and the congregation is fed from the table of God's living word by the reading of the Scriptures. This table needs very careful preparation by the reader.

Most people can read the words printed on the page. But much more is involved than simply reading the words in front of you. Lesson reading is an art, and the secret is to understand the spiritual meaning of the passage before you come out in front of the congregation to read.

No one should accept an invitation to read, unless he or she is willing to commit themselves to prepare it thoroughly. It is an awesome responsibility, because no less than God himself is speaking to the congregation through the words which are being read out. The reader will perhaps share the thoughts of Patrick Brontë, rector of Haworth, who felt 'power and humility when you fill the whole place with the sound of God's own voice'.

Here is a prayer to use silently before you start reading:

Cleanse me, O Lord, from all my sins.
Send your Holy Spirit,
and help me worthily to proclaim your holy Word
to all who are here today, through Jesus Christ our Lord. Amen.

In some parishes, those who are reading on the next Sunday meet (with the priest) and share thoughts and insights about the collect and three readings. This can be a great help to the priest to start his thoughts for his next sermon, and it can be a great help to those who are reading to start their preparation early. If this is not possible, each reader should do his or her preparation carefully and thoroughly by themselves. Then the Word can be proclaimed with authority on Sunday.

Much is expected from all who read, and of course it is a great privilege to read from the Sacred Scriptures in this way.

A prayer for use by PCC members and others for the person who is about to read:

Heavenly Father,
you make yourself known to us in the Scriptures:
give understanding and guidance to N (or this person)
and open all our hearts to receive your living Word. Amen.

Reading at special services This is an opportunity to invite outside or fringe members, instead of using regular church members. It is also a good way of finding new readers.

Prayers and intercessions Another ideal place for lay participation. The priest may decide to write the prayers himself.

Prayers should be addressed directly to God, and the phrase 'let us pray for' should not be used in each section. Intercessions are not a time for a spiritual current affairs chat with God, nor an opportunity to tell God what you think is the solution to the problem. A simple phrase is all that is needed – such as 'We pray for Africa'. This can be followed by silence.

One lay person can lead the prayers. Alternatively, a different person can read each section of the prayers. Prayers should not be too long. The temptation to give the congregation its 'money's worth' with unnecessary verbiage should be avoided at all costs. A short time of silence can be most effective.

Altar servers Young boys or girls, or adults, can be of great help to the priest during the service. In addition, using the young people in this way helps to keep them in church during a difficult period of their lives. *See* **SERVERS** on pages 180–1.

Administration of the chalice Lay people can be duly authorized by the Bishop, on the recommendation of the priest, and with the agreement of the PCC, to administer the chalice. Authorization usually has to be renewed every three years.

Offertory procession There is symbolic meaning in carrying the bread and wine in procession to the altar. Man's work is symbolized in the making of the bread, and his leisure activities in the wine, and these are offered to God. The offertory reminds us of our dependence on God – 'All things come from thee, O Lord, and of thine own do we give thee.'

Dignity is added to the procession if it is led by the crucifer and two processional candles – yet another way of involving young people.

Silence in worship The Quakers took the use of silence with them when they left the Church. Shared silence returned to liturgical worship with the Alternative Service Book. Silence is much more than absence of noise, and in moderate use, it helps us to be more aware of God's presence.

Midnight services These are popular in many parishes, but there can be problems. If most of the regular worshippers attend the midnight service, there can be a thin congregation to welcome the occasional worshippers who usually flock into church on Christmas morning. The young and the elderly cannot get to the midnight service. One solution is to encourage people to try to come to the main Christmas day service, even if they have already been to the midnight service.

The Peace This is a very ancient and meaningful sign, mentioned by St Paul. It is easy to say that you 'love your neighbour as yourself', but actually to turn to your neighbour during the service and shake hands reminds us of the saying, 'Actions speak louder than words'. The Peace is a positive way in which Christians can show that they do mean what they say in words.

The Peace of the Lord be always with you. This is a prayer that Christ himself will be with your neighbour. It is also a sign of friendship and Christian love. It is a sign of unity in Christ, and an expression of the love that exists amongst God's people. The Peace often has a powerful effect on occasional worshippers and visitors, and helps to draw them into the congregation.

The time of the early services Is 8 a.m. the best time for the early service? Would more people be involved if it were held at 9 a.m., and the main service at 10.30 a.m.? If Evensong is not flourishing, what about an occasional evening Communion service? Would Sunday evening be a good time to hold (monthly?) discussions after a shortened service?

Questions for discussion

1. How are new adult members integrated into the congregation? How much is left to chance as to whether or not they pick up the faith ('some seed fell on the stony path and died . . .')? Can the PCC help in any way?
2. How can the congregation be helped to grow in faith and love as a worshipping community?
3. Is it in any way necessary for the congregation to be 'converted' again and again (a term used by the Roman Catholics)?

HOME Something of a person's personality is reflected in their home. A good and stable home life is a great blessing and strength to the individual and also to the Church. Some people may be willing and able to lend their home to the Church occasionally, for a discussion or prayer group, a meeting or a social evening. A good home can be a powerful tool for evangelism.

Food for thought

1. Could you think of your home as an outpost for mission in the parish?
2. Has your home been blessed by a priest?

HOME COMMUNION Parishioners usually receive Communion every Sunday in church in most parishes. When they can no longer come to church through age or illness, it is right that they should keep in communion with Christ and the Church by receiving Communion at their home.

With the large (and growing) numbers involved, the priest is not able to conduct the whole service at each home. The usual method is to take bread and wine which have been consecrated in a service in church.

It is not wise for a priest to spend too much time administering Communion to the elderly. This is an area where lay people can exercise a valuable ministry after the main Sunday service – or during the week. Careful training is needed, and the appropriate written permission of the bishop. Lay involvement in this way can free the priest for mission and other tasks.

Those who receive Communion at home need to think about their own preparation. The aim of the visit is to receive the sacrament of Holy Communion. It is good practice not to chat before the service. Suggestions for preparation: read the Scripture readings for the day, and a psalm. Pray for the person who is bringing the sacrament; for the local church; for all who receive Communion at home; for the priest and bishop; and, of course, relatives, friends and neighbours. Work out those things for which you will ask for God's forgiveness. (The priest is always available to hear a private confession if this is requested.)

Christians who can no longer go to church can still play an active part in the mission of the Church through their regular prayers. A community and fellowship of prayer can be provided during the week in this way, and it is vital for the mission of the Church. A prayer book, written by the author, may be helpful for people who can no longer come to church: *Daily with God* (Canterbury Press, Norwich).

HOSPITAL VISITING Lay people can, after some basic training, supplement the work of the priest by visiting parishioners in hospital, and paying a follow-up visit after they are discharged. This is never instead of the priest, but in addition to the priest's visit.

One difficulty can be how to find out when parishioners are in hospital. Efficient street wardens can often pass on information in this connection.

Pray in church for those who are being visited. (*See* **GUILD OF ST RAPHAEL** on pages 89–90.)

Leave a parish magazine and a parish card with some prayers etc. when you visit a patient.

HOSPITALITY St Paul wrote: 'Be hospitable to one another.' His words are relevant today. To invite two or three people from church for a meal in your home is an act of Christian friendship, in addition to sharing the Body and Blood of Christ at the Eucharist. Hospitality was common practice in the early Church, and it is valuable (and enjoyable) today. It also has mission potential in this post Christian era. 'The way to a man's heart is through his stomach' and it might just possibly be a way to get near to his soul.

With the local church as host, there are many opportunities to invite outsiders and fringe members into a warm and friendly meal in the church community (*See* also **CATERING** page 27).

HOUSING ASSOCIATIONS (*See* **CHURCH HOUSING TRUST** on page 38.) Land not required in the future for a new hall, car park, curate's house or vicarage could be used for houses or flats for elderly or homeless people. A Housing Association can be formed by the PCC, or by the Deanery Synod, or by the local Council of Churches. Generous government grants are available to help to build and maintain these homes. Land can be leased (rather than sold) to the newly formed Housing Association.

The PCC is advised to contact the archdeacon at the initial stage, and before any money is spent on architect's fees. Selling or leasing the land to form a Housing Association is usually better than selling or leasing it to a local builder.

INSURANCE The PCC is responsible for providing insurance cover for all aspects of church life and church buildings. The Ecclesiastical Insurance Group (EIG) specializes in all forms of church insurance. Founded for this purpose, the company gives back profits to the dioceses, in proportion to the amount of business done with each diocese. EIG have a team of Insurance Consultant and Surveyors whose services are available without fee or obligation to advise on appropriate insurance for PCCs.

Insurance

The EIG surveyor visits the parish and provides a valuation figure for insurance purposes. It represents what the EIG regard as the minimum amount for which the building should be insured, as per the basis of cover shown below:

Buildings The figure for buildings represents an assessment of the approximate cost, using modern techniques and materials for:

(a) restoring or repairing the buildings to the extent described in the EIG's leaflet entitled 'Insurance Valuation for Churches' (ask EIG for a copy), or

(b) replacing the building with a modern equivalent.

In either case, the maximum liabilty of the Company will not exceed the sum insured. The cost of replacing the building in its present form, using original identical materials, could be a much greater. Therefore, if insurance cover is required on this basis, specialist advice can be obtained regarding the appropriate sums to be insured.

Contents Figures for contents have been assessed on the basis of typical costs for modern replacements.

As the cost of restoring historic buildings continues to rise, it is vital for the insurance to keep pace with these changes. Under the Parishguard policy the fire sums insurance is automatically adjusted monthly in line with the appropriate price index.

(In some diocese, it may be possible to arrange alternative levels of cover, without any penalty for under-insurance. Whilst these levels of cover may be available, the final decision rests with the PCC after consulting the Archdeacon.)

Property Damage Section Cover includes fire, lightning, explosion, earthquake, aircraft, impact, storm, flood, riot and malicious damage, theft, accidental glass breakage and other accidental damage etc, some automatic extension apply ie, raffle prizes and donated prizes, and Minor Buildings Works cover (subject to completion of questionnaire) for certain contracts up to £50,000.

Consequential Loss If serious damage occurs to the property by one of the risks insured under the Property Damage section, you may not be able to use your premises or hire out the property to other organisations. This section provides cover for loss of income and additional expenditure to cover costs.

Employers Liability Provides legal liability for accidents or illness of employees sustained in the course of their employment. This type of cover is a legal requirement and a certificate confirming it should be displayed on the Church notice board.

Public Liability Every parish *must* have adequate Public Liability insurance. With court awards reaching record levels, inadequate insurance can have disastrous financial consequences for a parish.

Other sections Loss of Money, Theft by Church Officials, Personal Accident and Legal Expenses.

Private Insurance The EIG provides insurance for private houses, cars, weddings, travel and life insurance. It is a friendly company, and quotations are given without obligation or charge. Details:

- By post: Beaufort House, Brunswick Road, Gloucester, GL1 1JZ
- By phone: 0845 777 33 22
- By email: Churches@eigmail.com

Food for thought
The majority of church fires are caused by electrical faults – particularly in the organ. Is your electricity supply for the organ on an independent system? Is it switched off at the mains every time after use? How safe is your church from someone deliberately trying to set it on fire?

The police are willing to help with the prevention of theft and vandalism. Has the local crime prevention officer inspected church property and reported to the PCC?

INTEGRITY What is absolute integrity?

INTERREGNUM (See **CHURCHWARDEN** on pages 46–7, para. 9) The interregnum is the period between the departure of the outgoing vicar and the institution and induction of the new one. Sequestrators are appointed by the Bishop, and they usually include the two churchwardens. The system varies, however, from diocese to diocese. The diocesan secretary, and sometimes the rural dean, are often appointed as sequestrators. Their task is to deal with the income of the 'living' – not to be confused with the income of the PCC. (*See **The sequestration account** on* pages 102–3). They are also responsible for maintaining the life and worship of the Church, and to look after all Church property during the interregnum, including the vicarage. The PCC will want to be certain that everything is being done that should be done in the parish.

The Rural Dean may call a meeting of the Churchwardens and the outgoing vicar to plan the arrangements for the interregnum. Careful preparation before the vicar leaves the parish is the best way of ensuring a smooth interregnum.

Length of interregnum Some PCCs expect the new vicar to arrive within days of the previous one leaving the parish. In practice, this does not happen, and an interregnum is often a matter of months rather than weeks.

Diocesan Pastoral Committee In these days of rapid change, the Diocesan Pastoral Committee usually considers the future of every parish whenever a vacancy occurs. They consider such questions as, What is the geographical position of the parish in relation to the centres of population in the deanery? Is the parish a financially viable unit – or does it depend heavily on the support of other parishes (through the Common Fund)? Does the PCC repay the expenses of office of the priest? Is the quota paid in full each year? Does the PCC have a good record in supporting the Church overseas? What is the condition of the church building, the hall and the vicarage?

Church services No priest can conduct a service unless he or she has the bishop's licence, or permission to officiate. The services may be reduced to one per Sunday and one during the week, and the times may have to be altered.

Provision has to be made for funerals, baptisms, weddings, calling of banns, home communions, and the pastoral care of the sick and elderly. Visits will have to be done for some of these services (by one of the churchwardens?). Where Holy Communion is 'reserved' in the church for use with the sick, then arrangements have to be made for its proper care.

PCC meetings and the Annual Meeting When a curate is appointed as minister in charge during the interregnum, he takes the chair at meetings. Otherwise, the vice-chairman of the PCC is the chairman.

The churchwardens should make sure that no changes are

made during the interregnum. Many bishops write to the churchwardens to this effect.

The Diocesan Handbook and Canon Law Every parish has a loose-leaf folder with diocesan instructions on various matters, and a copy of Canon Law. These belong to the parish, and should be left with the other papers and documents for the incoming vicar. It is helpful for the sequestrators and the incoming priest if there is an extra page in the folder with details of the house, drainage, electrical or plumbing systems and their oddities and idiosyncrasies.

The congregation It frequently happens that numbers drop off during an interregnum, and it is always hard work to get them back again. The best course is for the PCC to keep a close eye on the situation and see what action can be taken when necessary. The curate and the non-stipendiary priest, if there is one, cannot be expected to take over the work load of the outgoing vicar.

Care of the vicarage There may be diocesan instructions on this, but here are some suggestions:

1. The churchwardens – or someone else by arrangement – should check that all is well in the house each day.
2. If squatters occupy the house, immediately notify the archdeacon, the rural dean and the police. To prevent such occupation and to prevent vandalism, it may be possible to find someone willing to live in the vicarage during the interregnum – but the written permission of the archdeacon must always be obtained by the sequestrators.
3. If any immediate repair work is needed, it must be reported to the archdeacon as soon as possible.
4. The house should be properly ventilated, and the heating system put on for regular periods during winter months.
5. Security needs special attention. The risk of vandalism can be lessened by the following (assuming the locks and catches are working properly and are duly fastened):

     one or more lights on an automatic timing switch,
     curtains hung in all windows,
     grass and hedges cut regularly,
     mail, milk bottles and newspapers removed from the door.

6. The telephone should not be disconnected. The rental charge is paid from the sequestration account.

7. When a priest is offered the living, he (or she) visits the parish and vicarage. Before accepting the living, the priest will again inspect the house with the archdeacon, rural dean and churchwardens to discuss what repairs, alterations and decorations will be done before the priest moves into the house. The PCC will no doubt be asked to pay the cost, and a healthy vicarage improvement fund is useful for such occasions. Hopefully, the smell of paint will have vanished and the house will have been spring-cleaned days (not hours) before the furniture van arrives at the vicarage.

8. Any unofficial tenants living in the vicarage must leave on or before the day of departure of the vicar. The house is the responsibility of the sequestrators in all respects during the interregnum.

9. When a priest dies in office, the widow or widower is entitled to stay on in the vicarage for at least three months. The Pensions Board normally find accommodation for the family. The priest has given loving pastoral care to so many in the parish, and now it is the vicar's spouse who will need love and care and help and prayer.

The sequestration account   The income from the benefice (the priest's income) is not the same as the income of the PCC. The sequestrators are responsible for dealing with the income of the benefice (but not the fixed annuity, which was formerly endowment and glebe income, nor the additional money from the diocese). The sequestrators income comes from the 'incumbents' share of the fees for marriages, burials and other fees. The current fees are laid down in the Table of Ecclesiastical Fees, which is revised each year, and is usually found on the church notice board. These fees are usually insufficient to cover all expenses, and the deficit is repaid by the diocese.

A new bank account must always be opened, and the money kept completely separate from the PCC accounts. Thus it can be properly accounted for on the sequestration account balance sheet. Two people sign the cheques, and quite often the rural dean may be one of those who sign. A loan from the PCC to the sequestration account is useful to start the account, and it is repaid when the account is closed. Any rent from letting the vicarage garage is paid into the sequestration account.

Fees and expenses are paid from this account to all visiting clergy. Never ask 'What do we owe you?' Find out the current diocesan rate for fees and travelling expenses, and hand over the money or cheque in an envelope after the service.

The cost of heating the vicarage (or part of it – check diocesan regulations about this) is paid from this account. A balance sheet has to be prepared at the end of the interregnum, after all expenses have been paid. It is then duly signed by the two (or three) sequestrators, and certified by the bishop or his representative. The bank account is then closed.

Appointing a new priest   The person who appoints the new priest is called the patron. (When the Crown, the Duchy of Lancaster or Cornwall, or the Lord Chancellor is the patron, these rules do not apply. Nor do they apply in the case of a team vicar.) When a new parish ('Benefice') is created under the Pastoral Measure, e.g. by joining two or more parishes, the Pastoral Scheme provides the appropriate arrangements for patronage. (The PCC is always involved in any changes in respect of Patronage.)

Various procedures and consultations between the bishop, the patron and the PCC have to take place by law, which are laid down in the Patronage (Benefices) Measure 1986 (obtainable from HMSO – its contents are summarised below). Where the patron is an individual, he or she has to make a written declaration that he is an actual communicant member of the Church of England, or a Church in communion with the Church. When a 'corporate body' is the Patron, it must appoint a representative who can sign this declaration.

Procedure for appointing a new priest

1. The bishop is informed of the vacancy, and he informs the designated officer of the diocese, and the diocesan registrar (unless he or she is also the designated officer).
2. The designated officer writes 'as soon as practicable' to the patron and to the secretary of the PCC, and this notice shall include 'such information as may be prescribed' (para. 7(4)).
3. The PCC secretary convenes a meeting of the PCC (obviously, this should be done in consultation with the churchwardens). Much work has to be done at this meeting, and it may be wise to have no other items on the Agenda. This meeting has to be held within four weeks of the PCC secretary receiving the notice from the designated officer. Neither the retiring priest, nor the priest's spouse, nor the patron or patron's representative, can attend this meeting.

Decisions to be made by the PCC – under Section 11(1) of the Patronage Measure.

(a) 'Preparing a statement describing the conditions, needs and traditions of the parish.'

(b) 'Appointing two lay members of the PCC to act as representatives of the council to select a new incumbent.' (This is usually, but not necessarily, the churchwardens. A churchwarden who is patron of the benefice cannot act as one of the parish representatives.)

(c) 'Deciding whether to request the patron to consider advertising the vacancy.'

(d) 'Deciding whether to request a joint meeting with the patron, the bishop and the PCC, under Section 12 of the Measure.' (*See* (f) below.)

(e) 'Deciding whether to request a statement in writing from the bishop, describing, in relation to the benefice, the needs of the diocese and the wider interests of the Church.'

(f) 'Deciding whether to pass Resolution A or B (either or both) under Section 3(1) or 3(2) of the Priests (Ordination of Women) Measure 1993.' (*See* **WOMEN PRIESTS** on pages 210–13.)

After the meeting, the PCC Secretary must send the prepared statement about conditions, needs and traditions of the parish, and the names and addresses of the two parish representatives to the patron and to the bishop (unless the bishop is the patron).

A joint meeting of bishop, patron and PCC

1. The patron and the bishop (as well as the PCC) may request a joint meeting, and the bishop and patron may send a representative if either or both are unable to attend.

2. At least one-third of the members of the PCC must attend this meeting, and the retiring priest and the priest's spouse are excluded.

3. The purpose of the meeting is to exchange views on the PCC's prepared statement on the 'conditions, needs and traditions of the parish'. (Section 11(1)(a).)

4. The bishop (if so requested) must present a written statement of the 'needs of the diocese and the wider Church'. The meeting must be held within six weeks from the date on which the request for a meeting is made.

5. The meeting decides who is to act as chairman.

6. The PCC secretary must invite the rural dean (unless he is

the retiring priest) and the lay chairman of the Deanery Synod to the meeting.

Rejecting the priest whose name is put forward by the patron   The patron writes to ask the two parish representatives to approve the priest whose name has been put forward. If they wish to reject that person, the parish representatives must reply in writing within two weeks of receiving the letter from the patron. Unless they do so, the parish representatives 'shall be deemed to have given their approval'.

Some parish representatives may be fearful of turning down the first priest whose name is put forward. However, the Measure clearly states that the patron must not offer the benefice (parish) to a priest until the offer has been approved by the two parish representatives and the bishop (if he is not the patron). In other words, the two parish representatives (and the bishop) have the power to override or veto the priest chosen by the patron. (The patron does have the right to refer the matter to the archbishop, who can overturn the veto – but this does not happen very often.)

Time limits   It usually takes a long time to fill a vacant living. (The diocese will, of course, be saving money while the parish is vacant!) It is always in the best interests of the parish to get on with things as soon as possible. If no priest is appointed within nine months of the vacancy, then the patronage is passed to the archbishop of the province and the parish representatives lose their right of veto. The Archbishop must consult the bishop and the parish representatives, as well as anyone else he thinks fit, but he does not normally need their approval before offering the benefice to a priest of his choice.

The institution and induction service   If there is no newsletter from the church delivered free to every home in the parish, the arrival of a new vicar is an opportunity to send one out, together with an invitation to the service and reception, and other news of the parish can be included.

An official parish invitation list is drawn up by the standing committee or wardens. Include the Mayor and Lady Mayoress, Member of Parliament, trade union leaders, doctors, local government councillors, and representatives from local schools, hospitals and factories, the deanery clergy and clergy of the other denominations in the area. The rural dean should be consulted about the list, and the new incumbent will want to invite friends and relatives. Most parishes print formal invitation cards, and they should be sent out in plenty of time.

A rehearsal is arranged by the rural dean, and it is important that all concerned are present, including the organist, servers and sidesmen. Most institutions now take place within the setting of the Eucharist.

A copy of the Diocesan Service of Institution and Induction – or Service of Licensing – is sent by the bishop to the new priest. When the readings and hymns have been approved, a copy of the printed service is sent by the wardens to the patron(s) and the bishop, the archdeacon and the area dean, and the service should be in their hands at least ten days before the actual service.

The cost of printing this service is normally a charge on PCC funds, and must not be taken from the sequestration account, nor from the collection at the service.

The entire collection at the Induction Service is, in most dioceses, for the bishop's discretionary fund. A notice is usually printed in the Order of Service to this effect: 'The collection will be taken in the next hymn for the bishop's discretionary fund. You are invited to support this generously, as it is used to help clergy in special need and in emergencies.' In some dioceses, the collection is given to the Church overseas (the diocesan 'link').

Prayers for PCC meetings when there is no Priest or Reader at the meeting   PCC members meet together to do God's work. For this reason, we seek his will and guidance for our daily lives, and for all the items on the PCC agenda. Prayer also helps to provide a spiritual setting and a Christian atmosphere for the meeting. It is helpful if PCC members as a group can grow together in the faith. Dr Donald Coggan (former Archbishop of Canterbury) wrote: 'The most important part of your PCC meetings is that unhurried period of quiet thought and prayer which precedes the time you give to the consideration of the agenda – when you wait on God to discover His mind and will for the parish.' (This statement could be read out before the prayers.)

Leader   In the name of the Father, and of the Son, and of the Holy Spirit.
All   Amen.
Leader   O Lord, open our lips
All   and our mouth shall proclaim your praise.

Leader   Glory be to the Father, and to the Son, and to the Holy
         Spirit,
All   as it was in the beginning, is now, and ever shall be,
         world without end. Amen.
Leader   We say together – Almighty God,
         to whom all hearts are open,
         All desires known,
         And from whom no secrets are hidden:
         Cleanse the thoughts of our hearts
         By the inspiration of your Holy Spirit,
         That we may perfectly love you
         And worthily magnify your holy name,
         Through Jesus Christ our Lord. Amen.

A Psalm – (if books are available, the leader says the odd verses
and PCC members say the even verses. If no books with the
psalm are available, then the Leader reads the Psalm). Some
alternatives are given, in case the interregnum lasts for some
months:

April	Psalm 32
May	Psalm 37, verses 1–11 and 40–41
June	Psalm 39
July	Psalm 40, verses 1–13
September	Psalm 45
October	Psalm 48
November	Psalm 62
December	Psalm 67
January	Psalm 75
February	Psalm 84
March	Psalm 16

At the end of the Psalm, all say – Glory be to the Father, and to
the Son, and to the Holy Spirit, as it was in the beginning, is now,
and ever shall be, world without end. Amen.

Suggested Old and New Testament Readings – (use both, or
one – or choose your own).

March	Exodus 18,13–23	Ephesians 4,1–16
April	Joshua 1,1–9	Ephesians 6,10–20
May	Isaiah 6,1–8	Philippians 2,1–11
June	Isaiah 40,1–8	Colossians 1,3–14
July	Ezekiel 2,1–10	Colossians 3,12–17
September	Ezekiel 34,1–10	2 Timothy 2,1–13

Interregnum

October	Hosea 11,1–11	Hebrews 10,19–25
November	Joel 2,12–17	James 1,19–27
December	1 Peter 2,1–10	St Matthew 9,35–38
January	1 John 1,1–10	St Luke 14,15–24
February	1 John 4,7–16	St John 13,1–17

Leader – We have a short silence to think about the reading(s).

Leader Let us pray. Lord, have mercy
All Christ, have mercy
Leader Lord, have mercy

Leader Our Father, . . .

Leader We pray for the Church, especially here in the parish.
Pause
We pray for all involved in finding and appointing a new priest.
Pause
We ask God to bless and guide us in our meeting.
Pause

Leader Eternal God and Father,
You sent your Spirit to the Church at Pentecost:
Renew your gift of the Spirit in your servants gathered here
And help us to seek your holy will in all things;
We ask this through Christ our Lord,
Who lives and reigns with you, in the unity of the Holy Spirit,
One God, now and for ever. Amen.

One of the prayers below may be added here, before the Grace

Leader We say the grace together –
The grace of our Lord Jesus Christ, the love of God,
And the fellowship of the Holy Spirit,
Be with us all evermore. Amen.

Additional prayers – many others are suitable. (Use one per meeting.)

Leader Go before us, O Lord, in all our doings
With Thy most gracious favour
And further us with Thy continual help;
That in all our works, begun, continued and ended in Thee,

We may glorify Thy holy name,
And finally, by Thy mercy, obtain everlasting life,
Through Jesus Christ our Lord. Amen.

Leader　Remember, O Lord, what Thou hast wrought in us,
And not what we deserve,
And as Thou hast called us to Thy service,
Make us worthy of our calling,
Through Jesus Christ our Lord. Amen.

Leader　Teach us, good Lord, to serve Thee as Thou deservest,
To give and not to count the cost;
To fight and not to heed the wounds;
To toil and not to seek for rest;
To labour and not to ask for any reward,
Save that of knowing that we do Thy will,
Through Jesus Christ our Lord. Amen.

Prayers at the end of PCC meetings when no priest is present

Leader　Let us pray.
Let us ask for God's blessing on all our plans and decisions.
Lord, in your mercy
All　Hear our prayer.

Leader　O Lord God, when you give to your servants to endeavour any great matter, grant us also to know that it is not the beginning, but the continuing of the same, until it be thoroughly finished, which yields the true glory, through Him who for the finishing of your work laid down His life for us, our Redeemer, Jesus Christ. Amen.
All　Amen.

Leader　May the Lord give us His blessing, now and always. Amen.

INVENTORY　*See **The terrier and inventory** under **BUILDINGS** on page 21.

JEALOUSY　Jealousy and envy are the two curses of the ministry in the local church. Jealousy is a sign of immaturity and it has evil consequences for the individual and the church community. Pray regularly each day over a long period (years if necessary) for someone you dislike. This is strictly between you and God (unless you try to make a friendly approach to the person concerned). 'More things are wrought by prayer than this world dreams of.'

JOB IN THE PARISH   If your priest asks you to do a job in the parish, he has thought and prayed about it beforehand. Do not undertake the situation unless you are prepared to accept the responsibility involved, and are willing to put your best efforts into doing a good job. Consider all aspects carefully, and pray about it. Do not refuse unless there is a valid reason for doing so, as your priest obviously trusts you and thinks you are the right person.

There is another side to this question. Sometimes one individual has three or four jobs in the parish. Should one person accept all this responsibility? Would the results be better if the work were shared? The answers are obvious.

JOURNEY   When travelling through another parish, the sight of a church spire or tower can be a reminder to offer a silent arrow prayer: 'O Lord, bless the congregation, the PCC and the priest in this parish. Amen.'

KNEELING IN CHURCH   In those places where the congregation kneels to pray, actually kneel down, rather than pretending to kneel by leaning forward. There is surely a good reason for kneeling, and our joints will work just as well as those of our forefathers.

LAY READER   *See* **READERS** on pages 169–71.

LEARNING BY HEART   Former generations of Christians learned the collects, famous prayers, and well-known passages from the Bible. These passages became, as it were, an intimate part of the person's life, and they could be recalled and used whenever necessary. PCC members might find this a worthwhile idea for themselves.

LESSON READING   *See* **HOLY COMMUNION** on pages 91–3.

LIBRARY IN CHURCH   St Paul wrote, 'Know the reason for the faith that is within you'. People often become experts with their hobbies. Christianity is more than a hobby, and it is useful if the parish can build up a library of Christian books. A note-book is required to show the borrower's name, and the date when the book is taken out, and later returned. It may not be used every week, but it is a useful resource for every parish.

LUNCHTIME SERVICES AND MEETINGS   Churches in the centre of towns and cities have a good opportunity to minister to people who are regularly away from home at lunchtime. Various ideas are possible – worship, a series of addresses, discussions, music, hospitality, a place to sit and eat sandwiches, and cloak-room facilities.

What levels of support can PCC members give to organize these events?

MAGAZINE   The magazine can play an important part in the work of the church, as it goes regularly through the doors where priest and church members could not possibly go each month. There are three levels of communication through the written word:

1. *The weekly newsletter and notices*   This is given every Sunday to all the people at church, who are encouraged to take extra copies to other people who might be interested. A news-sheet avoids interrupting the worship with the notices.
2. *The traditional magazine*   Two problems constantly arise with the traditional magazine. First, how to increase the circula-tion. People die, move to another town, or simply do not wish to continue subscribing. Sending out a letter and free sample copies can help, but the best method to increase the cir-culation is by an organized sales drive with church members visiting every home in the parish.

    The second problem concerns the question of increasing costs. If the price is too high, the number of subscribers will fall. People will not buy the magazine if there are too many advertisements. The time may come when the PCC has to ask, Is it too expensive a luxury for such a limited circulation? Is there any alternative to the traditional type of magazine?
3. *Free magazine delivered to every home*   This removes all problems of how to increase the circulation! The local church has a mission to everyone who lives within the parish boundaries. A free magazine delivered every month to every home is in financial terms an important part of the Church's mission to

the parish. It requires ingenuity, planning and hard work – but everything worthwhile requires effort. To keep the costs to a minimum, most parishes will produce their own magazine – whatever copying or duplicating method is used. A traditional ink duplicator is still the cheapest method. But it must never be shoddy, nor badly produced, nor badly folded. Second best is not good enough for God.

One method used by the author is to have three pages of A4 paper, duplicated on both sides, folded and stapled with an electric stapler to form a twelve-page magazine. When there are several thousand homes in the parish, the task needs careful planning and many distributors, and a team of 'assemblers'. No advertisements are included, and the cost is seen as part of the Church's mission to the parish.

The contents   What is the aim of the magazine? Are the contents relevant for that purpose? Drawings, sketches, cartoons and plenty of blank spaces are helpful. Lists of sidesmen, servers, coffee and cake rotas, flower arrangers, brass cleaners, lesson and intercession readers – these are all irrelevant, irritating and of no interest to fringe members and those not connected with the church. If the contents are too 'churchy' people may not read it. How relevant are the contents for someone working in a factory, hospital, local school or shop? A different approach is needed when there is a general circulation to every home and place of work.

Magazine insert   Many parishes buy a pre-printed insert, with articles, news, profiles, topical features, reviews etc., which is used with their local parish material. There are three of these inserts (1) 'The Sign', which has eight pages, (2) 'Home Words', which has 16 pages. Details for both: The Subscription Office, 16 Blyburgate, Beccles, Suffolk, NR34 9TB. Tel: 01502 711171. (3) 'Christian Life', which has eight pages and can be supplied flat, folded or stapled. Details: The Additional Curates Society, Gordon Browning House, 8 Spitfire Rd, Birmingham, B24 9PB. Tel: 0121–382 5533.

Magazine cover   This is vital. If it is not appealing, the magazine will often only receive a quick glance before it is discarded. Attractive covers can be supplied by the above publishers. The same picture every month will not whet the appetite of any reader, especially if it has a view of the inside of the

Church with rows of empty pews! Why not design a home produced cover, with a different picture or words each month? Someone in the parish would no doubt have the appropriate skills.

We have to argue the case for the existence of God, and in simple terms. Many people today do not read the New Testament. Why not have one page per month with a passage from the Gospels, without any comment.

The distributors They are a vital link between the church and the homes of the parish. It is important to deliver the magazine carefully, and if possible without folding. Get them out as soon as possible, otherwise the events will be part of history before people read about them. When a new family moves into the parish, it is important to welcome them on behalf of the church, and to leave a magazine with them.

Editorial team Are there people with appropriate skills in the congregation or the community at large – e.g. journalists or artists?

Questions for discussion

1. Are magazines delivered free of charge to the local hospitals, schools, factories, police station, doctors' and dentists' surgeries, museum, libraries, hotels, hairdressers, etc.?
2. Does the PCC see the magazine in terms of its continuous mission to every home in the parish?
3. Is any diocesan material, e.g. the bishop's letter, included in the magazine?
4. If the magazine is delivered free to every home, is this a priority item on the annual budget?

MARRIAGE Marriage is an agreement between a man and a woman about love, money, a home and children, and it is a partnership of equals, which involves sharing. A Christian marriage includes all these, but has three things in addition. First, Christianity brings a deep understanding of love, shown in its most powerful way on the cross. God is the source of all love, and it is love which leads us back to God. Christian marriage is a sign which reflects something of Christ's love for the Church. It is a sacrament and a holy mystery, through which the Holy Spirit is given to the couple. Secondly, the Christian has a different understanding of forgiveness, again because of the cross. St Paul said, 'Do not let the sun go down on your wrath' (Ephesians 4,26). Thirdly, a Christian couple have the added spiritual dimension in their marriage. Jesus did not say that Christian marriage would be perfect, without tensions and rows, but there is much truth in the saying, 'A couple who pray together stay together'. Obviously, effort is needed every day to develop the marriage relationship.

Questions for discussion for married couples

1. Marriage has been described as the art of sustaining a relationship of love. What is your definition of love? What are the best ways of improving your marriage relationship?
2. How effectively do you communicate with each other?

MISSION – EVANGELISM – RENEWAL   Far from feeling any strong desire or motivation in these areas, many PCC members will no doubt feel embarrassed, unsuited for that kind of thing, or even afraid. You might even wish that this section had not been written, but whatever your feelings, please read on to the end. (The author might add that it was one of the most difficult sections to write.)

There are other problems connected with mission – apart from a reluctance by some Christians to be involved. These include the divisions between the different Christian Churches. The Bible is vital, but it is also a problem for the mission of the Church, because many people believe that the Bible has been 'disproved' by science.

The Church is faced with a desperate missionary situation of enormous proportions. Who is doing anything about it in your parish? Whose responsibility is it? Jesus created his Church so that his work would be continued by his followers after the Ascension. Whose ministry is it? It is Christ's apostolic and priestly ministry which is being continued by and through the whole Church; bishops, priests and lay people together. Many believe that mission and evangelism are the work of the vicar alone. According to the New Testament that is simply not true. All the gifts of the Spirit are not given to the priest alone. The Holy Spirit draws people together with different gifts and skills, so that the whole baptized membership of the local church can work together effectively as a single body – the body of Christ in the parish.

St Paul reminds us that some are called to be apostles, some evangelists, some prophets, some teachers, and perhaps we can add – some who make cups of tea, some to address envelopes, some to knock on doors, some to lead discussion groups or help to run the Sunday School, etc. The body does not say to the feet, 'I do not need you', nor does the hand say to the shoulder, 'I do not need you'. All parts of the body are needed for it to function properly, and they have to be co-ordinated under the head, who is Christ. Individuals are incorporated into the body of Christ by Baptism, not just to receive privileges from God, but also to serve him. The work of the local church is thus not a one-man band. It is a corporate ministry, involving the total membership of the church in one way or another, each according to the gifts and abilities he has received.

Jesus himself clearly intended it to be a corporate ministry, and he gave authority for every Christian to be involved in this work. It is helpful to think carefully about what the Bible actually says, particularly in passages such as Exodus 19,4–6; Isaiah 6,1–8; Romans 12,4–8; 1 Corinthians 12; 1 Peter 2,1–10; Revelation 1,6; 5,10; 20,6.

The Church clearly endorses this authority in its legislation about PCCs, and the Synodical Government Measure defines the function of the PCC – 'to co-operate with the incumbent in the whole mission of the Church, pastoral, evangelistic, social and ecumenical'. If we love and worship God, he in turn requires us to love our neighbour as ourselves. Some people believe that it is a spiritual matter to take the Christian gospel to all people in the parish and beyond its boundaries. Others see this love in terms of caring and action to meet the needs of society, but without any attempt to proclaim the gospel. The Church must never lose the quest for social justice in all spheres of life. Surely both these elements are needed, but in this book we concentrate on the spiritual mission of the Church. (The social gospel and mission of the Church requires another book on its own.)

Emil Brunner wrote the well-known words, 'The Church exists by mission as fire exists by burning'. The Church is not a closed club for the benefit of its members. Archbishop William Temple put it like this: 'The Church is the only society which exists for those who do not belong to it'. Mission involves 'crossing the boundaries' between the Church membership and those who have no faith in Christ and his Church. PCC members certainly have many opportunities which are not open to the clergy.

Large crowds attend football matches, but even larger numbers worship God in church every Sunday. Spectators enter the football stadium not in large groups but as individuals, one by one. This is the way in which people become members of the Church, one by one. At the beginning of his ministry, Jesus found Andrew. Andrew then went and found his brother and said, 'We have found the Messiah'. Andrew then actually brought his brother Simon (Peter) to Jesus. Imagine every member of your PCC bringing one other person to a faith in Jesus. Could it be the aim of every PCC member – to try to bring one new person into church membership per year? It requires patience, prayer, and waiting for the right moment to present itself. Perhaps only a few words will be required for this to happen, such as 'Let me tell you how I first came to the Church'.

Mission and evangelization – What is the difference? Mission is the whole outreach of the Church in its many forms and at many different levels in the parish. Mission can be divided into four areas – pastoral, evangelistic, social and ecumenical. It includes such trivial things as coffee mornings, committee meetings, clubs and countless things, inside and outside the traditional structures of the church community. It involves meeting human need in society.

Evangelization is much more specific and definite. It is the proclaiming or telling of the gospel – the good news – of Jesus Christ.

There may be a large 'evangelistic rally' when an evangelist proclaims the gospel to a crowd of people. This is a very specialized field, and perhaps not every PCC is able to gather a crowd of non-Christians together to hear the gospel.

For most PCC members, evangelization will take place quietly with another person, or perhaps in a small group. You may think that it is difficult and complicated, but in fact, it can be very simple: 'This is how I came to belong to the Church'. Then tell your faith story in a straightforward, sensitive and gentle way.

Once a person starts to respond, then appropriate help and training is needed – perhaps with another person. Careful thought and planning is vital, and Christian formation should not be left to chance. Perhaps a nurture group or starter group is needed?

The local church is in the long-term business of mission and evangelization. A free magazine delivered to every home in the parish – say, eight times per year – will sometimes produce some quick results. But on the whole, it is a question of sowing seeds for the future. Seeds usually take some time to germinate in the darkness of the soil, and your parish may, or may not, be difficult ground for the seeds of the gospel (*see* **MAGAZINE** on pages 111–13). What are the long-term alternatives? In what other way can the gospel message be delivered regularly to every home in the parish?

Door to door visiting by PCC members every third year may be appropriate in some parishes. It is certainly a challenge for PCC members, as well as for the parishioners. But it can be effective and useful. Training is needed, and a letter or leaflet can be left in each home.

Renewal The willingness of the PCC to be involved in mission and evangelization depends to a considerable extent on the spiritual health of the PCC and the congregation. This seems to go in cycles, and it is perhaps not unconnected with the ministries of successive priests in the parish. The renewal or the conversion of the congregation is the first step in many parishes.

What is involved in renewal? It involves repentance, a turning afresh to Christ, a call to holiness of life, taking the spiritual life seriously (*see* **SPIRITUAL LIFE OF PCC MEMBERS** on page 188). It is the Holy Spirit who calls us, and it is the Holy Spirit who teaches us and enables us to use the gifts which he has given to each PCC member for the work of the Church.

A praying community is a vital base for the continuing mission of the Church in the parish. PCC members are called to form the nucleus of that praying community. Elderly and housebound members of the Church can take part in front-line mission by praying regularly in their own homes for evangelism in the parish.

Inward and outward journey of the PCC Mission and evangelization involves PCC members travelling in two directions. The first is the inward and spiritual journey towards God. Spiritual renewal starts with individuals and, in time, the congregation grows in maturity towards the full stature of Christ himself. This can involve change, and perhaps surrendering something to God?

The outward journey into the parish is both spiritual and physical. The inward and the outward are perhaps inseparable, and one will not be fruitful unless progress is made in the other.

Renewal, evangelization and mission are the work of the Holy Spirit. They do not depend on human ingenuity, perseverance and goodwill alone – although these are vital ingredients. PCC members are channels for the work of the Holy Spirit. This they can frustrate or even oppose. Far better if they work in co-operation. God does not force himself on people in the majority of cases. There are, of course, exceptions, e.g. St Paul on the Damascus Road. God is looking for a free response to his love in Jesus Christ – and he is looking for this response first in PCC members, and then in the people of the parish.

In order to see the parish from God's point of view, we have to think about the nature of God. Long ago, the prophet Isaiah had a vision of God in the Temple (Isaiah 6). That vision was a turning point in his life. Today we have a fuller understanding of God, because we have what Isaiah did not have – the knowledge of the Resurrection of Jesus Christ. Isaiah waited on God in the stillness of the Temple. Jesus waited on God on the Mount of Transfiguration and elsewhere. The disciples waited on Jesus in the upper room after the Resurrection. The disciples waited for the coming of the Holy Spirit at Pentecost. This waiting on the Holy Spirit in stillness and quietness is an important part of renewal.

Christ entrusts the privilege and responsibility of continuing his mission on earth to ordinary PCC members (and others too), with all their hopes, fears, human weaknesses, and expectations. The task was completely beyond the Apostles, until they waited for the coming of the Holy Spirit. It will be beyond us too, unless we learn to wait for the guidance and help of the Holy Spirit.

The question is asked in the Revelation of St John: 'What is the Spirit saying to the Churches?' What is the Holy Spirit saying to the PCC and to the church in your parish?

It is helpful for the PCC to work out a parish policy about evangelization, to show what the PCC is trying to do in terms of evangelization. At what stage should the congregation be involved in this process? How can this include all organizations connected with the Church?

A high percentage of people are converted to Christianity because a friend or relative persuades them to come to a service or meeting at church. The appropriate words have to be chosen carefully. The telling of the faith story is the first step. This has to be followed by an invitation – 'Come and see'. 'Would you like to come with me?'

Outreach team The aims of this committee are:
1. To meet regularly (monthly?) to study, pray, and engage in evangelization.
2. To help and encourage all members of the congregation and

the PCC to engage in mission and evangelization on a long-term basis, as a normal part of church life, and to try to use every opportunity which is presented to further the work of the Church.

3. To report regularly to the PCC.
4. To study diocesan and national material about mission and evangelization, and to invite the diocesan missioner to the parish/PCC when appropriate.
5. To organize appropriate evangelization events, where members of the Church can bring friends and neighbours – special service, concert, party, etc.
6. How can the PCC work together with any other Christian Churches in the area?
7. What arrangements are there in the parish to nurture the faith of those who come forward?

The Church of God is like a ship of salvation. We all come on board through the waters of Baptism. At first we are passengers, and then in due course we start to help the crew with their work. Then we come to realize that God wants everyone who is baptized to become a member of his crew on the ship.

We can put this another way. One definition of the Church: it is the eucharistic community which gathers together for worship. When people go out through the doors at the end of the service, it becomes the scattered Church – the 'Church on legs'.

Mission audit   This is a time of great opportunity for mission and evangelization. How can the PCC respond to this situation? The first thing is to take a penetrating look at all the facts. Careful thought will be needed by the mission and evangelization committee about which facts will be useful for the audit. They will no doubt include communicants at Christmas and Easter, and perhaps the first Sunday in June and October, and also confirmations and baptisms, and other facts as are appropriate. The figures should be updated each year, in order to see if the Church is declining or growing in your parish.

After the facts have been collected each year, careful consideration and reflection is needed, which should lead on to planning and action. The purpose of mission audit is not to provide facts in a comfortable situation. The mission and evangelization committee needs to marshal all the God-given resources on the PCC and in the congregation to face the challenges and the opportunities in the parish.

Questions for discussion

1. Has your PCC discussed our Lord's call – 'Seek ye first the Kingdom of God'?
2. What is the quality of worship and fellowship like in your church? Is it something worth sharing with others? Could either be improved?
3. How should the PCC think about this difficult subject of evangelization? Could PCC members talk more about the Church to their friends?
4. How can the PCC be regularly renewed for its work?
5. Is it possible to co-operate with other Christian denominations in mission and evangelization?
6. It really is a great privilege – as well as a great responsibility – to share in Christ's mission to the world. How far is your PCC willing and able to take part in it?
7. What human factors in the local church can be used to co-operate with the Holy Spirit to bring people into the Church community?

MOTHERS' UNION   The MU is a large world-wide organization within the Anglican Communion. There are 750,000 members, who are mainly female, but it is open to all, both men and women, whether single, married or divorced, providing they have been baptized with water and in the name of the Holy Trinity. They also promise to uphold and support the aims and objectives of the Mothers' Union.

The aim of the MU is the advancement of the Christian religion in the sphere of marriage and family life. This is done through developing prayer and spiritual growth in families, studying family life and its place in society. The MU has high ideals of service to the community in general, and to the Church in particular, but it is not easy to translate these ideals into practice in today's secular society. The MU constitution requires that a branch programme is arranged to further the aims and objectives of the MU.

There is a great opportunity for MU members to influence those who are not members, and particularly young parents. The wisdom and experience of MU members can often help, and prayer and friendship are very important.

The divorce rate in society is very high, and there is an urgent need to provide Christian education about marriage and family life, and how to bring up children. The influence of the home and the influence of television are both very powerful, whether for good or ill. How can the MU help to strengthen Christian family life? If the MU is to be true to its aims, then great care is needed to work out what can be done by branches. How can the MU aims be translated into a branch programme. It will require much prayer and discussion, and the full support of all members of the branch. The programme should always be made with the priest, and not presented to the priest after it has been drawn up. It is vital that the priest and the committee meet to pray together, and plan the programme together. It can be useful to have a quick look at the past, and even to reflect on it in a mildly critical way, but always with Christian love. Good questions to consider are these: What does God want of us in our present situation? How far has the branch achieved the aims of the MU through its past programmes? How can it do so more effectively in the future?

The MU takes pride in calling itself the 'Handmaiden of the church'. Is this true in your parish? How can the MU be more effective in the parish? Here are some suggestions:

(a) The branch could help with baptism follow-up and pre-paration visits. A birthday card or 'MU anniversary of baptism card' could be delivered by a MU member living near the family. MU members could 'adopt' babies as they are baptized (whether known to the family or not). Friend-ship and also regular prayer could be offered for the families concerned.

(b) Sunday School recruitment. Help with the Sunday School?

(c) Organize a MU baby sitting circle, advertised through the church magazine. Could money raised be given for a MU overseas worker?

(d) Help or be involved with – or run – a mother and toddler group, pre-school playgroup, Pram Service, etc.

(e) Offer friendship, especially where there is loneliness amongst young mothers.

(f) The MU aims to develop prayer and spiritual growth in families. Could MU members pray together in church, per-haps using morning prayer or evening prayer in the Lady Chapel, but obviously with the agreement of the parish priest. Another suggestion – that MU members (who are able to do so) pray individually at home each day, say at noon.

(g) A meeting with an appropriate speaker talking about a sub-ject such as 'Staying together and growing as a family'. Invite young parents, and school contacts.

(h)   Organize parish Lent hunger lunches (with a speaker?).
(i)   Develop a link with a branch of the MU in a developing country.

The involvement of the priest in the planning is important at every stage. An MU branch cannot be started in a parish without the consent of the incumbent, and it should always be run with the incumbent's agreement. The incumbent is always instrumental in closing down a branch, which should only be done after consultation with the bishop, the PCC and the MU diocesan president. Obviously much thought, prayer and consultation is needed before closing a branch. The same is also true before a new branch is created in a parish. The MU can be a powerful force for good in the parish.

Details about the MU can be obtained from: The Central Secretary, The Mothers' Union, Mary Sumner House, 24 Tufton Street, London SW1P 3RB. Tel: 020–7222 5533. Fax: 020–7222 1591.

Email: mu@themothersunion.org Web: www.themothers union.org

MOTIVATION AND MORALE   The whole question of motivation is very important for the life of the local church, but motivation is not an easy matter to grasp and put into action. Certain basic factors are needed to motivate people and encourage them to share in the work and mission of the Church. These include a friendly and caring atmosphere, and the feeling that it is good to belong to the Church. Lines of communication are always important, and the actual worship of the Church must be good and meaningful. But these things in themselves will not motivate people.

A great deal depends on the vision and quality of leadership of the priest. However, the wardens and PCC members all have their part to motivate and encourage the congregation to do its work. What motivates the priest? It is easy to say that the priest has a vocation (all Christians have a vocation) – but more than that is needed.

As individuals, PCC members (and the priest) need to be secure in their daily lives and work, and to have sufficient money for a reasonable standard of living. People need to belong to a group (which is fulfilled by belonging to the PCC). People like to make progress as a group, and this can include bringing new people into the Church community. How do PCC members as individuals fit into the work of the Church? There needs to be an element of challenge, and a clear idea about what the PCC is trying to achieve. Daily work is not very fulfilling for some people, and the PCC can provide an exciting vision for them. The Church also provides opportunities for individuals to grow in a personal way and as a group, and to find fulfilment. One person said, 'I've done a great deal for the Church, but in return, I've had a great deal out of doing it'.

The actual content of the PCC agenda can have an important role in motivating people.

In addition, we must remember the work of the Holy Spirit, who inspires and motivates PCC members in their work. The extent to which all PCC members are open to the Holy Spirit is a vital factor. The whole question of motivation is not an easy one, but it does need careful consideration in every parish.

Questions for discussion

1. How can PCC members help with this whole question of motivation?
2. In what ways can PCC members accept some responsibility for the motivation and morale of the local church?
3. Is the love of God the best source of motivation for the PCC?

MOVING TO ANOTHER PARISH The population is more mobile today than in the past. Moving to another town can be the cause of a family losing touch with the Church. The priest writes to notify the parish about the new family's arrival, but the family itself must make an effort to join the new church, finding out where it is and the service times. Many things will be different: the relationship with the priest will be new, the building will be strange, and the service may not be the same in many ways. The congregation will all be unknown for a while. Perhaps no one will come forward and speak on the first Sunday.

Transfer your loyalty and adapt yourself to your new spiritual home 'without mental reservation or equivocation of any kind'. The Church somehow manages to make Christians into members of the local instead of the universal (catholic) Church. Joining a new church can be a real test of your spiritual life. All these thoughts bring home the importance of a warm welcome to strangers and visitors, and this will make up for many things which are different.

MUSIC IN WORSHIP   Music can be a very powerful factor in politics, emotions, entertainment and in worship. All the great religions have expressed themselves in song, and music has certainly played an important part in the life of the Christian Church. In the Bible, there are over a hundred references to musical instruments, and over fifty references to singing. Two well-known examples from St Paul on the subject of music: 'Speak to one another in psalms, hymns and spiritual songs; sing and make music in your heart to the Lord' (Ephesians 5,19). The other reference: 'Let the Word of God dwell in you richly as you teach and admonish one another with all wisdom, and as you sing psalms, hymns and spiritual songs with gratitude in your hearts' (Colossians 3,16).

The hymns and the musical sections of the service are a vital part of worship, and it is important that everyone in the congregation should try to do his or her best to make a worthy offering to God in terms of singing. Without music and singing, worship would lose much of its mystery (and 'otherness'). Singing is a powerful medium of communication between us and God, and, of course, also between God and us. Good singing can arouse awe and wonder in the congregation and it is a means of expressing prayer, penitence, praise and thanksgiving to God. It is also a channel through which the Holy Spirit encourages, rebukes, and exhorts the worshippers. St Augustine said 'He who sings prays twice'.

Good and lively hymn singing is the offering of another of our faculties to God. It can help to unite a congregation, and encourage visitors and fringe members to come again. Dull and uninspiring music, sung badly or played too slowly or too loudly on the organ, can have a bad effect on the worship, and it can be a factor which might keep some people away.

Music and singing are so important for worship that they should never be left to the choir alone, or to the choir and just those in the congregation who like singing. Worship is the primary concern of every Christian, and each member of the congregation needs to be helped and encouraged to give the very best they can offer to God in terms of music.

The Church of England has a unique musical heritage, particularly in the cathedrals. But in the parish church, it is important to remember that the choir is there to lead the congregation, and not to sing instead of the congregation. As people learn how to join in and 'have a go', so the congregational singing will improve. The more that people join in the singing, the more they will enjoy it. Every congregation needs to give some time (quarterly?) to congregational practices, and the results will soon be apparent.

A few practical points

1. Listen carefully while the organist plays the tune, and the speed at which it will be sung. Take careful note of any difficult parts in the tune, and keep up with the organist. Never drag behind the others.
2. Stand up as soon as the hymn number has been announced (or as soon as the organist starts to play over the tune if the hymns are not announced). You cannot be ready to start singing if you are using your energy and concentration on standing up. Be ready and prepared to sing the first note by taking two or three deep breaths before you start to sing. Deep breathing is good for your health, as well as for your singing. Breathe in and fill your lungs fairly quickly, but let it out slowly and in a controlled way as you sing.
3. Always attempt the high notes – even if you sometimes fail to reach them, and the range of your voice will gradually widen. For men with deep voices, try to sing the tune with other people, and not an octave below the rest. Remember that singing requires energy and effort, but it is most rewarding. The Venite (Psalm 95) encourages us – 'O come let us sing out to the Lord. Let us shout in triumph to the rock of our salvation' (Collins Liturgical Psalter). Enjoy your singing, for it is physically and psychologically good – and human voices singing together can make joyful music to the Lord.

Comfortable hymns?   To what extent is the congregation content to sing hymns which make them feel too comfortable? Does the congregation need some new hymns from time to time, which might stir them up from set ways? So often the music is a complete contrast with the music enjoyed by many people, and especially by young people. The music can present an enormous cultural barrier which no doubt excludes a large number of people. Should the local church give more thought to this matter? To change to modern 'pop' type music will probably not attract many – if any – to the congregation. It could well drive some of the present regulars away. But on occasions, the music for the Eucharist could be provided by a group of young people – perhaps a folk group formed in the youth club. It needs

125

expertise, proper training and rehearsal, and also the congregation will need encouraging too!

Questions for discussion

1. Could the congregational singing be improved?
2. How could the congregation be helped in singing?

Organist and choirmaster   Music is an important element in the worship of Almighty God, and it is sometimes one of the factors which influence visitors and occasional worshippers in deciding whether or not to return to the Church.

A written agreement with the organist/choirmaster is desirable *see* page 128. The main job of the organist is as follows:

1. To play at the main service on Sunday (and at the evening service). The PCC will pay the fees for a relief organist for four (or six) Sundays per year, the relief organist to be found by the organist.
2. To play suitable music for about fifteen minutes before the service begins, in order to set the scene and prepare the congregation for worship. (The name of the composer and the title of the music could be put on the church notice board, or printed in the duplicated weekly notices.) The organist is also asked to play for a suitable time after the service.
3. To take a weekly choir practice, except during the month of August and in the week following Easter and Christmas.
4. To recruit new choir members, and to look after the musical development of the choir, corporately and individually (RSCM scheme?), and to motivate the choir.
5. The organ is known as the king of musical instruments. Many organs have a considerable capacity to produce volume, which is excellent in an appropriate voluntary, but most discouraging when it drowns the singing of the congregation. It is better to err on the quiet side than to overwhelm the congregation.
6. The organist is probably the best judge of the choir's ability to sing anthems and to choose which would be appropriate and within the ability of the choir. But always consult the priest, and ask him before the choir practises the piece. It is unwise to choose an anthem for an ordinary parish church choir which really calls for the skills of a cathedral choir – the results can be unfortunate.

7. It is desirable that the organist is a communicant member of the church, who plays a full part in the life of the church family, and encourages the choir to do the same.
8. The starting and finishing times of every practice should be strictly observed.
9. A good organist/choirmaster can usually get the best out of the choir without using a long flow of words in explanation. Long-winded pep talks usually succeed in discouraging the choir.
10. It is much to be desired that the priest and the organist can work together in harmony as fellow members of the body of Christ, and it is hoped that disagreements and problems will not arise. When a decision has to be made, it is the priest who has the final decision – after listening carefully to all points of view. (*See Canon Law about music and musicians* on page 129.)

Singing competition   Music festivals are organized in many areas and it might be a good opportunity for your church choir to enter each year. When there is no suitable event in the festival for choirs, perhaps your PCC (or the Deanery Synod or a generous individual) could provide a suitable trophy and negotiate for a church choirs event in the local festival.

Suggestions
Have you tried any of the following – a verse of a hymn sung by the congregation alone – members of the junior choir singing one verse as a solo every Sunday, done by choir members in turn?

The Psalms   The Book of Psalms was the hymn book of the Jewish Church, and its lovely poetry has great spiritual value today. It is probably the best prayer book ever written. But the Psalms are difficult for the congregation (and some choirs?) to sing. It is always better to say them, rather than to leave them unused.

Here are two suggestions. Firstly, alternate verses can be said by a reader and the congregation. Secondly, a responsorial version, where the reader says (or a cantor or choir sings) the verses, and the congregation say or sing the simple response. Some hymnbooks, e.g. the *New English Hymal*, have a selection of responsorial psalms. Many parishes simply give the response on the notice sheet.

Music as the servant   Music in church is not an end in itself, but always the servant of the actual worship. It is also right and proper that the choir should sing an anthem or special setting of the Eucharist from time to time. This is an important side of the organist's job, but the other side is to encourage and involve the congregation. Occasionally it may help to have someone standing in front to conduct and encourage the congregation, especially at a congregational singing practice.

Other musical instruments   With the modern increase in leisure time, many people play a musical instrument to a reasonable standard. Instead of using the organ – say once per year – would it be possible for the organist to gather together and train some musicians in a small group or orchestra to lead the worship at the family Eucharist? Could the local schools provide young people and adults for this purpose? We certainly need to encourage the Church of the future, as well as the Church of today.

Agreement for appointing an organist/director of music   It is recommended that a written contract is drawn up when appointing a new organist or director of music. It can save problems and disputes if all concerned know exactly what is expected of the other. A Specimen Agreement is published on the authority of the Incorporated Association of Organists, The Incorporated Society of Musicians, The Royal College of Organists, The Royal School of Church Music, and the Legal Adviser to the General Synod of the Church of England. A copy can be obtained from the Royal School of Church Music (current charge £3.50).

The Royal School of Church Music   The RSCM promotes the use of music in worship, and provides musical and educational resources to train, develop and inspire clergy, church musicians and congregations of all denominations. A major part of the RSCM's work is connected with young people, through holiday courses, training schemes, awards and festivals. Details: Royal School of Church Music, Cleveland Lodge, Westhumble, Dorking, Surrey RH5 6BW. Tel: 01306 872800. Fax: 01306 887260. Email: cl@rscm.com, Web: www.rscm.com

Food for thought for the organist and the priest

1. How often is it desirable to have a congregational singing practice? What is the best time to involve as many of the congregation as possible?

2. Musically speaking, what will help the congregation to worship? What are the musical needs of the people in the pews?
3. It is quite an art to accompany the singing of the congregation on the organ – does the diocese or the deanery ever arrange courses or meetings for organists? Refresher courses are arranged.

Canon Law about music and musicians – Canon B20

1. In all churches and chapels, other than in cathedral or collegiate churches or chapels, where the matter is governed by or dependent upon the statutes or customs of the same, the functions of appointing any organist or choirmaster (by whatever name called) or director of music, and of terminating the appointment of any organist or choirmaster or director of music, shall be exercisable by the minister with the agreement of the Parochial Church Council, except that if the archdeacon of the archdeaconry in which the parish is situated, in the case of termination of an appointment, considers that the circumstances are such that the requirement as to the agreement of the Parochial Church Council should be dispensed with, the archdeacon may direct accordingly. Where the minister is also the archdeacon of the archdeaconry concerned, the function of the archdeacon under this paragraph shall be exercisable by the bishop of the diocese.
2. Where there is an organist or choirmaster or director of music, the minister shall pay due heed to his advice and assistance in the choosing of chants, hymns, anthems and other settings and in the ordering of the music of the church; but at all times the final responsibility and decision in these matters rests with the minister.
3. It is the duty of the minister to ensure that only such chants, hymns, anthems and other settings are chosen as are appropriate, both the words and the music, to the solemn act of worship and prayer in the house of God as well as to the congregation assembled for that purpose; and to banish all irreverence in the practice and in the performance of the same.

The 1992 Report – 'In Tune With Heaven'

Questions for everyone
Are we taking our music seriously enough
    — in our own worship?
    — in our relations with other Christians?
    — in our desire to be with those who are not yet Christians?

Music in worship

Questions for clergy and musicians
Are we doing our best to make good working relationships?
Are we giving an opportunity to members of our Christian community to talk to us about music and worship?
Are there enough opportunities for everyone to sing, to try something new, to participate?
Are we giving our musicians a chance to perform on their own?
Are we making the best use of silence in worship?
Are we making the best use of old *and* new material?
Is our worship concerned with quality – good language and music, good liturgical principles?
Do the Psalms have a decent place in our worship?
Are we honest about copyright and about supporting simple and fair copyright schemes?
Do we spend enough time and effort planning our worship?

Questions for clergy
Am I looking for, and training, other worship leaders?
Am I using the musicians in the right way, and giving them enough pastoral care and support?
If we have no competent musicians, should we try taped hymn accompaniments?

Questions for musicians
Are we good at enrolling new members in our choir or worship group?
Are boy and girl choir members treated equally and fairly?
Should there be more liaison with local schools?
If we only have a choir, should a music group be formed – or if we only have a music group, should a choir be formed? In either case, how would the two groups work together to complement each other?
Should we use instruments other than the organ?

Questions for PCCs
Do we have a worship committee?
Are we paying our director of music enough, and offering training?
Are we planning our overall expenditure on music, and deciding priorities?

NEVER GIVE UP   God in his mercy does not always allow us to see what he is doing through us at a particular time. God sometimes calls individuals, priests and lay people, and also groups of people such as the PCC, to do a job which seems difficult at the time. It is also strange how people will sometimes only hear just what they want to hear. In one sense, God is 'putting us to the time of trial'. Once you have put your hand to the plough, do not give up. God will provide the necessary strength and courage to finish the task.

Life can be difficult for a Christian at work, especially when the majority of people there do not belong to the Church. The same is true of home life and leisure activities. The Christian may meet mockery, hostility, or he may be ignored. Even in Church circles, Christians sometimes speak with malice and without considering the effect of their words on others. Do not give up, whatever the problems, and remember that Christ and other Christians have suffered before you, and finally triumphed in the power of Christ . . . 'Only be thou faithful until death, and I will give thee a crown of life' (Revelation 2,10).

Our Lord met strong opposition, which eventually put him on the cross. When the Church is active and alive, opposition must be expected. 'In all things we are more than conquerors through Him that loved us' (Romans 8,37).

NEW MEMBERS' EVENING It often happens that new members have to find out for themselves about prayer, the Bible, the faith and worship. Would a new members' evening be a help in your parish? Or a nurture group?

NOTICE BOARDS A notice board is an important means of communication, but it must always be kept neat, regularly painted, and only have up-to-date notices. It is a good idea to use four drawing pins for each notice.

The incumbent alone has the right to decide what notices may be exhibited on church notice boards, 'within and without' the church and in the church hall. The one exception to this is the official notices about rating, parliamentary elections and parish council notices, and these may not cover up nor replace the existing notices.

NURSES *See* **GUILD OF ST BARNABAS** on page 89.

ODD JOBS AND REPAIRS These frequently need doing in the church, the hall, the rectory, the house for the curate or semiretired priest. Inside and outside painting needs to be done regularly. Lucky the parish which has a man willing and able to do these jobs as his offering of time and talents to the church – but he should always be repaid the cost of the materials which he uses. If no such person is available, then the jobs must be done as soon as possible by a local builder or handyman.

ORDINATION Many clergy preach every year about vocations, because all Christians have a vocation to seek and to do

God's will in daily life. Some have a special vocation or calling to the sacred ministry. Do *you* ever have the feeling that God is calling you to be a priest? It may be as a full-time professional, or as a non-stipendiary minister where you continue in your present job during the week. It may be just a niggling feeling somewhere in the back of your mind, which will not go away. Pray about it, and talk it over with your priest, who may suggest that you see the director of ordinands, or the bishop. God often springs surprises on the people he is going to use, and it is not only the 'good' people that he calls to his service. Do not immediately reject the possibility of ordination simply because you feel unworthy for the priesthood.

In 1975, Dr Donald Coggan said at his enthronement as Archbishop of Canterbury – and his words are still relevant today – 'We must have a steady supply of parish priests who will give themselves wholly to this one thing – the thoughtful ministry of the word, the awesome ministry of the sacraments, the visiting of the homes of the people, the ceaseless ministry of intercession, the equipping of the laity for their witness ... There is no finer life than that of a parish priest. Covet this calling. Train for it. Put your best into it. Glorify in it. Count yourself thrice-blessed if you hear God calling you to it.'

The number of candidates offering themselves for ordination is a good barometer of the spiritual health of the parish.

Food for thought
When did your parish last produce an ordination candidate?

ORGANIST *See* **MUSIC IN WORSHIP** on pages 124–30.

OUTSIDE HELP When the PCC is planning a project, e.g. drama, concert, making a video for marriage, baptism or confirmation preparation, or doing a project which involves hard manual work, there is a vast field of skills and resources out there in the local community. When asked to help, many people are willing to give time and skills for the local church, if they think the project is worthwhile, and provided it is explained properly. Outside help is, of course, valuable in itself, but it may well be the beginning of a closer relationship for the people concerned with the Church.

PARENTS One of the most precious things which parents can give to children is their time. They often realize this when it is too late and their children no longer want them. Another precious thing which they can share with their children is their faith. Whether or not the children share the faith of their parents depends to a great extent on the quality of the parental faith. It is good to teach children how to pray from an early age, and to read something from the gospels before praying. It is much better for both parents to do this with their child each night. Suggestions: (1) 'Glory be to the Father, and to the Son . . .'; (2) Intercessions; (3) Our Father. (It is sad that many children today do not know the Lord's Prayer.)

PARISH POLICY   There is a saying, 'If you fail to plan – then you plan to fail'. It is so easy for the PCC to muddle along without having any definite policy.

It is helpful to work out and write down a parish policy. It is desirable to invite and encourage all members of the electoral roll and anyone else to take part in forming the parish policy. There are at least two basic questions which need to be considered.

1. What is the Church?
2. What is the Church trying to achieve in this parish?

It is useful to take plenty of time to do this (perhaps with help from the Diocesan Education Office?). The policy should later be written down and a copy given to every member of the church.

Once the aims have been worked out, then it is necessary to consider how to achieve these aims. Targets – or objectives to be achieved – can be worked out by the PCC, and presented to the Annual Meeting (by the churchwarden?). Obviously it is desirable to have as many as possible working to try to achieve the aims of the parish policy.

PAROCHIAL CHURCH COUNCIL   This is a complicated body, even before you take into account the personalities of the members. It is unlike other committees, for it has to carry out a mixture of spiritual, legal, financial, pastoral and missionary functions. The PCC shares the privileges and responsibility of making certain decisions with the priest, and in return it co-operates with the priest in the whole mission of the Church. This is not some clever arrangement worked out by the church lawyers. It is in fact an attempt to channel the teaching of the Bible into the life of the parishes.

What is the official 'job description' of the PCC? The answer
is clearly given in the Synodical Government Measure 1969,
which states:

1. It shall be the duty of the incumbent and the Parochial
   Church Council to consult together on matters of general
   concern and importance in the parish.
2. The functions of the Parochial Church Council shall include:

   (a) co-operation with the incumbent in promoting in the
       parish the whole mission of the Church, pastoral, evan-
       gelistic, social and ecumenical;
   (b) the consideration and discussions of matters concerning
       the Church of England or any other matters of religious
       or public interest, but not the declaration of the doctrine
       of the Church on any question;
   (c) making known and putting into effect any provision
       made by the Diocesan Synod or the Deanery Synod, but
       · without prejudice to the powers of the Council on any
       particular matter;
   (d) giving advice to the Diocesan Synod and the Deanery
       Synod on any matter referred to the Council;
   (e) raising such matters as the Council consider appropriate
       with the Diocesan Synod or Deanery Synod.
3. In the exercise of its functions the Parochial Church Council
   shall take into consideration any expression of opinion by
   any parochial church meeting.

This gives great emphasis on the part played by lay people in
the parish, and some further comment may be useful:

The incumbent and the PCC shall 'consult together'. The word 'consult'
is a legal process whereby the priest is required by law to discover
the PCC's views on all matters of importance in the parish. This
is done without prejudice to his or her own rights as incumbent.
It does not necessarily mean that the wishes of the PCC have to
be carried our after the consultation. In a similar way, PCC members cannot meet without the priest being present, so that they
may know his or her views. (The priest can, of course, withdraw
from a meeting for a particular item of business, and the PCC
can also meet without a priest during the interregnum).

Consulting together should bring to light any different opinions which exist, but progress in the parish cannot be made without consultation and discussion. Putting forward reasons for and
against a proposal will help to clarify what is best for the church.

Rights and responsibilities   Managing the boundaries between the rights of the priest and the PCC is not an easy area. Rules protect the Church from powerful individuals – whether ordained or lay – from misusing authority. Rules exist to help the Church to do its work more effectively. There will be occasions when the priest has to be firm, and occasions when the PCC will prevent something from happening. Hopefully, those occasions will be rare.

It is so easy for the priest and for the PCC to overreach their lawful authority. For this reason, everyone – especially the PCC secretary and wardens – should know and understand the rules. This prevents minor irritations, or perhaps worse. Those who created the rules have made a careful and wise balance of power between priest and PCC, and when the system is used rightly, exciting horizons are opened up in every parish.

Rights and responsibilities of the PCC   The following have been gathered together by the author from different sources:

1. The PCC has the right to be 'consulted' on all matters of importance in the parish. While taking into account the views of the PCC, the final decision, in some matters, may be taken by others, e.g. the Diocesan Bishop, the Diocesan Pastoral Committee, Diocesan Synod (about quota (Common Fund) payments), or the Church Commissioners. When considering major changes to the parish, the PCC has the right to express an opinion about it.
2. The PCC and the priest decide jointly how PCC money is to be used. A dispute is referred to the bishop.
3. The PCC is responsible for maintaining and repairing all church buildings, the contents, the churchyard and surrounding walls, hedges and lawns. It is responsible for raising the money for these purposes, and for making sure that the work is done properly.
4. The PCC has the right to receive a copy of the church architect's 'Quinquennial Report' made every five years under the Inspection of Churches Measure. It is the PCC's responsibility for carrying out the recommendations in the report. This usually means under the direction of the church architect, and it often involves a faculty or archdeacon's certificate.
5. The PCC is responsible for providing adequate insurance cover, particularly for paid and voluntary workers, and for coach outings, and for public liability claims.

6. The PCC has the right to be consulted about any proposed sale, demolition, or purchase of a parsonage house, or the building of a new one. The Church Commissioners must consider the views or objections of the PCC (made within 21 days) before they make any decision.

7. The PCC has the right to be consulted about the appointment of a new incumbent. The PCC can make a statement about the 'conditions, traditions and needs' of the parish. The PCC appoints two representatives who interview the priest or priests who have been sent by the patron. They have the right, on behalf of the PCC, not to accept the first person put forward. Obviously, there should be a good reason or reasons for using their veto in this way.

8. Decisions about which forms of approved services are to be used must be taken 'jointly' by the Minister and the PCC. If there is disagreement about the form of service to be used, there are set procedures laid down by Canon B3(2). (Hopefully, this will not be needed!)

9. Consultation with the PCC is required before any change is made in the priest's vesture in use in the church, e.g. from surplice and stole to chasuble, or vice versa. Disagreements are referred to the bishop. However, the priest can wear a cope on any suitable occasions without reference to the PCC.

10. The PCC is one of the 'interested parties' and has to be consulted about any major change which would affect the parish, e.g. the proposed creation of a group ministry or team ministry, or altering the boundaries, etc. The PCC has the right to meet a representative of the Diocesan Pastoral Committee (usually the archdeacon) about any proposed changes.

11. The PCC can acquire property, but with the permission of the Diocesan Board of Finance, which acts as Holding Trustees.

12. The PCC can purchase stocks and shares, or receive them as gifts or a bequest under the terms of a will.

13. The PCC is one of the legal parties in any agreement made for the sharing of the parish church with another Christian denomination (under the Sharing of Church Buildings Act 1969).

14. The consent of the PCC (and the diocesan bishop) is required for the incumbent or team vicar to continue in office beyond the retiring age of 70 years.

15. (Perhaps the most important responsibility of every PCC) –

'Co-operation with the incumbent in promoting in the parish the whole mission of the Church, pastoral, evangelistic, social and ecumenical.'

16. The PCC may have responsibilities under the Health and Safety Act, and the Data Protection Act, The Food Act, and Copyright legislation.
17. The PCC has clear and vital responsibilities under the Child Protection legislation. (*See* page 160.)
18. The agreement of the PCC is needed for the appointment, by the incumbent, of any organist, choirmaster or director of music. The agreement of the PCC is also required for terminating any such agreement. (Canon B 20 (amended)).

Rights and responsibilities of the incumbent

(1) The incumbent usually has the freehold of the parish church, which technically means that he or she is the legal owner of the church, who has control and use of the church and its contents, and also has 'custody of the key'.

   The incumbent cannot make any changes to the church and its furnishings without proper authorization, e.g. he cannot remove a stained glass window, nor put one in, without a faculty. (*See* pages 25–7.)

(2) The incumbent is responsible for the control and performance of divine services. The decision about which authorized service is to be used (other than 'occasional offices') must be taken jointly by the incumbent and the PCC. In the case of occasional offices (other than Confirmation and Ordination) the decision is to be made by the minister conducting the service, subject to the right of any of the persons concerned to object beforehand to the form of service proposed. (Canon B3)

   If there is disagreement, the forms of service shall be those contained in the Book of Common Prayer. The exception is where other authorized forms of service were in regular use during at least two of the four years immediately preceding the disagreement, and the PCC resolves that those other forms of service shall be used either to the exclusion of, or in addition to, the forms of service in the Book of Common Prayer.

   The minister who is conducting the service may, at his or her discretion, make and use variations which are not of

137

substantial importance in any form of service authorized. (Canon B5)

The incumbent may hold other authorized services and events in church, in addition to regular Sunday services, as he or she deems appropriate.

(3) The incumbent usually has the freehold of the churchyard (including certain ancient rights of herbage!). The incumbent may have delegated powers to authorize certain gravestones in the churchyard that fall within the parameters of the diocesan churchyard rules. The rules are for the benefit of all in the community, but great care is needed to prevent any possible dispute being aired in the local or national press. It may be wise to consult the archdeacon at an early stage if a problem arises, and also to suggest than an application is made for a faculty. Great harm can be caused to the reputation of the church over kerbstones, headstones and vases! The goodwill of the local community is surely important in parish.

(4) The priest has clearly defined rights and duties in connection with church music. See **CANON LAW** on page 129.

(5) The incumbent has a 'duty to consult the PCC on all matters of general concern and importance in the parish.' In some matters, the incumbent alone will be responsible for making the final decision. Obviously a wise priest will attach much weight to the opinions of the PCC.

(6) The priest has a joint responsibility – or equal say – with the PCC to decide how PCC money is to be used. No money can be voted for any purpose without his agreement. If a very serious disagreement arises, the matter is referred to the diocesan bishop (and, as a last resort, the account is frozen until the problem is resolved).

(7) The incumbent is an 'interested party' when a pastoral reorganization scheme has been proposed, and he or she is consulted separately about any proposed changes which will affect the parish or the living (such as a scheme to unite the parish with a neighbouring parish).

(8) The incumbent controls the assistant clergy, and, with the bishop, determines how many curates will be employed in the parish. The priest and the PCC together determine the proportion of money which the PCC shall pay towards the curate's stipend (salary) – but this obviously has to fit in with diocesan policy and needs.

(9) The Parish Registers belong to the churchwardens on

behalf of the parishioners, but their custody belongs to the priest.

(10) The incumbent has a duty to call at least four PCC meetings every year, in addition to the Annual Meeting (Annual Parochial Church Meeting). The incumbent is the chairman of these meetings, and as chairman has to give 'due heed to his (or her) own rights as incumbent'. The chairman is the person who is authorized to make decisions about 'points of order' which may arise in the course of a meeting. When a decision has been made about a point of order, it should be accepted by the meeting.

(11) The priest has the right to decide which notices may or may not be placed on all notice boards, inside or outside the church or church halls (apart from official government or local government notices, but these may not cover up or replace any existing notice).

(12) The priest allocates the seats in the chancel of the church.

(13) The incumbent controls the bells of the church.

(14) The incumbent must reside in the parsonage house of the benefice, and must also reside in the parish (unless he or she has an episcopal dispensation).

(Some of these items have been mentioned elsewhere.) In considering rights and responsibilities, whether of PCC members or of the priest, a good question to consider is this: 'What does God want in this situation?'

The functions of the PCC shall include co-operation with the incumbent The church lawyers did not include this as some kind of joke! Priest and PCC do co-operate and work together happily in many parishes, and this co-operation releases much energy and power for God's work. Other parishes experience difficulties in co-operating, for one reason or another. So what is needed to enable this process of co-operation to take place?

We will assume that the priest has learned, among other things, the necessary skills of a chairman, and that he or she has a certain understanding of human nature and of how people function in a group situation. People often act completely out of character when in a group – but there is always a reason for this (*see* **GROUPS – DISCUSSION GROUPS AND THE PCC** on pages 86–7). We also assume that the priest is willing to allow others to share in God's work.

What, then, is required of priest and PCC members to enable

this process of co-operation to take place? The answer includes a healthy spiritual life, a sense of humour, a willingness to listen to the point of view of others, a willingness to try to find out what God wants in the parish, imagination, foresight, commitment, humility, courage, a willingness to learn. Alertness to prevent the parochial blinkers obscuring the vision. Add to these an ability to see issues from a spiritual point of view; willingness to join in, to take part, and to be a full member; willingness to take responsibility; love and respect for other people.

It is vital to have a clear understanding of the aims of the PCC, which have been discussed and accepted by the PCC and congregation. The church is clearly God's instrument for bringing about his kingdom in the parish, and the PCC is the nucleus of the task force to help in this work. It is clear from the Old and New Testaments, and from the formulas and documents of the Church, that the Church is a community with a message. Those who allow their names to be put forward for election to the PCC need to be aware of the nature of the work to which they are committing themselves.

Co-operating with the incumbent in promoting the whole mission of the Church, pastoral, evangelistic, social and ecumenical Some PCC members may be worried by this clause, and even wish that it had not been included in the legislation about church councils. Others will be aware of the potential which exists, because two can achieve far more than one on his own. When twelve or twenty or more are involved, then the possibilities are enormous. Many vicars work on their own without a curate, but they are not alone if there is a good partnership with the PCC. There is a long tradition of putting responsibility on to one person, so that the rest do not have to bother. This happens most frequently at a subconscious level, and it reminds us of the saying, 'It is expedient for you that one man should die for the people'. There are many implications in that saying.

Mission is not an optional extra for those who like that kind of thing. Mission is part and parcel of the work of every PCC, and it is clearly written into the constitution of the PCC. The local church exists to worship God and to continue Christ's mission in the parish. Each person has his or her own unique contribution to make in the continuous mission of the Church, bringing their strengths, weaknesses, and possibly some hidden talents. Each person has some special skills from God. But there is only one ministry in the parish – the ministry of Christ himself, carried out through PCC members. Apart from Christ, PCC members can do nothing. Serving on the PCC is a call from God not just to co-operate with the priest, but to co-operate with the Lord Jesus Christ himself. There are no short cuts in mission, and it requires permanent commitment both 'in season and out'. This is dealt with more fully under the section **MISSION – EVAN-GELISM – RENEWAL** on page 114.

Some suggestions for PCC members

1. Study the agenda before coming to the meeting. Try to put God's will before your own likes and dislikes, especially when speaking or voting at the meeting.
2. In your prayers, ask God to bless and guide all members of the PCC and your priest.
3. Arrive in plenty of time, so that you can relax and chat to others before the meeting begins.
4. Keep to the point in a discussion, and address your remarks to the chairman. (Some PCCs find it helpful to arrange the seating in a circle, rather than in straight rows.)
5. The priest gives thought and prays about the business of the meeting. If he makes suggestions, it is because he believes that will be best for the parish. He will not always be right, but he will probably have a good idea of what is needed in the situation. Support his suggestions, unless there is a better alternative.
6. After the meeting, support the decisions made by the PCC and help to put them into effect (even if you voted against them).

The standing committee and other committees of the PCC
Every PCC is required to appoint a standing committee, which transacts business between PCC meetings. Many PCCs appoint other committees, so that there is more time to discuss certain subjects thoroughly in detail. The lay chairman can report and make a recommendation for action to the full meeting of the PCC. Sub-committees can co-opt people who will be helpful, and each sub-committee needs a secretary and minute book. The priest is *ex officio* a member of every committee in the parish, but he may feel it is not necessary to attend the meetings of committees. Close liaison with the priest is vital for the smooth running of the whole system.

Sub-committees of the PCC may be formed for the following: (a) finance, (b) stewardship, (c) education and youth, (d) mission in the parish, (e) the Church overseas, (f) the church building,

(g) the church hall, (h) the churchyard, (i) communications, (j) worship, (k) prayer fellowship, (l) Bible study.

Arranging PCC meetings   One method is to meet on the same day every month, e.g. the second Tuesday of every month (except August). Dates can then be entered into diaries at the beginning of the year.

Those who agree to serve should regard PCC meetings as top priority over other engagements. If you are unwilling to make such a commitment, is it right to stand again at the next election?

With an efficient sub-committee system, the PCC might hold a business meeting alternately with a discussion on a spiritual or biblical subject.

Husband and wife   It is usually better for the church not to have both husband and wife serving together on the PCC – not in case they disagree in public, but in order to involve another family in the work of the church.

Confidential business   It is fairly unusual for business of a confidential nature to appear on the PCC agenda. When it does, obviously it has to be treated as absolutely confidential.

In the normal course of events, it is helpful if PCC members do not gossip about who said what at the meeting with those who are not members of the Council. On the other hand, it may be a good idea occasionally to invite the congregation to a special meeting.

It is desirable to give wide publicity to the work of the PCC. One way is to display the minutes on the church notice board, and to make a report in the magazine.

Resolutions – opinions and action   Action is only required if a resolution on the agenda is formally passed by the PCC. Action does not have to be taken simply because someone has expressed an opinion at a meeting. It is only necessary to record the wording of the resolution, the proposer and seconder, and the voting in the minutes. Views 'for' and 'against' should not be recorded.

After the vote is taken, the PCC should then spend time deciding who will take the necessary action, and by what date (and record both in the minutes).

PCC members are responsible for the decisions made by the PCC, and for carrying out any action needed as a result of their vote. When, for example, the PCC decides to have a concert, play, discussion, social event, Sunday lunch, etc., then all PCC members (and not the priest alone) are responsible for organizing the event, supporting it themselves and actively encouraging others, organizing the selling and printing of tickets, etc. Corporate responsibility involves much more than sitting in a chair and voting 'for' or 'against' a resolution.

Sense of urgency   Mormons and Jehovah's Witnesses have a great zeal for winning converts to their faith. Sadly, neither of them are Christian. The Communists worked hard to achieve their objectives. Why is it that some people are fired with a strong zeal for their cause? How do PCC members get a similar zeal for God's work? The PCC often gets stuck in the rut of the past, ignoring burning issues of the day which are their proper concern. When the PCC wastes time on irrelevant and unimportant issues, then we should not be surprised if the Church is ignored by the rest of the world. Time is precious, and surely each PCC is a team with an urgent job to do in the parish. Is this reflected on the agenda, and is mission given priority?

Questions for discussion

1. What are the six most important things done by the PCC (as distinct from the priest)?
2. How can the PCC achieve a greater sense of dedication and urgency in its work?
3. How far do PCC meetings remind you of St Paul's words about being a 'new creation in Christ'?
4. How can the PCC help to make the truths about God more real in the parish?
5. Does the PCC rely too much on human methods, rather than on the power of the Holy Spirit?
6. One of the responsibilities of the bishop is the pastoral care of the clergy. Is it possible for the PCC to help?
7. Does the PCC try to do too many things at the same time? Would it be better to concentrate more effort on one matter for a year?
8. Are there any geographical areas of the parish which are neglected by the PCC?
9. To whom is the PCC responsible?
10. Would it be helpful to co-opt two young people to the PCC, and with full voting rights?
11. Is being a PCC member a call from God to grow in holiness?

12. To what extent is your PCC and church living off the financial and spiritual 'capital' created by Christians in the past?

The agenda of the PCC   A well thought-out and carefully planned agenda is not only necessary to get the work done, but it also helps to motivate PCC members.

Each meeting is an opportunity to think about God's will for the parish, and to learn how members can co-operate with the Holy Spirit to extend God's kingdom in the Church and in the area. God speaks through all members, and in one sense, the PCC is a school of applied Christianity.

From a legal point of view, a notice is put on the notice board ten days before the meeting to give its date, time and place. The agenda is sent to every member seven days before the meeting. This should list all the items to be discussed, and give any information which will be helpful in making a decision. Some people can make a decision quickly, while others need more time to think carefully about the pros and cons of each item. Thus the agenda has to be sent out seven clear days before the meeting.

Much more is needed than these two legal notices. Forward planning is vital, particularly if the standing committee is to be involved in drawing up the agenda. It is wise to plan the dates for the whole year in January, or earlier. For each PCC meeting, the following dates need to be reserved:

1. Date of standing committee – three weeks before the PCC meeting.
2. Notice put up about place, time and date of PCC meeting – ten days before the PCC meeting.
3. Agenda sent to every PCC member – seven clear days before the PCC meeting.
4. PCC minutes circulated to every PCC member – about ten days after the PCC meeting. (The sooner the better, as this reminds people not only of decisions, but of the actions to be taken, and by whom.)

The priest obviously plays a major part in the preparation of the agenda for every PCC meeting. It is a good idea for the standing committee to share fully in this preparation, and to work out who will introduce each item. The order of business is important, also making sure that there is enough business for the meeting (and not too much!).

Every PCC member is entitled to suggest items for the agenda. It is helpful if this is done in writing, and made available for the standing committee which arranges the PCC meeting. Items should never be brought on to the agenda through 'Any Other Business' – because proper thought and discussion cannot be given before a decision is made. The PCC is always responsible under God to give adequate and careful attention to each item, and this cannot be done if a surprise item is suddenly brought up through AOB. See *Any Other Business* below.

Certain items need to be put on every agenda. These include reports from the evangelization committee (or whatever it is called in your parish); the Deanery Synod report and future business; financial report and fabric report. It is good to keep mission and evangelism constantly before the PCC, even if only a short time is allotted to it on the agenda of each meeting. Many PCCs keep these reports brief, and sometimes the person may say, 'Nothing to report, Mr Chairman, for this meeting'. It is helpful to have a main item or subject on the agenda, perhaps with an outside speaker, or recorded talk or video.

It is wise to work out a proposed timetable for the PCC meeting, and include it on the agenda. Some PCCs have a definite time for ending PCC meetings. This helps to clarify thoughts and stop things dragging on endlessly.

Food for thought
What are the priorities of the PCC? Do these priorities appear regularly on the PCC agenda?

Any Other Business   No business which is not on the agenda shall be transacted at a PCC meeting unless three-quarters of those present agree to this. Even when this agreement is given, 'the Chairman might reasonably, when the matter is important, rule that it is adjourned to a future meeting' (quoted from *Handbook for Churchwardens and Parochial Church Councillors*, published by Mowbray).

Any Other Business allows a genuine matter of urgency to be discussed, which has arisen since the agenda was sent out to PCC members. However, AOB is definitely not an occasion for PCC members to bring up additional items of business at the end of the meeting when everyone is tired. It is unwise and undesirable that any item should be brought to the PCC in this last-minute way. The PCC has a responsibility under God to consider all the options carefully and prayerfully, and then to make a responsible decision. This cannot be done on the spur of the moment and without adequate time and thought being given to the matter. There is a proper channel for every PCC member to bring an item to the agenda, and exceptions should not be made to this procedure. When something urgent arises, an exception can be made, and it can be dealt with at the meeting; or alternatively, an emergency meeting of the PCC could be arranged.

Many PCCs do not include Any Other Business on their agenda, and people soon get into the habit of using the proper channel for bringing something to the PCC.

Membership of the PCC (Summary of Church Representation Rules (as amended) Rule 14(1)). The PCC shall consist of

(a) All Clerks in Holy Orders beneficed in – or licensed to – the parish.

(b) Any Deaconess or Lay Worker licensed in the parish.

(c) If a Team Ministry, all members of that Team. (Where there is a group ministry, details of PCC membership are normally laid down when the Group is established)

(d) The churchwardens (and deputy churchwardens, see Rule 18(4)).

(e) Such, if any, of the readers licensed to the parish, as the Annual Meeting may determine.

(f) All on the electoral roll who are lay members of any deanery synod, diocesan synod or general synod.

(g) Co-opted members, if the PCC so decides, not exceeding in number one-fifth of the lay representatives elected under (g) above, or two persons, whichever shall be the greater, and being either clerks in holy orders or actual lay communicants of 16 years or upwards. The term of office of a co-opted member shall be until the conclusion of the next Annual Meeting, but without prejudice to his or her being co-opted on subsequent occasions for a similar term, subject to and in accordance with these rules.

General Provisions relating to PCCs (Church Representation Rules, Rule 15 Appendix 2)

1. ***Officers of the Council***
    (a) The Minister of the parish shall be chairman of the Parochial Church Council (hereinafter referred to as 'the Council').

(b)   A lay member of the Council shall be elected as vice-chairman of the Council.

(c)   During the vacancy of the benefice, or when the chairman is incapacitated by absence or illness or any other cause, or when the Minister invites him to do so, the vice-chairman of the Council shall act as chairman and have all the powers vested in the chairman.

(d)   (i)   The Council may appoint one of their number to act as secretary of the Council. Failing such appointment, the office of secretary shall be discharged by some other fit person, who shall not thereby become a member of the Council, provided that such person may be co-opted to the Council in accordance with the provisions of Rule 14(I)(h).

(ii)   Where a person other than a member of the Council is appointed to act as secretary, that person may be paid such remuneration (if any) as the Council deems appropriate, provided that such person shall not be eligible to be a member of the Council.

(iii)   The secretary shall have charge of all documents relating to the current business of the Council, except that, unless they are the electoral roll officer, they shall not have charge of the roll. The secretary shall be responsible for keeping the minutes, shall record all resolutions passed by the Council and shall keep the secretary of the diocesan synod and deanery synod informed as to their name and address.

(e)   (i)   The Council may appoint one or more of their number to act as treasurer, solely or jointly. Failing such appointment, the office of treasurer shall be discharged either by such of the churchwardens as are members of the Council, or, if there is only one such churchwarden, by that churchwarden solely, or by some other fit person who shall not thereby become a member of the Council, provided that such person may be co-opted by the Council in accordance with the provisions of rule 14(I)(h).

(ii)   Where such a person other than a member of the Council is appointed to act as treasurer, that person may be paid such remuneration (if any) as the Council deems appropriate, provided that such person shall not be eligible to be a member of that Council.

(f) The Council shall appoint an electoral roll officer, who may be, but need not be, a member of the Council, and may be the secretary. If such person is not a member, the Council may pay to him such remuneration as it shall think fit. The electoral role officer shall have charge of the roll.

(g) If an independent examiner or auditor to the Council is not appointed by the Annual Meeting, or if an independent examiner or auditor appointed by the Annual Meeting is unable or unwilling to act, an independent examiner or auditor (who shall not be a member of the Council) shall be appointed by the Council for a term of office ending at the close of the next Annual Meeting. The remuneration (if any) of the independent examiner or auditor shall be paid by the Council.

(h) For the purposes of this paragraph, where a special care of souls in respect of the parish has been assigned to a vicar in a team ministry, or where there has been no such assignment but a special responsibility for pastoral care in respect of the parish has been assigned to a member of the team under section 20(8A) of the Pastoral Measure 1983, that vicar or that member, as the case may be, shall be deemed to be the minister unless incapaciated by absence or illness or any other cause, in which case the rector in the team ministry shall be deemed to be the minister.

2. **Meetings of the Council** The Council shall hold not less that four meetings in each year. Meetings shall be convened by the chairman, and if not more that four meetings are held, they shall be at quarterly intervals so far as possible.

3. **Power to call meetings** The chairman may at any time convene a meeting of the Council. If they refuse or neglect to do so within seven days after a requisition for that purpose, signed by not less than one-third of the members of the Council, has been presented, those members may forthwith convene a meeting.

4. **Notices relating to meetings**
   (a) Except as provided in paragraph 8 of this appendix, at

least ten clear days before any meeting of the Council notice thereof specifying the time and place of the intended meeting, and signed by or on behalf of the chairman of the council or the persons convening the meeting, shall be posted at or near the principal door of every church, or public building licensed for public worship in the parish.

(b) Not less than seven days before the meeting, a notice thereof specifying the time and place of the meeting signed by or on behalf of the secretary shall be posted or delivered to every member of the council. Such notice shall contain the agenda of the meeting, including any motion or other business proposed by any member of the Council of which notice has been received by the secretary. The notice required by this sub-paragraph shall not be required for a Council meeting immediately following the Annual Parochial Church Meeting which has been called solely for the purpose of appointing or electing any officers of the Council or the members of the standing committee thereof, provided that the notice required by sub-paragraph (a) has been given.

(c) If for some good and sufficient reason the chairman, vice-chairman and secretary, or any two of them, consider that a convened meeting should be postponed, notice shall be given to every member of the Council specifying a reconvened time and place within fourteen days of the postponed meeting.

5. ***Chairman at meetings*** Subject to the provisions of rules 22 and 23 the chair at a meeting of the Council shall be taken

(a) by the incumbent of the benefice, if present;
(b) if the incumbent is not present, or the benefice is vacant, by any clerk in holy orders duly authorised by the bishop with the clerk's agreement to take the chair at meetings of the Council, following a joint application made by the minister of the parish and the Council for the purposes of this sub-paragraph.
(c) if neither the incumbent nor a clerk in holy orders duly authorised as aforesaid is present, the minister of the parish as defined in (b) or (c) of the definition of 'minister' in rule 54(1) provided that at any such meeting the

chairman presiding shall, if they think it expedient to do so, or the meeting so resolves, vacate the chair either generally or for the purposes of any business in which they have a personal interest, or for any other particular business.

Should none of the persons mentioned above be available to take the chair for any meeting or for any particular item on the agenda during a meeting, then the vice-chairman of the Council shall take the chair or, if they are not present, a chairman shall be chosen by those members present from among their number and the person so chosen shall preside for that meeting or for that particular item.

6. **Quorum and agenda**   No business shall be transacted at any meeting of the Council unless at least one-third of the members are present thereat and no business which is not specified in the agenda shall be transacted at any meeting except by the consent of three-quarters of the members present at the meeting.

7. **Order of business**   The business of a meeting of the Council shall be transacted in the order set forth in the agenda, unless the Council by resolution otherwise determines.

8. **Short notice for emergency meetings**   In the case of sudden emergency or other special circumstance requiring immediate action by the Council, a meeting may be convened by the chairman of the Council at not less than three clear days' notice in writing to the members of the Council, but the quorum for the transaction of any business at such meetings shall be a majority of the then existing members of the Council, and no business shall be transacted at such a meeting except as is specified in the notice convening the meeting.

9. **Place of meetings**   The meeting of the Council shall be held at such place as the Council may direct, or in the absence of such direction, as the chairman may direct.

10. **Vote of majority to decide**   The business of the Council shall be decided by a majority of the members present and voting thereon.

11. ***Casting vote*** In the case of an equal division of votes, the chairman of the meeting shall have a second or casting vote.

12. ***Minutes***
    (a) The names of the members present at any meeting of the Council shall be recorded in the minutes.
    (b) If one-fifth of the members present and voting on any resolution so require, the minutes shall record the names of the members voting for and against that resolution.
    (c) Any member of the Council shall be entitled to require that the minutes shall contain a record of the manner in which their vote was cast on any resolution.
    (d) Minutes of meetings of the Council shall be available to all members of the Council. The members shall also have access to past minutes, which the chairman and vice-chairman jointly determine to be relevant to current Council business.
    (e) The auditor of the Council's accounts, the bishop and the archdeacon or a person authorised by one of them in writing, shall have access to the approved minutes of the Council meetings without the authority of the Council.
    (f) Other persons whose names are on the church electoral roll may have access to the approved minutes of Council meetings held after the Annual Parochial Church Meeting in 1995, except any minutes deemed by the Council to be confidential.
    (g) Other persons may have access to the minutes of Council meetings only in accordance with a specific authorization of the Council, provided that where minutes have been deposited in the Diocesan Record Office, pursuant to the Parochial Registers and Records Measure 1978, the authorization of the Council may be dispensed with.

13. ***Adjournment*** Any meeting of the Council may adjourn its proceedings to such time and place as may be determined at such meeting.

14. ***Standing committee***
    (a) The Council shall have a standing committee consisting of not less than five persons. The minister and such of the churchwardens as are members of the Council shall be

ex-officio members of the standing committee, and the Council shall by resolution appoint at least two other members of the standing committee from among its own members and may remove any person so appointed. Unless removed from office, the appointed members shall hold office from the date of their appointment until the conclusion of the next Annual Meeting of the parish.

(b) The standing committee shall have power to transact the business of the Council between the meetings thereof, subject to any directions given by the Council.

15. **Other committees**   The Council may appoint other committees for the purpose of the various branches of church work in the parish, and may include therein persons who are not members of the Council. The minister shall be a member of all committees *ex-officio*.

16. **Validity of proceedings**   No proceedings of the Council shall be invalidated by any vacancy in the membership of the Council, or by any defect in the qualification or election of any member thereof.

17. **Interpretation**   Any question arising on the interpretation of this appendix shall be referred to the bishop of the diocese, and any decision given by him or by any person appointed by him on his behalf shall be final.

PASTORAL CARE   Difficulties and personal problems arise from time to time in any community. Friends and neighbours often provide care and support but sometimes a talk with a responsible person outside the immediate circle of friends is helpful. A wide variety of problems arise, including family and marital problems, depression and anxiety, guilt, bereavement and loneliness.

Pastoral care of the congregation   Is there an awareness among PCC members of the pastoral needs of the congregation? And by whom are these needs met? Traditionally, people through the centuries have brought their problems to their parish priest, in confidence that whatever they say to him will not be repeated to anyone without their express permission. The pastoral care of the congregation and of the PCC is still an important part of the priest's work, but he surely needs help. For example, he may not have noticed that the little old lady who sits near the back of the church has not come for four or five weeks. A PCC member could ask the vicar 'Do you know how Mrs X is – she hasn't been to church recently?'

Quite often, the only help that is required is for someone to call and have a friendly chat. A pastoral care group in the parish can keep an eye open for people who are ill, lonely or who have a problem. They can visit as appropriate, and call in the priest when necessary.

Pastoral care of the people in the parish   The Church of England is in a unique position to help in many ways, perhaps through a street warden system. This provides a communication link between the people in need and the church. The simple act of calling at a lonely person's home is important in itself. Often the street warden can deal with many problems, but if not, other help can be found.

Pastoral care of the priest and his family   Who looks after the shepherd? Traditionally, this is the work of the bishop, but most bishops have many other problems to deal with, and it is not always possible for the bishop to know when a priest is under extra pressure and stress. Today, far too many clergy have breakdowns, heart attacks or marital problems, all largely due to long working hours every week, and pressures and problems in their work. Apart from prayer and an awareness of the problem – in what ways can the PCC help?

Food for thought
Is there an effective pastoral care system in the parish?

PASTORAL REORGANIZATION   What is pastoral reorganization? It covers all changes connected with the reorganization of parishes, the abolition or suspension of livings, creation of team or group ministries, new parishes, boundaries and making a church redundant. It is a subject which causes much emotion, and consumes a great deal of time.

Why does the diocese want pastoral reorganization from time to time? There may not be enough clergy to run the parishes, or not enough money to pay and house them, or a church may be situated away from the population of the parish, or the state of the building may be so bad that the parish cannot raise the money to save the church.

153

The whole situation has to be considered both from the circumstances in the parish, and also from the point of view of the diocese as a whole. When a parish falls vacant, representatives of the Diocesan Pastoral Committee usually consider the situation in the parish. What is the size of the electoral roll? The spiritual health of the congregation? Has the parish paid its Parish Share in full and on time? Is the building such a burden that there is no time and energy left for spiritual work? Some dioceses use three categories when considering the future. Is the parish healthy – sick – or terminally ill? Having a new vicar can often save a church from being closed, and bring new life to the parish.

When a major change is proposed for your parish, the PCC will be consulted in the initial stages. Perhaps the PCC may wish to consult the archdeacon or his representative, or the diocesan registrar. The Church Commissioners (Address: 1 Millbank, Westminster, London SW1P 3JZ) handle all major changes, and they send the draft proposals to all 'interested persons and parties'.

When the PCC is not happy about the plans, an amendment should only be sent if there is a better alternative available. The PCC can obtain a copy of the Pastoral Measure 1969 and the 1975 Code of Practice. The PCC would be well advised to make its views and suggestions known at the beginning of the negotiation procedure, and not when matters are about to be finalized. It is as well to remember that formal 'appeals' can be very costly, and they always involve many people in a considerable amount of extra work. Quite obviously the PCC must make its views and wishes known, but a scheme is always put forward for the good of the Church, after the Diocesan Pastoral Committee, the archdeacon and the bishop have considered the matter carefully, and consider that the proposed course of action is the best one available.

PILGRIMAGES   A pilgrimage is a journey to a holy place, and it plays an important part in many of the great religions of the world. In one sense, every Christian is on a pilgrimage throughout life, following in the steps of the Lord. In fact, Jesus went on a pilgrimage to Jerusalem when he was only 12 years old. Since very early times, Christians have made special journeys to the Holy Land to see and pray at those places connected with our Lord's earthly life.

Pilgrimages had become quite popular by the Middle Ages. The Crusades (1095–1291) were both pilgrimages to the country where God chose to become man, and also 'holy wars' to recover

Jerusalem and other holy places from the Muslims. During the Reformation in England (which started in 1534) the spiritual value of pilgrimages was rejected. The Blessed Virgin Mary was closely connected with many holy places, and the reformers were unhappy with this special association. It is impossible to prove or disprove the truth concerning the visions of Mary which people claim to have seen, but whatever your views about visions, Mary was given a privileged part to play in God's plan of salvation for mankind.

During the twentieth century, the Church of England has rediscovered the joy and spiritual value of a pilgrimage, which is both a holy day and a holiday, and often with a joyful carnival atmosphere. It is an occasion when Christians metaphorically stand up to be counted. As pilgrimages become increasingly popular, it is encouraging to see Christians gather together in such large numbers – and return again, year after year.

Some questions, however, have to be faced. Is there any spiritual value in a pilgrimage? Prayer and devotion, penitence and intercession, and an element of self-sacrifice are important parts of every pilgrimage. Prayer is always answered, but not always in the ways we hope or expect. A pilgrimage is both an outward and physical journey, and also an inward and spiritual journey, lifting heart and mind to God.

Another question: Can one place be more holy than another? God became flesh, and Christianity (more than any other religion) attaches importance to both the physical and the spiritual side of life. Bethel is a holy place in the Bible, where a pile of stones became for Jacob the meeting place of earth and heaven. The command was given to Moses at the burning bush: 'Take off your shoes, for the place where you are standing is holy ground'. T.S. Eliot in his play *Murder in the Cathedral* wrote:

> For wherever a saint has dwelt, wherever a martyr has given his blood for the blood of Christ,
> There is holy ground, and the sanctity shall not depart from it
> Though armies trample over it, though sightseers come with guidebooks looking over it.

Is it true, then, to say that a place of pilgrimage is even more holy than your own parish church? Just as God calls and sets apart individuals to do special work for him, so it seems that God also uses certain places for special purposes.

The Church is on a pilgrimage, in a similar way to the individual on his or her pilgrimage through life. The pilgrim Church (and the parish church?) has moved from one stage of spiritual and doctrinal development to the next one, through succeeding centuries. Changes take place in individual Christians as well as in the Church. And for both the individuals and the Church, the pilgrim way is always along the path trodden by the Lord himself, who is the way, the truth and the life.

Two of the main places of pilgrimage in England are Walsingham and Glastonbury.

Walsingham (near Wells on Sea, North Norfolk) The shrine was founded in 1061 in response to a vision of the Blessed Virgin Mary. It was destroyed in 1538 at the Reformation under Henry VIII, and restored in 1922 by Father Hope Patten, the vicar of Walsingham. It is now England's premier place of pilgrimage. There are lovely grounds and accommodation for pilgrims, and a very good restaurant. Special accommodation is available for the sick and handicapped people. There is a full-time education officer at Walsingham, who will facilitate visits for schools and parish young people's pilgrimages.

The National Pilgrimage is held every year on the last Monday in May with Mass at 12 noon in the grounds of the ruined abbey (near to the present shrine) There is a Youth Pilgrimage near the beginning of August each year, Sunday to Thursday for 11–18 year olds, and a Children's Weekend Pilgrimage (Friday to Sunday) in the Spring each year for 6–11 year olds. The Pilgrimage for the Sick is on the last Monday of August at 12 noon.

Details about pilgrimages, accommodation, youth work, the Pilgrim's Manual, individual and parish membership: The Shrine Office, Shrine of Our Lady of Walsingham, Norfolk, NR22 6EE. Tel: 01328 820255.

Email: education@olw-shrine.org.uk

Glastonbury The main pilgrimage is held every year on the second Saturday of July in the grounds of the lovely ruined abbey. At 12 noon, there is a concelebrated Eucharist (with a bishop and a number of priests consecrating the bread and wine). There is an annual Young People's Pilgrimage, as part of the main Glastonbury Pilgrimage. Many young people walk to Glastonbury (or part of the way). There is a youth event on the Friday night. On Saturday morning at 10.30 a.m. there are various separate activities, teaching and a Sunday school, as the first part of the Pilgrimage Mass.

There is a procession, with singing of hymns down the

high street at 3.30 p.m. followed by Book of Common Prayer Evensong and Benediction.

Details: Mr Robin Thwaites, Secretary of The Glastonbury Pilgrimage Association, 37, Devonshire Buildings, Bath, BA2 4SU. Tel & Fax: 01225 446670.

Egmanton (Nottinghamshire) The Society of Our Lady of Egmanton organises pilgrimages as follows in the Egmanton Parish Church, starting with Mass at 12 noon: there is usually procession and benediction in the afternoon. Details from the vicar of Egmanton: tel 01623 860522.

Last Saturday in June

Saturday after the Feast of the Assumption (15 August)

Second Saturday in October.

There is a Youth Pilgrimage on the First Monday in May – (singing practice at 11.30 a.m.)

Llanthony (in the Black Mountains between Hay-on-Wye and Abergavenny) Mass at 12 noon, usually on the last Saturday in August. Service in the afternoon at ruined monastery higher up the valley.

There are other pilgrimages in addition to the above. Details can usually be found in the Church press.

Food for thought

1. Where is the nearest place of pilgrimage to your parish?
2. Have you as an individual – or a group from your parish – made a pilgrimage there yet?
3. When did you last read Bunyan's book *Pilgrim's Progress*?

PLAYGROUP The appropriate legislation has to be complied with, and a qualified leader is required, in order to start a playgroup in the parish.

An alternative, if there is no one with the appropriate qualifications, is to have a mother and baby group. No laws or regulations at present affect this, as the babies and toddlers are in the care of their mothers.

Equipment is needed, and space is required for storage; this can be a problem in some halls. (Problems are there to be overcome.)

Whether a playgroup or a mother and baby group is started by the PCC, it is desirable for the group to be a 'church' group, which reports each year to the APCM. Either or both provide a service for the community, and a great pastoral and evangelistic opportunity for the church.

POSTER SECRETARY   *See* **PUBLICITY AND COMMUNICATION** on page 165.

PRAYER   *See* **SPIRITUAL LIFE OF PCC MEMBERS** on page 188.

PRAYING THE NEWS   A suggestion made by USPG. A silent prayer can be offered to God in the middle of listening to the news on radio or television, or whilst reading the newspaper on the train. The prayer only needs to be short, and offered to God for those injured in some disaster, or for a statesman with a difficult task in hand. Praying the news must never be a substitute for a regular time of prayer each day.

PRIESTHOOD   (*See* **ORDINATION** on pages 131–2.) There are two types of Christian priesthood – the 'priesthood of all believers' and the ordained priesthood.

Priesthood of the Baptized   St Peter wrote this in his first Epistle:
   'So come to him, our living Stone – the stone rejected by men but choice and precious in the sight of God. Come, and let yourselves be built, as living stones, into a spiritual temple; become a holy priesthood, to offer spiritual sacrifices acceptable to God through Jesus Christ. For it stands written:

   I lay in Zion a choice corner-stone of great worth.
   The man who has faith in it will not be put to shame.'
   (1 Peter 2,4–6 NEB)

   The priesthood of all believers is given to every Christian by virtue of Baptism and Confirmation. This is not something which can be quietly forgotten, for it forms the basis of the ministry of every Christian. We may feel inadequate, but the love and forgiveness of God are more than enough for our weakness.
   God calls every Christian to be 'kings and priests unto God the Father' (Revelation 1.6). All Christians are involved in this royal priesthood, and all are mediators between God and men through their daily work, home life and leisure activities.
   St Thomas Aquinas (1225–74) developed the idea of the priesthood of all believers at a time when the Church was firmly in the hands of the bishops and clergy. He wrote, 'We are

responsible for the working for our own salvation and also by sharing in the priesthood of Christ, to act as his apostle in the salvation of the world' (*Ministry and Sacrament* 1937. Acknowledgement SCM Press).

The ordained priesthood   The threefold ministry of bishops, priests and deacons has existed in the Church from very early times. Ordained priests are given authority by God, and are set apart as 'ministers of Christ and stewards of the mysteries of God'.

Here is a quotation from *Ministry and Ordination, An Agreed Statement of the Anglican-Roman Catholic International Commission*: 'The Christian community exists to give glory to God through the fulfilment of the Father's purpose. All Christians are called to serve this purpose by their life of prayer and surrender to divine grace, and by their careful attention to the needs of all human beings. They should witness to God's compassion for all mankind, and his concern for justice in the affairs of men. They should offer themselves to God in praise and worship, and devote their energies to bringing men into the fellowship of Christ's people, and so under his rule of love.

'The goal of the ordained ministry is to serve this priesthood of all the faithful. Like any human community, the Church requires a focus of leadership and unity, which the Holy Spirit provides in the ordained ministry.' (Reproduced by permission of SPCK.)

PRIEST-IN-CHARGE   When a change is being considered for the existing situation, it is sometimes necessary to appoint a priest-in-charge, instead of a vicar or rector. The priest-in-charge is deemed to be the incumbent of the parish for all purposes of the PCC (Powers) Measure and the Church Representation Rules.

PRISONS AND THE PCC   Is there any opportunity for the PCC to be involved in caring for prisoners, their families or the victims of crime, or with young people caught up in a cycle of crime and punishment? There are many problems connected with this whole subject, but crime is certainly on the increase. What would our Lord want his Church to do, apart from learning to forgive?

Prisoners need to have their confidence and self-respect restored by having an opportunity to show that they can do something useful for other people and which the recipients value. When discharged, they often need somewhere to live, otherwise they are usually inside prison again before very long. (Perhaps there is need for a church-sponsored hostel in the area?) Prisoners are increasingly going out to assist in local community activities and in community service of all kinds, including work with the blind and handicapped. Can the PCC help in any way? Even if there is no prison, open prison, youth custody centre, etc. in the vicinity, perhaps the PCC could consider another question – is our local church doing all it can as a serving and caring community to help to prevent people, young and old, from being involved in crime?

PROTECTION OF CHILDREN FROM ABUSE The Children Act 1989 highlighted the importance of protecting children and young people from abuse. The House of Bishops has issued a revised policy. Every PCC is required to have a written Child Protection Parish Policy, and to take appropriate action to protect children and young people, and the adults who work with them on behalf of the church. Every PCC is required to make an annual review of the policy and how it is working. Some of the following (based on the policy in the author's parish) may help when the subject is being considered:

The PCC's policy statement
1. The PCC attaches great importance to the nurture and care of children and young people in the parish. We recognize our responsibility to guard against the possibility of physical, emotional and sexual abuse of children and young people, and those who work with them on behalf of the church. We require all new workers to sign the PCC's declaration form.
2. The PCC will take up references for each new worker, and ensure that training is undertaken by all who act on behalf of the church.
3. The policy and practice will be renewed by the PCC each year.
4. The PCC is committed to providing a safe, supportive and nurturing community for all children (and adults) in the parish.
5. The PCC aims to minimize the risks, and thereby to safeguard the children and all who serve in the name of the church. The care and welfare of children is paramount in such matters.

Recruiting policy guidelines

1. Those applying to work with children and young people in the parish must complete the application form and the confidential declaration, and provide two referees. The applicant is required to state his or her relationship with each referee. A birth certificate must be submitted with the application.
2. Applicants may be screened by the Department of Health Consultancy Service Index (mandatory for all paid workers). Any information received from this screening will be reported to the diocesan bishop.
3. Applicants are required to attend an interview by a panel, consisting of the vicar, one of the churchwardens and a third member chosen by the vicar and churchwarden from a panel of six persons nominated by the PCC. The interview is confidential, and a record will be securely kept by the vicar.
4. The application, confidential declaration and references, together with comments by the interviewing panel, must be kept securely by the vicar, and retained indefinitely. During an interregnum, these records must be handed to the rural dean, who shall retain them until a new priest is appointed.
5. No person under the age of 18 years may act as a worker. Persons between 16 and 18 years may assist with activities involving children, but they must sign the confidential declaration, which must then be counter-signed by a parent or other responsible adult.
6. Temporary helpers need careful consideration. Where help is being provided on a reasonably regular basis, the above guidelines must be followed. This is not required for occasional or casual helpers, but such persons must not be left alone with children or young people.

Statement of good practices

1. A safe physical environment shall be provided for work with children and young people (and adults too). Safety guidelines shall be followed by all workers in respect of fire safety, food hygiene, and the inspection and safe use of any equipment.
2. Any accident on Church premises must be recorded in the accident book, including accidents to visitors and those hiring the hall. The first aid box must be regularly examined and supplied.
3. Careful arrangements are needed for dropping off and collecting children at the church or hall. Children under

8 years of age must not be allowed to leave the premises without a known, responsible adult carer. (Should this age limit be raised higher than 8 years of age?)

4. At least two workers should be present with each group of children, or, where this is not possible, at least be within sight or hearing of another group. Every effort should be made to have a leader of each gender for a mixed gender group of children.

5. If transport is needed, there should be at least two adult passengers in each vehicle. Two or more workers should be present when taking a group of children away from church premises. Written parental consent is required for all such outings when a child is not accompanied by a parent or guardian.

6. When it is not possible to have two workers who have attended a training course to be present, the leader of the group should have access to the telephone numbers of other workers who have had formal training for use in emergencies.

7. So far as is reasonably practicable, a worker should avoid being alone with a child or young person. Where this is unavoidable, then a second worker or other appropriate person should be told of the situation, and for how long it will last.

8. The following are signs of possible abuse, but it should be noted that they might be due to other explanations. The worker should never jump to conclusions, as it is more than possible, if not probable, that they may be due to some other cause. The list includes: unexplained injuries; signs of neglect; stomach pains with no medical reason; a 'don't care' attitude; sexually explicit behaviour inappropriate for a child of that age; an aggressive attitude; inappropriate sex play; unsocial behaviour; child only being happy when away from home; self-inflicted injuries; reverting to young behaviour; relationship between adults and children are secretive and exclude others; severe sleeping disturbance with fears and phobias; running away from home and unusual behaviour.

9. If the signs are constant and habitual, the worker should consult the person to whom he or she is responsible, or the person he or she is authorised to inform. It is important that no unauthorised person is told of the worker's concerns. The Worker should not undertake any investigation into the

alleged abuse, as, in the end, the Social Services are legally the only body allowed to deal with reported abuse. They will follow up every reported incident.

10. The worker should make accurate notes of his or her suspicions, recording dates, times and places. It is important that the language of the child is used, and not a sanitized version.

11. When a child or young person wants to talk about abuse, it is important that the worker should try to keep calm, and not look shocked, and accept what is said. Make a note of what is said in the child's own words. The worker should not ask any leading questions, but try to reassure the child that he/she was right to tell the worker, and also to tell the child that they are believed. The worker should pass no judgement on either the child or on anyone else. It is vital that confidentiality is maintained at all times.

12. In the event of an actual allegation of abuse, by children, on their behalf by parents, carers or other responsible adults, it must be reported at once to the Child Protection Unit of the Social Services, and at the same time to the diocesan bishop, and to the vicar.

13. It is vital that confidentiality is maintained, and that full and proper records are kept in a secure place about actual and potential areas of injury or abuse. This should include times, dates, things said, and action undertaken by the child. All conversations, telephone calls, decisions taken, as well as by whom and the reason for them, should be recorded and dated and retained indefinitely, together with any correspondence and other relevant papers. Such records should be kept under lock and key by the vicar.

14. Arrangements will be made for the pastoral care of all those affected by an allegation of abuse. The bishop's representative will provide support and advice. Pastoral care will not be offered by the same person to all parties to the allegation.

Training and monitoring   All new workers should be asked to attend diocesan training sessions on child protection as soon as possible and, in any event, within 12 months of taking up their new position (and existing workers, if they have not already done so). Until the training has been completed a worker should not be allowed to be in charge of children, unless they have appropriate prior experience (at least 2 years). Alternatively, a fully trained worker should be present. Training will also provide guidance to workers about protecting themselves from the risk of untrue allegations.

It is the responsibility of the vicar and churchwardens to ensure the appropriate training courses have been attended by all workers in the parish. All workers are expected to sign a declaration that they have attended a course, and that they will attend any further courses if required.

Church hall and the protection of children   Anyone who hires the church hall for activities involving unsupervised contact with children and young people shall have a child protection policy which is similar to the requirements of the PCC policy. This should be clearly stated on the hall hiring application form and the hall rules.

Questions for the confidential declaration

1. Have you ever been convicted of any criminal offence?
2. Have you ever been cautioned by the police, or bound over to keep the peace?
3. Have you ever been found by a court exercising civil jurisdiction (including matrimonial or family jurisdiction) to have caused significant harm, ill treatment, sexual abuse or impairment of physical or mental health and development to a child or young person under the age of 18 years, or has any such court made any order against you on the basis of any finding or allegation that any child or young person was at risk of significant harm from you ?
4. Has your conduct ever caused, or been likely to cause, significant harm to a child or young person under the age of 18 years, or put a child or young person at risk of significant harm, or to your knowledge has it ever been alleged that your conduct has resulted in any of those things? This relates to any conduct, whether in a paid capacity, as a volunteer worker, or otherwise.
5. Has a child in your care, or for whom you have or have had parental responsibility, ever been removed from your care, been placed on the Child Protection Register, or been the subject of a Care Order, a Supervision Order, a Child Assessment Order, or an Emergency Protection Order under the Children Act 1989, or a similar order under other legislation?
6. Have you any health problem(s) which might affect your work with children or young people under the age of 18 years?

7. Have you, since the age of 18 years, ever been known by any name other than that given below?
8. Have you, during the past five years, had any home address other than that given below?

Applicants should be asked to give full details in all answers.

PUBLICITY AND COMMUNICATION   Personal contact is by far the best form of communication. Could the PCC encourage the congregation to chat about the events at the church as much as possible to their friends and neighbours? Obviously, the Church needs other forms of communication, and the PCC might consider how effective are all its forms of communication and publicity.

Notice boards should be fixed in the best possible position, and always kept in good order and well painted. Remove all notices as soon as they are out of date.

Posters should be carefully planned, and well produced. Posters are always much more effective if a number of them are displayed around the parish, all with the same design and colour. Can we learn anything from publicity at a general election in terms of posters? Many notice boards appear in people's gardens and on fences. Thirty or forty small notice boards can easily be made from wood, 18 × 30 in, nailed to a 5-ft stake. These could be used by members of the congregation when publicity is needed. A poster secretary arranges the printing – or produces the posters.

A good relationship with the Press and local radio is desirable.

QUINQUENNIAL REPORT   *See* **BUILDINGS** on page 24.

QUOTA   (now usually called Common Fund or Parish Share) *See* **FINANCE** on page 82.

QUOTATIONS FOR PCC MEMBERS   Here is a random selection:
The unsearchable riches of Christ. (Ephesians 3,8 AV.)

The harvest truly is plenteous, but the labourers are few. Pray ye therefore the Lord of the harvest, that he will send forth labourers into his harvest. (St Matthew 9,37 and 38 AV.)

The Church is the only society which exists for those who do not belong to it. (Archbishop William Temple.)

Seek ye first the kingdom of God. (St Matthew 6,33 AV.)

God loved the world so much that he gave his only Son, that everyone who has faith in him may not die but have eternal life. (St John 3,16 NEB.)

Go ye into all the world, and preach the gospel to every creature. (St Mark 16,15 AV.)

Follow me, and I will make you fishers of men. (St Matthew 4,19 AV.)

You are a chosen race, a royal priesthood, a dedicated nation, and a people claimed by God for his own, to proclaim the triumphs of him who has called you out of darkness into his marvellous light. You are now the people of God, who once were not his people; outside his mercy once, you have now received his mercy. (1 Peter 2,9 and 10 NEB.)

Lo, I am with you always. (St Matthew 28,20 AV.)

The essential equipment of mission is made up of humility, service, sacrifice. Evangelism is essentially one beggar telling another beggar where food may be found. (Bishop Sadiq.)

The world wide task of evangelism is not an 'optional extra'. It is the high calling of every disciple. (Lambeth Conference Encyclical Letter in 1958. Acknowledgement SPCK.)

The evangelization of England . . . is a work that cannot be done by the clergy alone. It can only be done to a very small extent by the clergy at all. There can be no widespread evangelization of England, unless the work is undertaken by the lay people of the Church. (Archbishop William Temple in *Towards the Conversion of England* – 1945 Report.)

Of one thing I am certain; the One who started the good work in you will bring it to completion by the Day of Christ Jesus. (Philippians 1,6 NEB.)

Come to me, all whose work is hard, whose load is heavy, and I will give you relief. Bend your necks to my yoke and learn from me, for I am gentle and humble-hearted and your souls will find relief. For my yoke is good to bear, my load is light. (St Matthew 11,28–30 NEB.)

A Christian is either a missionary or a misfortune. (Source unknown.)

Be ye doers of the word, and not hearers only, deceiving your own selves. (James 1,22 AV.)

The Lord appointed other seventy also, and sent them two and two before his face into every city and place, whither he himself would come. (St Luke 10,1 AV.)

166

You will receive power when the Holy Spirit comes upon you, and you will bear witness for me. (Acts 1,8 NEB.)

Life is only for Love. Time is only that we may find God. (St Bernard.)

Blessed are the pure in heart: for they shall see God. (St Matthew 5,8 AV.)

Attempt great things for God. Expect great things from God. (Inscribed on the Lectern in Westminster Abbey.)

There can be no participation in Christ without participation in his mission to the world. (The Willingen Conference 1952.)

What can I give him, poor as I am?
If I were a shepherd I would bring a lamb;
If I were a wise man I would do my part;
Yet what I can I give him – give my heart.
(Christina Rossetti.)

A handful of men and women, mostly uneducated, mostly poor, but strong in the Lord and in the power of his might, men of the resurrection, men of the Spirit, went out into the pagan world – and won it for Christ. Let them shame our faithlessness! Let them be our example. (The Archbishop of Canterbury's Christmas Sermon, 1977.)

The most important part of your PCC meetings is that unhurried period of quiet thought and prayer which precedes the time you give to consideration of the agenda – when you wait on God to discover His mind and will for the parish. (From *Convictions* by Dr Donald Coggan, acknowledgement Hodder & Stoughton.)

RACIAL PROBLEMS   This is not always a comfortable subject. The Anglican Communion has many more black members than white ones. General Synod has asked PCCs to consider what can be done to promote better relationships between people of different racial groups. There is a great deal that is wrong in this whole area, and our emotions are often quickly stirred up by it. There is much anger, violence and guilt, both in the world as a whole, and sometimes hostile feelings are only just below the surface even in Church members.

Racism is an ugly sin. The kingdom of God is about justice and peace, and our Lord wants us to 'Love your neighbour as yourself'. We are all equal in the sight of God. We belong to the one human race. We are all made in the image of God. And Christians are all brothers and sisters in Christ.

We need courage to examine our own attitudes. Are they still affected by our past history with all its pains as well as glories? It is said that there is a certain amount of racial prejudice in most (all?) of us. If we can admit that, then we have taken the first step on the path to doing something positive about the problem.

Self-examination is a Godly discipline. Although it is not good to wallow in guilt, we do need to take a cool and steady look at the problem. In this way we become more aware of the sin of racism, and we grow towards unity between the races.

You may protest that the PCC is already a civilized and Christian group, and that the PCC does not act in a racist and discriminating way. If this is true, it is, of course, a good thing. Black people, however, are a disadvantaged group, not because of a deliberate policy, but because of subtle forces and attitudes in society as a whole. There is also such a thing as institutional racism.

The pressures of racism have great consequences, especially for young people. Some black people feel they have no role to play, and that they are of no personal significance. They often have a deep sense of hopelessness, and feel that the Church does not care about the problem.

The eradication of racism is a serious task, and a challenge to all Christians – whether it exists in the heart, in the parish or in the world.

A serious commitment to be involved does require a willingness to listen, to discover the facts, and to pray for racial harmony and unity between different racial groups, both within the Church and in the world. Pray that we may grow towards God's purposes and to work for the establishment of a more just society in the world. We have a long way to go to achieve this.

What can PCC members actually do? Make an opportunity for the PCC, together with the congregation, to discuss this subject. The diocesan office or the archdeacon could suggest an appropriate person to come to a parish meeting to introduce the subject. In this way we can become more racially conscious and sensitive. Each PCC member is capable of effecting some change, however small it may be. We are not alone. Read Ephesians 2, verses 11–16. There are plenty of other relevant references. But the matchless vision of the Church in Revelation is particularly appropriate – 'After this I looked and saw a vast throng, which no one could count, from every nation, of all tribes, peoples, and languages, standing in front of the throne and before the Lamb' (Revelation 7,9 NEB). PCC members have the resources of the gospel to bring healing into this situation.

Questions for discussion

1. Who is my neighbour?
2. How can we love God, if we do nothing to help our neighbour in his hour of need?

RAPHAEL   *See* **GUILD OF ST RAPHAEL** on pages 89–90.

READERS   The office of Reader is open to men and women, and the selection procedure for Readers is similar to that for the sacred ministry. Each candidate has to be nominated by the priest, and with the support of the PCC. If accepted for training, the candidate embarks on a course of study to take the Central Readers' Conference Certificate. Training is on a part-time basis – usually one evening per week during university 'terms' in many dioceses. The course normally lasts for three years. Readers are examined about both their knowledge and their competence.

With the widespread popularity of the Parish Communion, and with the increased participation of lay people in the Eucharist, the 'liturgical' role of Readers is limited in some parishes, apart from Evensong. Lay people can be authorized to do most of the things which Readers do in the Eucharist, apart from preaching a sermon. Careful preparation is required to prepare a sermon. Preaching is also very closely connected with the spiritual life of the Reader. *See* **SERMON** on pages 182–3.

Readers can conduct funeral services in church, or at a cemetery or crematorium, but they can do this only with the goodwill of the relatives and at the invitation of the priest. During an interregnum, this is at the invitation of the area/rural dean.

Many clergy have been withdrawn from the countryside through pastoral reorganization schemes, and often a number of churches are now grouped together in a team or group ministry. There is a vital role for the Readers in the countryside, to lead the worship and to share in the pastoral work. In other parishes, the way in which Readers exercise their ministry seems to vary enormously. In all cases, this depends on the amount of time which the Reader can offer for this work, the relationship between the Reader and the priest, and the needs of the parish.

The pastoral and educational role of the Reader   In addition to the 'liturgical role', a Reader can exercise an effective pastoral ministry in every parish, providing he or she is willing to do this, and the time can be given for this work. The Readers can share with the clergy particularly in the following areas:

1. The pastoral care of the bereaved – *see* **BEREAVEMENT** on pages 13–14.
2. Baptism Preparation and follow up after the service – *see* **BAPTISM** on page 11.
3. An educational role in leading discussion groups and Bible study groups.
4. The preparation of Confirmation candidates.
5. 'Home Communions'. When regular worshippers can no longer come to church to receive Communion, then the sacrament has to be given to them at home or in hospital. Readers can be authorized by the bishop, with the agreement of the PCC, to administer Communion to people at home or in hospital. The wafers and wine are consecrated by the priest in church, and often the wafer is 'intincted' with a very small spot of wine. This avoids the danger of spilling the wine, or passing on infection in cases of sickness. (*See* **HOME COMMUNION** on page 96.) With increasing numbers of people requiring Communion at home or in hospital, Readers can exercise a very important role in this ministry. In some parishes, the sacrament is taken out of the church with an appropriate prayer just before the end of the service. Readers sharing in this work can help to relieve pressure on the priest's work-load, and enable those concerned to 'share in the communion of his Body and Blood' in a regular way.
6. The daily offices. The effectiveness of a Reader's work depends to a very large extent on his or her spiritual life. It can be a great help to the Reader to share in saying Matins and Evensong with the clergy in church. This can also be a help to the clergy.
7. It may be appropriate to take part in staff meetings with the vicar and curates etc.
8. To co-operate with the priest in the whole mission of the Church. The involvement of Readers in the mission and work of the Church will vary considerably from parish to parish. Much depends on time available, willingness and ability to co-operate and work with the priest and to work under the priest's authority, and also on the situation in the parish.

A Reader is not automatically (*ex officio*) a member of the PCC. This depends on the Annual Parochial Church Meeting.

Some feel it is a good idea to elect the Readers in the same way and at the same time as other lay people. In other parishes, Readers are elected to the PCC for a certain number of years.

When being admitted to office, every Reader makes a declaration of assent, to give due obedience to the bishop. In the parish, the Reader undertakes to support the priest, and to work under the direction and authority of the priest. The theological, liturgical and pastoral training gives a tremendous potential for the effectiveness of a Reader's ministry. The need is clearly there in every parish, but so much depends on the relationship and the personalities of those concerned.

A Reader's licence does not continue automatically year after year, and it is reviewed periodically. The priest has to sign the form to renew the licence, which is annually in some dioceses. The bishop may revoke or withdraw the licence at any time.

Two thoughts for Readers
1. Could a Reader be more involved in the mission and work of the church in your parish?
2. Is God calling you to the ordained ministry?

A thought for PCC members
Is God calling you to be a Reader?

REDUNDANT CHURCHES The Pastoral Measure 1969 updated the arrangements needed to close a parish church, and quite a number of churches were declared redundant as a result. Now, however, most deaneries have the right number of church buildings, and there should be fewer redundancies in the future, particularly where priest and PCC can work together effectively. Now is the time for the PCC to have confidence in God, and in its ability to co-operate with the work of the Spirit in the parish.

If the diocese does propose a redundancy scheme, there might be a good reason for it. To fight such a proposal could be a costly business, and the question has to be asked – Who will pay the costs? Details about redundancy procedures can be obtained from the diocesan secretary or from the diocesan registrar (address and telephone number in the local telephone directory).

Now is the time to fight off any possible redundancy scheme, by repairing the roof, keeping gutters and drains in good order, and paying the Common Fund by monthly instalments, co-operating with the priest, and getting on with the rightful work of the PCC before it is too late.

Redundant Churches Fund Certain churches of historic or architectural interest which are no longer required for worship may be vested in the Redundant Churches Fund for preservation, if no suitable alternative use is available. When this happens, arrangements can be made for the church to be used on special occasions. A church vested in the Fund can be brought back into use as a parish church if there is a major change in the local situation.

RELIGIOUS COMMUNITIES OF MONKS AND NUNS

This section briefly considers the origins and place of communities in the Church today.

Religious communities did not begin with the Christian Church. The Essenes were a Jewish community with a highly organized monastic life at the time of John the Baptist (Dead Sea Scrolls). From very early times, Christian men and women have not married so that they could devote their lives to God in prayer and in works of charity.

Christian communities were started as early as the third century by hermits in the Egyptian deserts. One of them – St Anthony – organized a simple community life about AD 303. The idea spread, and during the later Dark Ages, the light of learning and devotion was only kept alive by the monasteries. By the sixteenth century, many communities had forgotten the high ideals and the rules of their founders. Some were undoubtedly corrupt and in need of reform. King Henry VIII used this excuse to seize the great wealth of the monasteries, and he ordered them to be 'dissolved' (1534–39). The spiritual life of the Church of England was undoubtedly poorer as a result of this action, but during the nineteenth century religious communities were refounded within the Church as a result of the Oxford Movement. Many obstacles were put in the way of this remarkable growth of religious communities at the time, but happily the situation is very different today. Now there are ten religious orders for men, 45 for women, and two mixed communities within the Church of England.

The main activities of a religious community are prayer, work and hospitality. Most community houses have a place where people can go for a retreat, either alone or with an organized retreat, whether for a single day, or a few days. The call of Christ to join a religious community comes to people of all walks of life, and from all shades of churchmanship. The normal age for applying is between 21 and 45, and applicants need to be physically and psychologically robust. There is usually a probationary training period of three years before the first vows are taken. Anyone who thinks he or she may have a vocation to the religious life is advised to consult their own priest, and then to visit perhaps more than one religious community to experience their way of life. The *Anglican Religious Communities Year Book* is published by Canterbury Press. Details about the different communities from: The Rev'd Father Aidan Mayoss CR, St Michael's Priory, 14 Burleigh St, London WC2E 7PZ. Tel: 020–7379 6669. Fax: 020–7240 5294. Email: amayoss@mirfield.org.uk

Is there any value in having a traditional monastic community when so much has changed in modern life? The simple answer is – prayer is just as vital as ever. These communities provide a wonderful powerhouse of regular prayer. Some believe that the next great Christian advance will come through the religious communities.

Questions for thought or discussion

1. Where is the nearest monastery to your parish?
2. Would it be possible for the parish to have a prayer link – parish retreat – and other involvement with the community?
3. What about having a visiting speaker or preacher from one of the religious communities?

REPENTANCE   Sin can be a very real problem in the Church, both the sins of the individuals and the sins of the Church. This section is not about personal sins, but about the corporate failures and sins of the local church. No parish is perfect. To mis-use Saint Paul's words: 'all have sinned, and all fall short of the glory of God'. Does your church need to repent, because it does not take mission seriously, or it is indifferent to strangers and visitors, or there is pride, in many forms, lack of charity, unkindness to the priest, lack of preparation before Communion . . . ? Perhaps an annual Service of Repentance in Lent or Advent? Repentance is needed before renewal will come.

RETREAT   Not in a military sense of an army retreating because of pressure from the enemy. We grow primarily in the Christian communities to which we belong, but there are outside resources such as a retreat, which can help from time to time. A Christian retreat is withdrawing from the pressures of daily life in order to have a period of quiet reflection with a group of people in a shared silence. Usually a retreat conductor gives two – or perhaps three – talks during the course of a day.

Silence is kept for the duration of the retreat, and this can be a wonderful experience which produces inner peace and tranquillity, and refreshes the soul. Daily life is often full of noise, chatter, pressures and distractions. Sometimes even our prayers are full of 'chatter' to God. The silence of a retreat provides a wonderful opportunity for God to talk to us and for us to listen to him, and to think of his purposes in our lives. This is much easier to do during a retreat than it is at home.

A retreat is an opportunity to pray, and also to learn more about prayer. The conductor usually puts up a list of times when individuals can make an appointment (by an anonymous tick) to talk about any problem, or to talk about prayer itself, or to make a private confession. A retreat is also an opportunity to read, and a time for physical rest, refreshment and a walk in a quiet garden.

Many people are afraid of silence, and thus they always carry a transistor radio playing loud music. The Christian is never alone, for Jesus said, 'Lo, I am with you always, even to the end of the world'. If someone is bursting to talk on retreat, they can always go and talk to the conductor. But it is strange how so many people say at the end of a retreat that they enjoyed the silence, and that they were sorry when it ended.

From time to time, Jesus took his disciples away from the crowds for a time of quietness, rest and prayer. The invitation of Jesus still stands today, 'Come ye apart, and rest awhile'. Could you who are reading this section respond to this invitation? For a retreat is strongly recommended for all PCC members – and people return from retreat in a relaxed state and with a new vision of the faith, and a new zeal for life. Many who are searching for something in life often find it on retreat.

The number of people going on retreat is steadily increasing year by year, and this in itself is a good testimony to their value. Special retreats can be arranged for PCC members, for young people, the MU, or a general one for the congregation.

Association for promoting retreats APR fosters spiritual growth in the Church of England and Anglican Communion by promoting retreats. It welcomes into membership all Christians who are in sympathy with its aims. Details: The Administrator, Association for Promoting Retreats, Central Hall, 256 Bermondsey St, London, SE1 3UJ. Tel: 020 7357 7736. Fax:

020 7357 7724. Email: apr@retreats.org.uk. Web: www.retreats. org.uk

Retreat association   This is ecumenical and is made up of six official bodies from Baptists, Methodists, Quakers, Roman Catholic, United Reformed and Anglican Churches (APR above). There are about 160 Retreat houses throughout the country. Details – the same as APR above.

Details of most retreats can be found in the Church press, or from the APR or Retreat Association.

ROUTINE JOBS   (*See also* **VERGER** on page 206.) Volunteers can help in a variety of ways, just as routine work is shared out in many households today. Help in this way will free the priest for the work for which he was ordained. It is an act of Christian kindness to relieve the priest of some of the heavy work-load. 'Charity begins at home.' Due care needs to be taken with all routine work, and it is wise to consult the priest about methods.

Church heating   Another routine job which does not need a priest to look after it is the heating system. Surely a lay person can do this, with an understudy for holidays and sickness. An automatic switch can be fitted to many systems which will operate only on Sundays (or as required). It is important to have a warm church – it is so much more encouraging. A cold church will not tempt those with a lukewarm faith.

Hymn boards   Put up appropriate numbers for the service and take them down afterwards. Never leave the numbers on the board during the week, as this gives the impression of slackness.

Church cleaning   Instead of paying a cleaner, some churches have a rota of volunteers to clean each week. It is easier if two adults, or a family, work together each time.

ROYAL SCHOOL OF CHURCH MUSIC   *See* **MUSIC IN WORSHIP** on page 128.

RURAL DEAN (AREA DEAN)   The rural dean was an ancient appointment in the Church, but the duties were gradually taken over by the archdeacon. The office was revived in 1836, and more and more work now seems to come to them.
    The rural dean is the chairman at the meetings of the deanery

clergy chapter. He presides at meetings of the Deanery Synod if he so wishes, or he may choose to hand over the chairmanship to the lay co-chairman. The rural dean is appointed by the bishop, usually after consultation with the deanery clergy. The appointment is for a period of three or five years, and can be renewed.

The main responsibility is one of leadership. He shares the bishop's pastoral care of the clergy and their families, and he is a vital channel of communication between the bishop, the clergy and the parishes. General Synod and diocesan synods sometimes send matters to the parishes through the rural dean, and he is also involved when PCCs send matters up to the Diocesan Synod.

During an interregnum in any parish in the deanery the rural dean is sometimes appointed as one of the parish sequestrators. He has general oversight of all vacant parishes in the deanery, and he is the co-ordinator of arrangements for the institution and induction service. He also carries out parish visitations (inspections) on behalf of the archdeacon, and he is involved in various deanery committees and events.

The work of a rural dean is demanding, and it always requires attendance at additional meetings outside the parish. In order that the rural dean's parish does not suffer, how can PCC members help to 'fill the gap'?

SACRAMENTS   A sacrament is an activity of the Church which expresses the presence of Christ. It is an 'outward and visible sign of an inward and spiritual grace' (BCP). There are two sacraments of the gospel – Holy Baptism and the Eucharist. In addition, there are Confirmation, Penance (personal confession before a priest, who then gives Absolution), Orders (ordination), the Anointing of the Sick, and Matrimony.

There is a distinction between the 'matter' and the 'form' of the sacrament. The bread and wine in the Eucharist are the 'matter', and the 'form' is the use of the correct words. To have a valid sacrament, the right form and matter are needed, together with the right intention. The validity of the sacrament is independent of the worthiness or unworthiness of the minister who celebrates the sacrament.

Canon Law requires that only a priest, duly ordained by a bishop, can celebrate the Eucharist.

SACRISTAN   This is the person who looks after the sacred vessels and vestments, and who prepares the altar for a service of Holy Communion.

There is a saying, 'Cleanliness comes next to Godliness', and perhaps that saying is only partly true. Cleanliness and neatness are certainly needed for all work in the sacristy.

The cruets for the water and wine need cleaning regularly. Any stain on the glass can be removed with tea leaves or grains of rice, and some water, briskly shaken.

The priest will explain what is needed. When a new priest arrives in the parish, do not be surprised if there are some changes, and you are asked to do things in a different way.

After the service, the chalice (cup) and paten (plate) and ciborium (chalice with a lid for the wafers) are washed, dried and locked away in the safe. Never put silver on silver without a purificator between them, as silver is a soft metal which scratches and quickly wears away.

The silver does not need cleaning with silver polish very often, provided it is regularly washed and rubbed with an ordinary soft tea cloth. When silver polish is used, always wash it afterwards with very hot water and washing up liquid, and rinse well. Unless this is done thoroughly, the silver polish can react with the wine to produce a most obnoxious taste. Even the slightest trace of polish can be detected. In addition, unless the washing has been very thorough, small droplets of wine will cling to the side of the chalice during the administration.

The sacristan also looks after the church vestments (if any) and the robes, and also takes action when they need cleaning, repairing or replacing (after consultation with the priest). Perhaps there is another person willing to do the repairs?

The purificators (small cloths used to wipe the chalice) and the small Lavabo towel (used to dry the priest's hands in the middle of the service) all need washing and ironing (with a little starch) each week. The 'fair linen cloth' (as the 1662 Prayer Book describes the altar cloth) and the corporal (the square linen cloth on which the sacred vessels stand) and other cloths need washing from time to time. The altar cover has a dust cover to keep the fair linen cloth clean, and this of course needs laundering from time to time.

The altar frontal(s), the pulpit fall and the priest's vestments are changed to the appropriate colour for the seasons and saints' days of the church year. The appropriate colours are given in a diary called the lectionary. The colour green is shown by a G, red is R, white is W, and violet or purple is V. The lectionary can be purchased from any religious bookshop. Buy a copy in November, when the church year begins (*see* **CHRISTIAN BOOKSHOPS** on page 217).

Sacristan

The sacristan orders fresh supplies of wine, the priest's and people's wafers, candles, incense (where used), and oil for the candles. Also new linen as required.

In parishes where there is a daily Eucharist, perhaps it may be necessary to have an assistant sacristan – who would also be able to help during holidays.

In this very secular age, we need to remember that the sacred vessels and vestments are used to further God's kingdom here on earth. Sacristy work is a vital service to the church, and is it not a privilege for the person concerned?

One final thought – each time you prepare the altar, could you offer a prayer to God for the priest taking the service, for all who come to it, for the people of the parish, and also for yourself? (*See* **SPIRITUAL LIFE OF PCC MEMBERS** on page 188.)

Sacristan's traditional prayer

Almighty God, who through thy most holy Son didst ordain and set in order all things in the upper room, that we might receive the inestimable benefits of his most precious body and blood, grant unto us thy servants that in true humility and fervent recollection we may serve thee in thy sanctuary here on earth, and finally adore thee with thy holy angels in heaven, through the merits of the same, our Saviour Jesus Christ. Amen.

ST LUKE'S HOSPITAL FOR THE CLERGY   This is a small surgical and medical hospital in one of the loveliest squares in London. It has accommodation for 28 patients and provides treatment entirely free for clergy of the Anglican Communion, their spouses, widows, dependent children, monks, nuns, deaconesses, overseas church workers, members of the Church Army, theological college students, and all full-time church workers licensed by a bishop.

The main advantage of this hospital is that the date of admission can usually be arranged to fit in with the events in the parish – unless the vicar is rushed to hospital as an emergency case. There is also privacy and the quiet atmosphere of a friendly Christian hospital.

St Luke's Hospital was a gift of the laity to the Church in 1892. Today, over 150 leading London consultants keep up an old tradition and give their time and talents entirely free of charge, which is a wonderful offering to the servants of the Church.

There are over 850 deanery representatives whose task is to

remind PCC members from time to time of the great work done by St Luke's Hospital, and to invite PCCs and individuals to make an annual donation for the hospital. Enquiries and donations to: The General Secretary, St Luke's Hospital for the Clergy, 14 Fitzroy Square, London W1T 6AH. Tel: 020–7388 4954. Email: stluke@stlukeshospital.org.uk, Web: www.stlukeshospital.org.uk

Food for thought

1. Who is your deanery representative for St Luke's Hospital?
2. When did the deanery representative last approach your PCC, and with what results? Does your PCC consider making a donation to St Luke's Hospital when preparing the annual budget?

SCHOOLS   *See* **CHURCH SCHOOLS** on pages 39–40.

SECRETARY FOR THE PRIEST   An endless flow of paperwork comes to the priest's office, and not all of it can go straight in the waste-paper basket. The priest's ministry will be much more effective if too much time is not spent on paperwork and administration. A good secretary can be a tremendous help with much of the routine work, and in this way, free the priest to concentrate on new initiatives and on all the other jobs done by the priest. It is said that a good secretary can be of more use to the priest than a curate – although it would not be wise to pursue that thought.

The secretary is in some respects a personal assistant to the priest. A job description would include the following – someone who is trustworthy, because confidential papers will sometimes be involved; reliable; efficient; methodical; able to deal with routine administration, filing, typing, a word processor and photocopier/duplicator; ability to think and plan ahead, and to remind the priest of things which need to be done.

Some PCCs are able to pay for a secretary for the priest. If this is not possible, then a volunteer may be willing to offer time and secretarial help to the church without charge. In this case, the PCC could give an honorarium.

SECRETARY OF THE PCC   The PCC appoints its secretary at the first meeting after the APCM. The secretary is normally appointed from among the PCC membership, but it is possible to appoint someone who is not a member. In the latter case, the person could either have to be co-opted to the PCC, or be a non-voting member.

Much more is involved in the work of the PCC secretary than taking notes at the meeting, and writing the minutes afterwards. The following is a summary of the work involved:

1. Ten clear days before the PCC Meeting, put a notice on the notice board, signed by – or on behalf of – the chairman, to announce the date, time and place of the meeting.

2. Seven clear days before the meeting, send a copy of the agenda to every PCC member. *See **Agenda*** on pages 144–5, ***Any Other Business*** on pages 5 (para. 3), 6 (para. 16) and 145–6, and ***Standing committee*** on pages 141–2.

3. During the meeting, take careful notes of the discussions and decisions, and the numbers voting for and against a resolution if the vote is close. Record the names of all present, or circulate an attendance list or attendance book. Record and announce any apologies for absence during the meeting. Be aware of all matters which will arise from the minutes. Consult with the chairman, preferably two or three days before the meeting, about which correspondence is to be read out at the meeting.

    A good secretary can be a great help to the chairman during the meeting, and for this reason it is helpful if they sit next to each other. *See **Rights and responsibilities*** on pages 135–7.

4. After the meeting, prepare a draft copy of the minutes as soon as possible, and certainly while they are fresh in the mind. Submit them to the chairman for approval, and then put them in the minute book. They can be pasted in the minute book, and trimmed to size. When the minutes are photocopied and kept in a loose-leaf file, it is wise to initial and number each page.

    The minutes should be brief, accurate and adequate. They are not a record of a debate, but a record of the decisions made by the PCC. Sometimes it is helpful to have a brief summary of the arguments for and against. Clear headings in capital letters are desirable. The right-hand column of the minutes should have a heading, 'Action'. This is to record who is to take action and by what date the action is to be taken. The wording of all resolutions should be recorded, and whether they were carried or rejected.

5. Circulate the minutes to all PCC members as soon as

possible after the meeting. This will be a reminder of who is doing what, as a result of the meeting.

6. There is a whole range of jobs which have to be done before and after the meeting, including letters to write, lists to prepare, and other administrative jobs.

7. The PCC secretary is an obvious candidate to be elected each year to the standing committee. Otherwise, who else will do the agenda, minutes and other paperwork involved? The secretary has an important role in the standing committee in planning ahead and in foreseeing problems which might arise.

8. Work out the dates for the whole year for PCC meetings and standing committee meetings, with the chairman (for approval by the PCC). Also the dates for putting up the legal notices in the porch, and sending out the agenda.

9. Prepare the notice, the agenda and the various reports for the Annual Parochial Church Meeting. Order a supply of the necessary official Synod notices and voting papers in good time. (*See* **ANNUAL PAROCHIAL CHURCH MEETING** on page 4.)

   Take notes during the meeting. Prepare a draft of the minutes for the chairman's approval, and then put the final copy in the minute book.

   After the APCM, put on the notice board a list of the names of the new churchwardens, the Deanery Synod representatives, and those elected to serve on the PCC for the coming year.

   Each year, it is wise to read through all the rules governing the PCC and the APCM, and particularly before the APCM. It can be helpful on occasions to remember the appropriate rules, and to quote them when necessary.

10. After each meeting, write a report for the magazine (a job for another PCC member?).

11. Not every parish is lucky enough to have a verger or caretaker. The committee room or church hall has to be prepared, and the heating put on well before the meeting, so that the room is adequately warm. Soon after being appointed as secretary, it is wise to discuss this with the churchwardens and the priest or standing committee, and also to work out who should deal with the refreshments for meetings.

12. The PCC secretary must inform the secretary of the Diocesan Synod and the secretary of the Deanery Synod, of his or her name and address on appointment.

13. The PCC secretary has an important administrative role when a new priest is being appointed. Detailed instructions are sent by the diocese about procedures, but the parish loses its legal rights about the appointment unless all time limits are strictly observed. (*See Appointing of the new priest* under **INTERREGNUM** on page 103.)

SECURITY OF CHURCHES A rota of volunteers to look after the church is one method. Another is to form a Church Neighbourhood Watch Scheme. All the people living around the building may not want to come to church, but if approached, they may be willing to help with a watch scheme. How about a social evening and slide show to launch it?

Children love to climb on a church roof. If this is a problem in your parish, one answer is to take a photograph of them! It usually works.

SEQUESTRATION *See* **INTERREGNUM** on page 102.

SERMON Every preacher has an awesome responsibility. What, then, do you think the preacher is aiming to achieve? To proclaim the gospel – to convert the congregation – to rebuke on occasions – to encourage – to strengthen and build up the faith of the Church – to draw out and expound God's word in the Scriptures?

A former Archbishop of Canterbury, Dr Michael Ramsey, said, 'Preaching creates and re-creates the Church'. Think for a moment how God's living word is at work in your parish, and also at work when the Church gathers together to worship God.

The sermon plays a very important part in our worship each Sunday. A preacher cannot arrive in the pulpit and hope for sudden inspiration! If the preacher is true to this high calling, then much time is needed for careful preparation. Those who are present will to a large extent be the same people in the congregation week by week.

A priest cannot produce good sermons regularly when the work-load is impossibly heavy. The quality of the sermon will play an important part in determining whether the occasional worshipper in church comes again next week.

The preaching of the gospel was made a priority in the lives of the Apostles. 'The Twelve called the whole body of disciples together and said, "It would be a grave mistake for us to neglect the word of God in order to wait at table. Therefore, friends, look out seven men of good reputation from your number, men full of the Spirit and of wisdom, and we will appoint them to deal with these matters, while we devote ourselves to prayer and to the ministry of the word." This proposal proved acceptable to the whole body' (Acts 6,2–5 NEB). See also Acts 2,2–4 and 2 Timothy 4,1–5.

What message is the preacher delivering? Careful listening is important for all present, for PCC members, and especially 'Know the reason for the faith that is within you'.

A suggestion for every PCC member (and for the congregation too): pray for the preacher just before the sermon. A suggested prayer:

Almighty God, bless this your servant,
and open all our hearts to receive your living word,
through Jesus Christ our Lord. Amen.

Food for thought

1. A sermon is much more than a lesson or lecture – but is it the only form of Christian education for the congregation week by week?
2. An occasional alternative to a sermon – a dialogue, or a question and answer session between two people, or a discussion after the service about the sermon on a special subject such as Christian stewardship, mission and evangelism, church music, etc.

SERVERS There are two sayings about trying to keep young people in the Church:

1. 'Use me, or lose me'.
2. 'The boy holds the candle, but the candle holds the boy.'

How many parish priests have discovered their vocation to the sacred ministry through serving at the altar? Quite a thought!

It is a great privilege to serve at the Eucharist, and for this reason, servers should do their utmost to make their part of the worship as perfect as possible.

The hallmark of a good server is to be unobtrusive, and all movements should be carried out quietly, efficiently and with the minimum of fuss. Whenever two servers are required to move together, they should do so in harmony. Careful training is obviously needed to achieve this.

It is helpful if servers are in church at least twenty minutes before the service (ten minutes on weekdays?). The first thing to do on each occasion is to offer a short prayer to God for the priest, for those present, and for yourself. A suggested prayer (to learn by heart?):

Heavenly Father,
your Son is our great High Priest in heaven:
bless us all with the gifts of your Holy Spirit,
make us worthy to serve you in this holy sacrament,
and unite us in your everlasting love,
through Jesus Christ our Lord. Amen.

As a member of the Church community, it is desirable that every server should join in the worship as far as is possible. The offering of the servers, however, is first of all to do the work of serving to the glory of God, and to the best of their ability.

After the service, help to clear away. Always use the extinguisher to put out the candles. Never blow them out, as this spreads the candle wax. It then has to be removed by someone! This is not always an easy task.

A prayer to be used by the server before leaving church (to learn by heart?):

O God, you have given so much to me.
Give me one thing more – a greatful heart,
for Christ's sake. Amen.

SERVERS GUILD   Mr Roy Creswell, The General Secretary, The Guild of the Servants of the Sanctuary, 20 Doe Bank Rd., Ocker Hill, Tipton, West Midlands, DY4 0ES. Tel: 0121–556 2256.

Food for thought
Does anyone from the parish belong to the Guild of the Servers of the Sanctuary?

SHOES   A suggestion: if walking on uncarpeted aisles before or during a quiet service, try to walk quietly.

SIDESMEN – SIDESWOMEN   In choosing sidesmen, effort should be made to include people from all walks of life, young and old, men and women, rich and poor, black and white. People need to feel included in the life of the Church. What are the duties of sidesmen?

1. About 20 minutes before the service, prepare the books, service and notice sheets, so that they are all ready to hand to people as they arrive.

2. The greeting and welcome given to people as they come in is the most important part of the sidesmen's job. It is good to look directly at each person as the books are handed over to them. Never turn your back on people when they come in, in order to pick up the books. A smile works wonders. It is a good thing for the sidesmen to learn the names of the congregation so that they can all be greeted by name. Some churches have a special welcome team, who look out for visitors and strangers. If a visitor comes alone, it is helpful and friendly if someone from the welcome team can sit with them during the service. After the service, invite them for coffee, and introduce them to some other members of the congregation.

3. The sidesmen play a vital role in helping to provide the right tone and spiritual atmosphere in the church before the service. A warm and friendly greeting is good, providing it is done quietly. If the sidesmen talk loudly with each person, this will disturb those who are trying to pray and to prepare for worship. Lack of thought and concern for others can very quickly destroy the peace and quietness that are needed. The sidesmen have a great potential for helping the whole church to prepare for its worship, or for destroying the prayerful and quiet atmosphere that is so vital in preparation. 'How awesome is this place. This is the House of God. This is the Gate of Heaven.'

4. When strangers or visitors come to church, try to find out their names and addresses – but always in a tactful way. Write it down later on, and hand it to the visiting committee or to the vicar. Cards are available from church bookshops – 'Visitors and Newcomers' cards.

5. Take the collection during the service – if that is the tradition in your church. It seems to produce more money than leaving the plate at the back of the church! Count the money and open the envelopes, record the amounts in the Register of Services, and sign the book. It is customary to have at least two sidesmen counting the money in this way.

6. In most parishes, the sidesmen are asked to perform other duties before the service. These usually include putting on the light and heat, lighting the candles, and, if there is no server, preparing the altar. After the service, put out the

candles and lights, and turn off the heating once the church is empty.

7. It is important that the sidesmen come early enough to do the jobs properly. It is more important that they prepare themselves spiritually for the service. It is wrong to forget their own spiritual preparation because they are busy doing other jobs. Canon Law states 'It is the duty of the sidesmen to promote the cause of true religion in the parish' (Canon E2(3)). Their own example and practice is an important part of it.

8. It is the duty of the sidesmen to assist the churchwardens in maintaining order and decency in the church and church-yard, especially during an act of worship. Perhaps it is not very common in your parish for the preacher to be booed during the sermon, but a good team of men may be needed to keep out the drunks at the Midnight Service.

9. After each service, most clergy try to shake hands with all members of the congregation as they leave the building. (They are busy praying before the service.) A friendly word from the sidesmen as people leave is a good thing – 'Hope you enjoyed the service, and that we'll see you again next Sunday'. The sidesmen should never turn their backs on people in order to put the hymn books away.

A prayer for use by the sidesmen before the service

Almighty God,
you have called us to serve you as sidesmen in your Church:
fill us all with your Holy Spirit,
bless all who come to your House this day,
and help us to worship you with reverence and devotion,
through Jesus Christ our Lord. Amen.

If there is an opportunity, read the collect, the appointed Psalm and the three Scripture readings, as part of your own preparation.

A prayer for use by sidesmen after the service

Heavenly Father,
the hosts of heaven ceaselessly proclaim your glory,
and we have joined with them in praising your holy name:
Make us mindful of all your blessings,
and guide all of us in this coming week,
through Jesus Christ our Lord. Amen.

SILVER   All silver, gold, brass and pewter vessels are valuable and it is wise to have them photographed for identification purposes, in case they are stolen. It is a simple matter to have a parish identification 'mark' engraved, or the police have an ultra-violet pen (needs re-doing periodically). *See* **SACRISTAN** on pages 176–8.

SINGING   *See* **MUSIC IN WORSHIP** on page 124.

SOCIAL EVENTS   It is not possible for the priest to know more than a small percentage of the people in a large parish. Any social event organized by the church is an opportunity for PCC members and others to invite fringe members and outsiders. The PCC – or the entertainments committee – can organize 'open' social events on numerous occasions, e.g. Shrove Tuesday party, New Year party, dance or dinner dance, barn dance, harvest lunch or harvest supper, wine and cheese party, coffee morning and so on.

Much more than social gatherings is required to draw people into church membership, but these events certainly do help. How can PCC members help to follow up any contacts apart from prayer?

SOCIAL RESPONSIBILITY AND CONCERN   The spiritual gospel and the social gospel are closely linked together, and they are both an important part of the life and work of the Church. God created all people, and his Son took flesh for the redemption of the whole world. This is shown in the sacraments. We demonstrate his love not only in our words, but also by our deeds. This includes working for justice and peace in the world, trying to meet human need, working for the relief of suffering, and trying to do our share for the whole of God's creation.

The Church will lose much of its cutting edge if it fails to do something about the problems of the modern world – apart from praying about them. What would the prophet Amos say about modern injustices, poverty, unemployment, depression, crime, drug addiction, the problems of the elderly and the young, the lonely, the mentally handicapped, the disabled?

The state has done much to improve the lot of many people, when compared with former years. But the whole system is a partnership between the state and various voluntary organizations, including the Church. Quite often, the system needs prodding, questioning, a new vision and encouragement. It is part of

187

being a Christian in the world to take an active interest in society, and to help whenever possible. The parable of the good Samaritan shows us who are our neighbours. Who then are the modern equivalent of the despised Samaritans? The parable also shows how Christians should be involved, and Jesus himself was constantly helping other people.

The PCC as a Christian organization responds because of its understanding of what God is like. God does not love only the rich and the privileged. He also loves the poor, the oppressed and those who are the outcasts of society today. When God entered the human scene, it was among the poor of the earth that he came. It is so easy for a PCC to be preoccupied with the actual life of the church. It is so easy for Christians to be detached and isolated from the problems of society in general – or even the problems of the local secular community. The basis of Christian love and concern for others comes from the fount of all love, God our loving creator and redeemer.

General Synod has a Board for Social Responsibility, which produces official reports on issues of concern from time to time. These reports are debated in General Synod and widely reported in the media. The reports can be studied, and then discussed at PCC meetings to give a clearer understanding of the issues involved.

The problems of modern society are large and even frightening. They may well seem beyond the ability of the PCC in a small parish to do anything about them. But a concern for justice, for freedom and truth are surely high ideals which a Christian believes should be enjoyed by everyone. Justice and peace are important parts of the kingdom of God.

SPIRITUAL LIFE OF PCC MEMBERS Prayer has been described as 'the lifting of the heart and mind to God'. There is a saying, 'all activity compared with prayer is as nothing', and this is particularly true for PCC members. This section on the spiritual life is probably the most important part of the *ABC*. Every PCC member can make a far greater contribution to the life of the local church through prayer than through any amount of activity. However efficient, caring and responsible a PCC member may be, he or she is failing unless prayer and Christian love are given high priority in their daily lives.

Some people want religion without discipline. 'God will not accept a divided affection' (William Wilberforce), and Evelyn Underhill reminds us that 'there are no short cuts in the spiritual life'. There are different ways of praying, and each PCC member has to work out which is the best for them. Each has to work at his or her spiritual life, and start again after each failure. Continual discipline is needed, but the day will come when prayer is not so much a duty as a delight. Prayer is about developing a relationship with God, and no one else can do this for you. Prayer is your search for God – but remember that God has been searching for you long before you started your search for God. Prayer is deliberately putting yourself into God's presence, and exposing yourself to his love.

Personal prayer Christians are formed by the way in which they pray. Your views about what God is like will powerfully affect your spiritual life. Jesus taught us to think of God as Father. Whatever faults your earthly father may have had, your Heavenly Father is a God of mercy and love, and he really does love you, and all other people too. How then do you respond to God's love for you on the cross, and how do you develop a personal relationship with someone you cannot see or touch? It can be done, but it requires time and commitment each day. Prayer is a journey of discovery.

Many people find it helpful to say the Lord's Prayer very slowly. Go through it phrase by phrase, and with a definite pause between each phrase. This is a particularly good way of starting – or beginning again in the spiritual life.

Praying for ten minutes on your journey to work each morning is a good habit. It is certainly helpful to be aware of God's presence during the journey. But if you are serious in your desire to pray – (and this must surely include every PCC member) – then you need to make additional time for prayer each day in a quiet place, preferably in your home. It is said that 'silence is the gateway to the spiritual life'.

Still your mind, and relax your body, and only when you have done this, try to put yourself into the presence of God. Each person is a complex being, and our emotional and mental side can have a powerful effect on our prayer life and worship. We usually come to God with what we might call our own special personal baggage – our fears, guilt, hopes, expectations, and a whole host of things which will distract us from God. In some ways, our prayer time can rapidly change from being 'God-centred' to 'self-centred'. In the Confirmation service, we say, 'I turn to Christ' – and we have to turn to Christ again and again, especially after being distracted. Learn to develop an inner stillness and to focus all your attention on God. Choose a position which you can maintain without moving. Whether you sit, stand or kneel, be still, and be aware of your breathing, which should be deep, regular and slow. Hymns of the Holy Spirit are helpful, or simply ask for God's help: 'Heavenly Father, you sent your Spirit to the Church at Pentecost. Renew your gift of the Spirit in us, and teach us how to pray'.

Learn to wait in silence, and do not be in a hurry to begin your prayers with words. God is always trying to help us to get to know him better. His Spirit is always with us, and we have to try to be open to his suggestions and promptings. Reading books on prayer helps you to find out what other people have discovered about prayer before you. Your aim is to find God in your prayers, so try to find a way of praying which works for you. Each person must try and work out what is best and most helpful.

Praying with the Bible   Many people soon come to the end of their own resources in prayer, but God offers us help, for example, through the Bible. By all means use the King James Authorized Version if you glory in good English, but it is helpful to have another more modern translation as well. Compare the old with the new version. Buy a Bible with good clear print. The Bible is one of the important ways in which God's word comes to us today. Become aware of God's presence, and imagine that you are part of the scene in the Bible passage. Reflect on how God is speaking directly to you through the passage. You may feel happiness, sadness, guilt or anger, but try to turn your feelings and thoughts about the passage into prayer.

Praying with a mantra   A mantra is a word or phrase which is repeated many times whenever appropriate during the day or night. It is a very ancient method of prayer from the East, and it quickly makes you aware of God's presence. Choose your own mantra carefully, and then use it as required. Here is a selection:

> Lord Jesus Christ, Son of God, have mercy on us (The Jesus Prayer).
> Jesus is Lord.
> Jesus Christ is risen indeed.
> My God, I love thee. Help me to love thee more and more.
> I am loved by God more than I can either conceive or understand (Henri de Tourville).
> Jesus, I love you.

Using a book of prayers   Ask your priest for suggestions. (It may be helpful for the PCC to spend a whole meeting, with no other business on the agenda, to discuss the subject of prayer.) When using a book of prayers, it is important actually to *pray* the prayers, rather than just read them. The day will come, as you grow in your prayer life, when you will want to use your own words. Here are some suggestions for prayer books: *When You Pray* compiled by John Gilling and Sister Patricia (Darton, Longman and Todd); *Some Daily Prayers for Church of England People* compiled by Harry Ogden (St Denys Bookshop, 11 Oak Street, Manchester M4 5JP); *A Diary of Private Prayer* by John Baillie (Oxford University Press); and *Daily with God* by the author (Canterbury Press).

Praying and breathing   Pray one line of (say) the Lord's Prayer, with each intake of breath, and with a silent pause as you breath out. It will seem strange at first, but effective when you have mastered it. This can be helpful in the early stages of learning how to pray. Other prayers can be used in this way too.

Learning to meditate   Become still, and aware of God's presence. Then spend time thinking about one word only, which describes Jesus or God, e.g. holy Jesus, loving Jesus, merciful Jesus, forgiving Jesus. Each time, use only one of these words. 'If a man love me, he will heed my words and my Father will love him, and we will come and make our dwelling with him.'

Cross or crucifix   Some people find it helpful to conduct their prayer time in front of, or near, a cross or crucifix, e.g. in their room. A lighted candle is also helpful.

Saints' days   Receiving Communion on the major Saints' days is part of the rule of life of a Christian (a 'day of obligation').

We ask people to pray for us during our life on earth. Do they stop praying for us after they die? Many people (but not all) feel it is right to ask the Saints to pray for us. Probably the most widely used prayer (apart from the Lord's Prayer) is the Hail Mary, which is used in the Orthodox and Roman Catholic Churches, and by many Anglicans too. People do not pray to the Saints, but ask the Saints to pray for them.

Food for thought
Which of the Apostles, Saints or Martyrs do you feel are close to you?

A busy life?   If the answer is yes, then think about Martin Luther's words: 'I have much to do today, therefore I shall have to pray for a long time'.

Arrow prayers   These are short, quick prayers, offered to God at any time on the spur of the moment. It is important to remember that arrow prayers are always 'extra' prayers, and they must never be used as an alternative for a regular time of prayer. Arrow prayers help you to become aware of God's presence during the day or night, and they help you to seek God's will in every situation. They are also asking for God's help, particularly when there has been an accident, or when you are watching the news on television. Here are a few examples:

> O Lord, bless this person here with me now.
> O Lord, bless all who are travelling on this plane/train/ship/bus.
> Father, forgive me for those unkind words/for that unkind thought.
> Thank you, Lord, for all your blessings, and especially . . .
> Lord, help this person.
> Heavenly Father, bless and help all who are connected with this emergency (at the sound of ambulance, fire engine or police car).
> Lord, help us to see what you want in this situation.

Making the sign of the cross   From the way in which Tertullian (AD 160–225) writes about it, the making of the sign of the cross appears to be as old as Christianity itself. The cross is the 'standard' of Christ, and making the sign of the cross is a very ancient way of showing our loyalty and dedication to Christ to those who are near to us, (and also to ourselves?). It reminds us of God's work of salvation on the cross to save us from our sins. It is a shorthand prayer to bring this to mind. It is normal to say (aloud or to yourself) the words: 'In the name of the Father and of the Son and of the Holy Spirit. Amen.' And this, of course, also reminds us of the nature of God as the Holy Trinity.

The sign is made with the right hand, marking the letter 'I' from the top to the bottom of the chest, and then crossing it out, from left to right. It is saying – 'I turn from myself and I turn to Christ.' It is normally made at the beginning and the end of our prayers, and an act of worship. It is also made at the end of the Creed, and at certain places in the Eucharist. Using our body in this way in our worship reminds us of the words, 'and here we offer and present unto Thee our souls and bodies, to be a living sacrifice. . . .'

What to say in your prayers Prayer is not a time to give a catalogue of your wants and desires to God. Not much of a relationship can be built up if all you do is to say what you want from God. As we grow in our spiritual lives, so we come to realize that there are different kinds of prayer, and these are represented in the word PACTS. Each letter of the word PACTS stands for a different aspect of prayer. P stands for Preparation for prayer. A stands for our Adoration and praise of God. C stands for Confessing our sins to God. T stands for Thanking God. S stands for the word 'Supplications' – which means praying for others and, lastly, praying for yourself. 'PACTS' reminds us of the different parts of prayer, and some people find they can base their daily prayers on the word PACTS. But it is not easy, and it is wiser not to try this in the early stages.

Prayer should always be 'God-centred' rather than 'self-centred'. The praise and glory of God is followed by the needs of men and women (as in the Lord's Prayer). Always avoid telling God what you think he should do, as though you know best. It is sufficient to bring the person or situation to God in prayer – and 'kept in your heart' while you are praying.

God's love flows endlessly towards the world, and our prayers for others are one channel of his love. Prayer is about God and his kingdom, his will and his justice.

Pray each day for your bishop and your priest by name. Pray regularly for the mission of the Church in your parish, in your deanery, and in the nearest town or city. Pray for PCC members in the parish and in the deanery – for all who have been baptized and confirmed, and their families – for all who have lapsed – for all on the electoral rolls of the deanery – for diocesan officials – for those who serve on diocesan committees or Diocesan and Deanery Synods – for those who live near to you – for all who live and work in the parish – for all who are ill or dying, the bereaved, those who have died, and for those whose anniversary of death falls during the week.

Include 'outward'-looking subjects such as those who influence public opinion – those who administer the law – the unemployed – homeless people and all refugees – all in authority, locally and nationally – the leaders of the nations – police, probation and prison officers, prisoners and their families – the Royal Family – the disabled and their families – all involved in education, especially Christian education. Could you make your own '31-day cycle of prayer'? Pray for your friends, family, and finally for yourself – including those 'dark corners' in your life (if any exist). Prayer is all about bringing our wishes into line with God's wishes.

One way to conclude your prayers is with the Lord's Prayer, the collect for the day and the Grace. Do not then get up and rush away from God's presence. He is your friend, and he is always with you. If you do want to rush away, then ask yourself what is wrong. Also consider: could my prayers have been better?

Difficulties in prayer Prayer is sometimes joyful and peaceful, while at other times you may not feel like praying. Your thoughts wander or you do not even want to start praying. At such times, keep on praying 'as a duty', even though it is difficult and God does not seem to be there. He is always there, even though you are not aware of his presence. Always try to pray before you are too tired, because you cannot offer your best to God when you are half asleep. However, a prayer last thing at night, in addition to your regular time of prayer, is a good thing.

One way to deal with difficulties in prayer is to try to turn them into prayer – even your wandering thoughts. You may well experience difficulties in the early stages, and also in later stages too. Perhaps the difficulties indicate that you need to change your method of praying. Consult your spiritual adviser about it.

Sin and forgiveness We all have to learn the difficult lesson of how to forgive other people. 'Forgive us our trespasses (sins) as we forgive those who trespass against us.' This is vital for your spiritual life, and it will also teach you something about God's love and mercy and forgiveness for you.

Any form of sin kills spiritual growth, and separates you from God. Every Christian needs God's forgiveness regularly, and it can be received in three different ways. First, by asking God in your own private prayers to forgive you. Secondly, you can confess your sins Sunday by Sunday in the general confession at church, and the priest pronounces God's absolution. Thirdly, you can make a private confession to a priest, if you feel this is necessary. The 1662 Book of Common Prayer states, in the visitation of the sick: when a person's 'conscience is troubled with any weighty matter' he is to make a private confession to a priest, who will absolve him with the authority of Christ, and in his name. Sacramental confession gives us the assurance of God's forgiveness. There is a saying in the Anglican Church about confession – 'None must, all may and some do'. Whatever the priest hears during confession is always kept with absolute secrecy.

Parish days of prayer Ask people to spend 30 minutes in prayer in church on a rota list through the day. Just because one person is in church e.g. from 1 to 1.30 p.m., it does not mean that others cannot be present at the same time. The important thing is to have the chain through the day. There is usually a special 'intention' for the prayers, e.g. the mission of the Church in the parish, and prayer material can be provided for those who wish to use it. How often should a day of prayer be held? Four times a year? Monthly? Opportunity should be provided for those who work to come in the early evening.

Parish prayer fellowship This is arranged with a daily list of intercessions for each month, and a teaching letter on prayer for use by people at home. Each member prays each day for all the other members of the prayer fellowship, and for the priest and the parish. Could this be organized by a lay person?

Three-parish prayer links Each parish prays for the other two parishes every day. A town parish, a country one and an inner city parish? Dare one say – an evangelical (low Church) linked with a catholic (high Church) parish?

Husband and wife What a strong team if husband and wife can pray together! This is not always easy. An alternative – to read a passage from the Bible together each day or night, followed by silent prayer (or saying the Lord's Prayer together). The Psalms may be added, one saying even verses and the other doing the odd verses.

Parish library A collection of books about the spiritual life is a good resource for every local church. Every PCC member should aim to read one book on prayer each year (during Lent?).

Spiritual director (soul friend) Whatever name is used, it is helpful to talk about your prayer life with another person at least once a year. Have you fallen back or made progress in your prayer life during the year? What are the problems? Spiritual blockages?

Choose someone steeped in prayer, whether ordained or lay, but someone you can trust and with whom you would be happy to share the secrets of your spiritual life. 'Spiritual direction' is at the heart of spiritual growth. The way you live your life during the day affects your relationship with God and your whole prayer life. Your body is a 'temple of the Holy Spirit'.

A retreat An annual retreat forms part of the life of many PCC members. What about a PCC retreat or quiet day? (*See* **RETREAT** on pages 173–5.)

God's will Prayer is not offered to God to try to persuade him to change his mind, and to alter the course of events. You pray to discover God's will, and to bring your will into line with God's will. 'Thy kingdom come, thy will be done, on earth as it is in heaven.' How far do you really mean that, when you say the Lord's Prayer?

Regular worship The Church is the eucharistic community, which gathers together on its knees to receive the body and blood of Christ in the Eucharist. Then it becomes the 'Church on legs' as PCC members and others go out into the world to love and serve God during the coming week. Worship is not a question of going to church only when you feel like it. Your presence shows how much God is worth to you (worship means worthship). Invite visitors to come with you, and allow nothing to keep you away, except illness or an accident. PCC members should set an example to the congregation in this matter of regular worship, which is essential for personal growth and the growth of the congregation. God wants you to worship him and to show your love to him in this way. If you stay away, you are rejecting his love, and also causing weakness in his body the Church. Your absence shows that you do not appreciate the cost of God's love for you on the cross. Jesus said, 'You shall love the Lord your God with all your heart, with all your mind, with all your soul and with all your strength'. In the ten commandments, we are exhorted to 'keep holy the Sabbath', i.e. by worshipping God. See also St John 15,5.

Holy Communion During the week a parish is fortunate if it can have a daily celebration of our Lord's death and resurrection. 'Give us this day our daily bread.' Without any shadow of doubt, a daily celebration of the Eucharist makes a tremendous difference for the spiritual life of the priest. It is also good for the parish to have a daily celebration of the Eucharist. After all, the

Church is the Eucharistic community. Receiving Communion regularly is a vital part of Christian formation.

Preparation for Holy Communion   Noise before the service can be a problem in some congregations. The 'General Notes' in Common Worship state: 'Careful devotional preparation before the service is recommended for every communicant' (proposed at General Synod by the author). St Paul puts this in a different way: 'Anyone who eats the bread or drinks the cup of the Lord unworthily will be guilty of desecrating the body and blood of the Lord. A man must test himself before eating his share of the bread and drinking from the cup' (1 Corinthians 11,27–28 NEB).

The Eucharist means the Thanksgiving. Thank God for his blessings given to you, to your loved ones, and to . . .

Confess your sins. Before the service, go back over the past week and work out exactly what you will confess to God in the service. Remember, we only receive God's forgiveness if we forgive those who sin against us. The cross is about our sins. Penitence (sorrow for sin) is needed for spiritual growth. 'Drink this, all of you; this is my blood of the new covenant, which is shed for you and for many for the forgiveness of sins. Do this, as often as you drink it, in remembrance of me.'

Offer each Eucharist to God with your own special intention – whether for some person, institution or cause. Do this in addition to the intention which is (usually, but not always) offered by the priest. Work out your intention before the service begins.

Arrive early, and if possible about fifteen minutes before the service. As a PCC member, you have a responsibility to give a lead to the congregation in prayer and preparation. By arriving early, you can make your own preparations in an unhurried and worthy way, and learn to grow in the spiritual life. It is not easy to put yourself in the presence of God especially if you arrive in a hurry or late. Obviously, it is much more difficult for a family with young children.

Are there other Christians kneeling and praying in church when you arrive? If so, what secret about the spiritual life have they discovered that you have not yet learned?

Another suggestion. Very quietly say 'Hello' to the sidesmen, but do not chatter before the service. You are there to worship your Creator and Redeemer, and you need to prepare yourself to come into the presence of the King of Kings. To chatter before the service is harmful to the spiritual life of the Church, and it prevents you and others from making careful preparations. Voices carry in a church building, and your talking, however quiet, will disturb those who are trying to pray. Noise certainly lessens the spiritual effectiveness of the Church. Two old sayings: 'Silence is the gateway to the spiritual life.' 'Before the service, talk to God. During the service, listen to God. After the service, talk to each other.'

In former years, people had a greater respect for the Church. Today, this respect seems to be much less evident, even among Church members. Jesus said, 'My house shall be called a House of Prayer'. Perhaps we need to rediscover a sense of awe and mystery for what is sacred and set apart for God in a building consecrated to his holy name. God said to Moses, 'Take off your sandals, for the place where you are standing is holy ground'. Muslims take this literally. Is there a message which we can learn from this? A church building often has an atmosphere of prayer, and many find it is a good place for their own private prayers. People come early not only to make their own preparation, but also to say their prayers in the peace and quietness of God's house.

When you have made your preparation, use any spare time to read the Scripture readings appointed for the day. Think about their meaning, and what God is wanting to say to you through them. Work out what is the common theme of the readings. Can you turn any parts of the Scripture passages into prayer?

The hymn 'Come, Holy Ghost, our souls inspire' is good for personal preparation. Could you learn it by heart and use it as your prayer before the service begins? Many Communion hymns are good for personal preparation.

The Book of Psalms is the greatest prayer-book ever written, and the Psalms were loved and used by Jesus. They are excellent for our preparations. Use the Psalms and get to know them, and work out which are helpful in preparation.

Another suggestion: pray for all who are near you in the building, the priest, and all who will lead the worship. Pray for the whole congregation at this and the other services today. If you have offended anyone, or if you have been offended by anyone, or you find it hard to like someone, then pray for God's healing love, and for his blessing on them and on you. Pray for the deepening of the spiritual life of the congregation, and for an extension of God's kingdom in the church and in the parish.

Another thought – as you walk up to the church door, say a prayer to yourself. 'Lord, bless us and all who will worship in your house today.' Or the well-known prayer, 'Lord, teach us how to pray'.

In one sense, we receive from the service in proportion to what we put into it in terms of personal preparation. In another sense, we receive everything, unworthy though we are, through the grace and love of God.

A powerful way to help the mission of the Church is through prayer – and to make our worship a spiritual powerhouse.

Worship means 'worthship' – how much God is really worth to us. Jesus asked Peter, 'Do you love me?' If God asked you to what extent do you love him, how would you answer? One way we show our love for God is by the care and effort with which we prepare for our worship.

Before receiving Communion   Many people, as they walk up to receive Communion, repeat to themselves the words: 'Lord, I am not worthy to receive you, but only say the word, and I shall be healed'.

After the service   Kneel quietly and thank God for all the benefits you have received, and particularly the gift of his Son in the sacrament.

A 'rule of life' for PCC members   PCC members are all at different stages of their spiritual journey. Whatever stage you have reached, you need to think about what you are doing and why. Prayer is difficult, and if you find you have stopped for a few days or years, then start again, and ask God to help you to persevere. The basic principles of the spiritual life remain unchanged, despite all other modern changes.

Think about what God has done for you through his Son on the cross. In making a rule of life, we try to respond to God's love for us. We give our time to acknowledge that all our time is a gift from God.

1. *To receive Communion every Sunday.*   This should be central in the life of every Christian. 'The Lord's service in the Lord's house on the Lord's day.' Regular worship changes us from being self-centred to God-centred people. Sunday worship should be the first duty in the life of every Christian.
2. *Daily prayer.*   Prayer is not easy, but it should have a central part in the life of every PCC member. Usually it is a matter of setting aside a time each day for prayer. Even if it is only to say the Our Father (and some would add Hail Mary) it is very

important. How could you improve the quality of your prayers?

3. *Read your Bible.* Once you get into the habit each day, it becomes part of your daily life. Go through the four Gospels, and later the New Testament, in a systematic way, with a book marker. If you read your Bible carefully and prayerfully, it will give you a deeper knowledge and love of Jesus. What does God want to say to you through the Scriptures?

4. *Money.* One way to measure (or test) our love for God and his Church is in our sacrificial giving. Work out in a prayerful way what is a responsible proportion of your income that you could give back to God and his Church each week. Do this in thanksgiving for his many blessings, and for all that he has given to you. PCC members who have not yet considered this as a spiritual matter should consult **Stewardship of time, skills** and **money** on pages 30–2.

5. *Our time and talents.* It is good to thank God for the time and the skills which he has given to each of us, and to work out how we can use some of our time and skills in the service of Church, neighbour and community.

6. *Daily life.* Are you satisfied with the part which your faith plays in your daily life, work and leisure?

Some people find it is helpful to write down their rule of life on paper, using the above headings, and add the date. They can be revised later, again adding the date of the revision.

Questions for discussion

1. Do you make adequate preparation before you receive Communion?
2. Do you read the Bible each day? Do you try and work out how it is relevant for you?
3. Are you satisfied with the progress you are making in your spiritual life?
4. Do you have a spiritual director (soul friend)?

SPRING CLEANING   The church building, and the hall, need to be thoroughly cleaned once a year, apart from their regular weekly or daily cleaning. Members of the congregation can be invited to help. If this is done in the evening, or on Saturday, it enables those who are at work to help. Do not forget the tower and those dark corners where things are 'dumped', and especially on top of cupboards in the vestry. Someone is needed to organize the spring cleaning. (Is it a good time to think about timber treatment after the spring clean?)

STEWARDSHIP   *See* **CHRISTIAN STEWARDSHIP** on page 29.

STREET WARDENS   A warden system has been adopted in many parishes. There are different ways of doing this, but always the whole of the parish is divided into areas. Each area has its own warden, who is the church representative for that area. The warden's job is to be the communication link to take information from the church to every home, and this can be done verbally, by duplicated letter, or (free?) magazine. The warden is also the communications link between the home and the church, and particularly to report back sickness, someone in hospital, death, a problem, departures and new arrivals.

SUNDAY SCHOOL   Whatever name is used instead of Sunday School, children and young people are an important part of today's Church. It is an absolute gift when children actually come to Church (without the Church trying to get them there). How can the Church keep them and make sure they will be there in the years to come? If the Church fails to win the children at an early age, the task is very much harder later on. If the opportunity is not grasped to help them to grow in the faith, the Church may never have a second chance with them.

Here are some suggestions to help the PCC in its discussions:

(1) Most parishes have a Sunday School at the same time as their main Sunday service. The Sunday School spends the first half of the main service in the hall (if there is a hall) or in the vestry or Lady Chapel, when there is not hall. They come into church during the Offertory Hymn, and they come to receive a Blessing when the congregation comes to receive Communion. The sidesman or churchwarden can tell the Sunday School teachers that it is time to come into church, and also assist with their entry.

(2) It can be good for the parents to stay in the Sunday School with the children (up to a certain age) and be involved with the worship and lessons.

(3) What is needed from the local church to assist with the spiritual formation of the children entrusted to its care?

(4) Parents of children can sometimes be persuaded to help, and hopefully become involved with teaching the children.

(5) Not everyone can teach the faith, and some help and training is essential. The diocesan education director may well provide suitable training, either in the parish or at a deanery centre. Perhaps the diocesan education team could be invited to an open meeting, with PCC members, parents, Sunday School Teachers and members of the congregation.

(6) Many resources are available to help the parish in its work. Ask the diocesan education director what is available. The church building and the church hall are great resources in themselves. In addition, there must be people who will help with the Sunday School. Perhaps a rota system?

(7) It can be difficult to keep the interest of children, with so many other interests powerfully competing for their attention. Boredom is the great enemy, but a church – with some imagination and prayer – does have the resources to counteract boredom. Interesting lessons are needed. The children belong to an organisation which circles the globe and spans the centuries. We are not alone! We belong to a friendly organization where there is an opportunity to meet others. How can we use this to the benefit of the Church, as well as to the benefit of young people?

(8) Children can be lost to the faith when they finish their time at Sunday School. An important part of the Sunday School work is to prepare the children to be baptized (if they have not been baptized already), to be confirmed and become regular communicants. (*See* **CONFIRMATION** page 55 ff.)

(9) Jesus said, 'Allow the children to come to me. Do not try to stop them. The Kingdom of God belongs to such as these.' Hopefully, members of the congregation can be encouraged to get to know the children, and take an interest in them. Perhaps some of their work could be displayed on a board for the congregation to see each Sunday.

SYNODS OF THE CHURCH   The word 'synod' comes from two Greek words which mean 'the way' and 'together'. Synodical government is built on the principle of a partnership between bishops, clergy and lay people. Synodical government does not mean that the Church is a democracy in the full and more usual sense of the word. It is sometimes called 'government by discussion'. The bishop exercises a guardianship of the

Church, and to a lesser extent this guardianship is also one of the functions of the parish priest.

The Deanery Synod This is made up of two 'houses' – the house of clergy (all incumbents, assistant clergy, clergy holding the bishop's licence, and semi-retired clergy who are 'resident and working') and also the house of laity. The Deanery Synod has at least one lay representative from each parish (depending on the numbers on the electoral roll) who is elected for three years by the Annual Parochial Church Meeting. Deanery Synod members are *ex-officio* members of their own Parochial Church Councils.

It is important that the lay representatives make a report on the proceedings of Deanery Synod at every PCC meeting. When a PCC representative cannot attend a Deanery Synod meeting, it is important to arrange for an observer to attend the meeting.

A PCC can send a resolution to the Deanery Synod, or to the Diocesan Synod, or indeed to the local government council if appropriate.

The Diocesan Synod This has three 'houses' and the house of bishops forms one of these houses. The house of clergy forms another house, which includes the dean or provost, archdeacons and the clergy elected by Deanery Synods. The house of laity forms the third house, and it is elected by the lay members of the Deanery Synods. On important matters, a resolution has to be carried in all three houses, voting separately by houses. In other words, each house has the power of veto. Items on the Diocesan Synod agenda are normally discussed and voted upon by all three houses sitting together in full synod, and require only a simple majority vote.

The General Synod This has three 'houses', bishops, clergy and laity. General Synod is a legislative assembly, a financial authority, and an administrative centre for the Church of England. It was created by the Synodical Government Measure 1969. The houses of clergy and laity are elected mainly by Deanery Synod members. They are elected for five-year periods.

Convocations The two ancient Convocations of Canterbury and York are much older than Parliament itself. Convocation has two houses – bishops and archbishops, and secondly the clergy.

General Synod has taken over most but not all of the functions of the Convocations, and meetings of the Convocations are now held only occasionally.

The Anglican Consultative Council   The Anglican Church came into existence mainly through the work of the missionary societies of the Church of England in the different continents of the world. The Anglican Church has no legislative body, and the Church in each province is constitutionally independent.

As recently as 1971, the Anglican Consultative Council was created. Three representatives from each province throughout the world meet every other year. The Council has no power to make any laws, and its functions are mainly advisory, and a platform to exchange opinions and information.

TEAM MINISTRY   *See* **GROUP AND TEAM MINISTRIES** on page 84.

TELEPHONE   Is your church listed in the directory under the name of your Church?

TERRIER AND INVENTORY   A terrier is a list of lands, goods and possessions of the parish church and any chapels. Every parish is required to have an up-to-date terrier and inventory.

The archdeacon or rural dean inspects the terrier every three years, and it has to be signed by the archdeacon (or rural dean) and the churchwardens, two members of the PCC and the minister. This is to ensure that a proper inspection is made to check that nothing is missing. A copy of the terrier and inventory can be obtained from any religious bookshop.

THANKSGIVING FOR THE GIFT OF A CHILD   There are a number of reasons why parents chose this service: (a) to celebrate the birth or adoption of a child. (b) Some parents regard it as a preliminary to Baptism. (c) Some parents may not wish to have their child baptized at present. (d) Parents who do not want to make the Promises required for Baptism, but who do want to give thanks to God for the birth of their child. (See also **BAPTISM** on page 11).

TRANSPORT   Elderly and disabled people often need transport to and from church and for other journeys too. This can often be organized with volunteer help from the congregation. A transport organizer is required, with his or her name, address and telephone number clearly in the magazine, and on the notice board. He enlists the drivers and arranges lifts as and when needed. The demand will vary from time to time. Each driver is advised to check his insurance policy.

TREASURER OF THE PCC *See* **FINANCE** on pages 81–2.

TROUBLE-MAKER Occasionally, there is someone in the parish whose main aim is to cause trouble. There is strong legislation to deal with a priest who 'goes off the rails'. The situation has recently been balanced with legislation to deal with a lay person who is a persistent and deliberate trouble-maker. The bishop now has the power to ban such a person or persons from holding office for a number of years. It is wise to consult the archdeacon at an early stage when a problem of this nature arises.

UNIFORMED ORGANIZATIONS A major part of Church youth work is done through uniformed organizations. But how much thought does the PCC give to this most important aspect of Church life? Does the relationship of the uniformed organization depend entirely – or largely – on the relationship of the priest with them? If so, would it not be wise for the PCC to be involved?

The largest groups are the Scout Association, and the Guide Association. Each member is required to make a promise. . . . 'to do my best to do my duty to God. . . .' The Scout Information Centre, Gilwell Park, Bury Rd., Chingford, London E4 7QW. Tel: 0845–300 1818. Fax: 020 8433 7103. Email: info.centre@ scout.org.uk, Web: www.scoutbase.org.uk. The Guide Association details: The Guide Association, 17–19 Buckingham Palace Rd., London SW1W 0PT. Tel: 020–7834 6242. Fax: 020 7630 6199. Web: www.guides.org.uk Email: chq@guides.org.uk. Anglican Fellowship in Scouting and Guiding, 31 Losely Rd., Farncombe, Godalming, GU7 3RE. Tel: 01483 428876.

The Church Lads' and Church Girls' Brigade is for young people between the ages of 5 and 21. It is a uniformed organization within the Church of England seeking to encourage faithful membership of the Church. Through a wide range of recreational, educational, cultural and spiritual activities, it seeks to offer its members fun, challenge, discipline and increasing responsibility, all within a Christian setting. Details: National Headquarters, 2 Barnsley Rd, Wath upon Dearne, Rotherham

S63 6PY. Tel: 01709 876535. Fax: 01709 878089. Email: generalsecretary@clcgb.org.uk Web: www.clcgb-org.uk

One difficulty is how to find suitable leaders who are competent to take charge of young people, and who also have a strong Christian faith. Some uniformed organizations have departed from the original intentions of their founders in respect of the Christian faith. This is partly due to the problem of finding Christian leaders.

Another problem is how to encourage young people to come to church parade without too much pressure (assuming the worship is bright and attractive). Many will come from families with little or no connection with the Church, but a church parade may well sow seeds which will flourish later on in life.

How much should the PCC expect from church-sponsored organizations – bearing in mind their stated aims? The church provides a hall. It is good, of course, to provide a service for the community in this way too. But apart from the hall, is anything further required from the PCC? What about a meeting of the leaders with the PCC – followed by refreshments? The encouragement, support and interest of the PCC and congregation are surely vital to build up good relationships with the uniformed organizations. Involvement of young people in worship and in parish activities is also helpful, so that they feel that it is their church, and that they belong to it.

Food for thought
Could more be achieved with the uniformed organizations by the PCC?

VERGER The person who carries the verge or mace (staff of authority) in processions, and also looks after the church. Most churches no longer enjoy the luxury of a paid verger. They either have a paid cleaner, or church members help to clean the church on a rota system.

A schoolboy definition of a verger – 'someone who minds his keys and pews'.

VESTRY MEETING Until 1894, the Vestry Meeting was a meeting of parishioners (ratepayers) who fixed the rates for the coming year. They appointed the churchwardens (or overseers), who administered relief to the poor of the parish. In 1894, all the civil functions of the Vestry were transferred to the local government authorities. The church functions of the Vestry were transferred to the PCC by the Parochial Church Council (Powers) Measure 1956. The churchwardens are now appointed under the Churchwardens' Measure 2001. (*See* **CHURCH-WARDENS** on pages 41–52.)

VICARAGE MAINTENANCE Apart from the committed members of the congregation and the priest, the most important assets and resources of the parish are surely the church building, the hall and the vicarage. It is important to remember that the vicarage is the private home of the priest and his or her family, as well as a place of work. If the house seems too large for a single priest, the next incumbent may well be married with four or five children.

The diocesan architect or surveyor inspects the vicarage every five years, and the repairs are carried out under diocesan supervision. The bills are paid by the Diocesan Board of Finance, and a proportion of the parish Common Fund goes towards vicarage maintenance. Sometimes, a PCC is asked to pay towards some particular improvement in the vicarage.

VICARAGE – SALE OF The PCC does not own the vicarage (nor the church). The ownership is vested in the priest for the period when he is vicar of the parish. Any scheme to sell or alter the vicarage requires his or her formal consent. The PCC also has to be notified of any proposal to sell or to demolish the parsonage house, or to buy or build a new one. The PCC is given 21 days in which to object – but in practice this is usually much longer. The diocese takes professional advice, but it is possible that, with the benefit of local knowledge, or by seeking another opinion, a better scheme could be found. Christians have to be as 'wise as the children of this world' in their property dealings.

Certain questions need consideration: Is the vicarage in a good position? Next to the church is ideal. If it is old and has stood the test of time, it will probably outlast any new building. Most of the large and rambling parsonages have now been replaced.

It is the Church Commissioners who have the final responsibility of upholding or overruling any objections. The Commissioners fortunately have much experience and wisdom in this whole subject.

VIDEOS There is a wide range of religious subjects available for church use. Many parishes have a video recorder and screen installed in the hall or committee room. A parish videos library needs a well organized index.

VISITING   The old saying is still true today – 'a house-going priest makes for a church-going people'. Nothing can replace personal contact; but it is an impossible task for one person to do single-handed. But the vicar is surely not the only person who can do visiting on behalf of the Church? Roman Catholic congregations often do a great deal of visiting on behalf of the Church, and so too do the Mormons and Jehovah's Witnesses. At general election time, think how many people visit homes in the constituency. What a difference if such numbers from the Church did visiting to extend the kingdom of God!

Many congregations and PCCs do in fact undertake visiting. The magazine distributor, for example, can knock on the door of a lonely person and say, 'Hello, I've called to deliver your church magazine and to see how you are today'. An annual visit can be made to the homes of the Sunday School children, the choir, the uniformed organizations, the youth club, etc., to invite parents and children to special functions at the church. The church-warden, or whoever is in charge of the sidesmen's rota, could visit fringe people in their homes to recruit new sidesmen. The church is the whole baptized membership, and there is great value in the church going out into the community in these and other ways.

When visiting a home, knock boldly three times, and as you do so, say to yourself 'In the name of the Father, and of the Son, and of the Holy Spirit. Amen'. Another silent prayer may be appropriate, e.g. 'Peace be to this house and to all who live here.'

There is much value in a general visitation of the parish, undertaken every five years – if there are sufficient people willing to undertake this work. A final thought: Remember the call of the prophet Isaiah, 'Whom shall I send?' 'Here I am', I answered, 'send me.'

WHERE TO SIT   Unless allocated a seat by the churchwarden or his representative, worshippers can choose where to sit in church, and it is strange how people will sit near the back. Are Christians afraid of each other? Is the love of God locked so firmly in their hearts that it cannot radiate out even to fellow Christians? God wants the 'ice' to melt so that Christians can be friendly with other Christians, and so that his love can go to non-Christians. The outside world is desperately crying out for fellowship and (Christian) love, and the Holy Spirit wants to create a friendly family atmosphere especially in the congregation.

At the last supper, Jesus was not at one end of the upper room with his back to the twelve, and they were not scattered over the length of a long building. The best conditions for worship will be created if the congregation is the 'gathered community' because it is gathered and not scattered around a large building. The disciples gathered around a table for a meal in the upper room.

PCC members can set an example by sitting in any empty pews at the front when necessary.

LAST WILL AND TESTAMENT   *See **Diocesan Board of Finance** (DBF)* (d) page 76. Not an easy subject, but one which should not be neglected. The rubric in the visitation of the sick states: 'and if he hath not before disposed of his goods, let him then be admonished to make his Will'. This is good advice from the 1662 Book of Common Prayer.

Christians usually leave most of their money and possessions to their nearest and dearest when they die. But, in addition, many leave a proportion of their estate to the Church. Presumably you would only leave a small proportion of your money to the Church if you have a family. But if you have no relatives, then you might consider leaving the whole of your estate to the Church.

Money or property can be left to the Diocesan Board of Finance, the Clergy Pensions Board, the Church Commissioners, a missionary society (which your church supports?), or to your own parish church. All of these are charitable bodies. This means that they are exempt from inheritance tax or gift tax, thus allowing your gift to go that much further in helping the Church. Non-Christians frequently leave *all* their money to a particular charity, but it is only Church members who leave money to the Church. Should not every Christian think seriously about including a bequest for the Church in his or her will?

Many people do not want flowers at their funeral, and they specify 'Family flowers only. Donations invited for St John's Church'. This can be included in the will, and also that you want a requiem Communion (if that is your wish). It can help your relatives if you choose the hymns for the service.

Here are some suggested clauses for a will:

1. *When you wish to leave a percentage of your estate to your parish church (or to the diocese)*: 'I give ___ per cent of my residuary estate to the Parochial Church Council of the parish of ___ in the diocese of ___ free of duty to be applied as to both capital and income by them for such of the purposes specified in Section 5 of the Parochial Church Councils (Powers) Measure 1956 as are charitable and I declare that the receipt of the PCC treasurer or other proper officer of the Council shall be a sufficient discharge to my Trustees.'

In order to carry out your exact wishes, and to avoid the effects of inflation, it is wise to leave a 'percentage' of your estate in this way, rather than a fixed sum of money.

A bequest can of course be made for a specific purpose in the church, e.g. for the roof or fabric fund, for the restoration of the bells etc., or to set up a trust fund, e.g. to pay the choir. In many cases, it can be more helpful to the PCC if no conditions are placed upon the bequest.

2. *When you wish to leave a fixed sum to your parish church*: 'I give to the Parochial Church Council of the parish of ___ in the diocese of ___ the sum of £ ___ free of duty to be applied as to both capital and income by them for such of the purposes specified in Section 5 of the Parochial Church Councils (Powers) Measure 1956 as are charitable and I declare that the receipt of the PCC treasurer or other proper officer of the Council shall be a sufficient discharge to my Trustees.'

Making a will avoids problems concerning the disposal of your property. It also provides you with an opportunity to help with the work of the Church in the future.

If you have already made your will, it is a simple matter to add a codicil, in order to include a bequest to the Church. It is always wise to do this through a solicitor, and to tell your family about your wishes.

WOMEN PRIESTS   Some people are in favour of women priests (and women bishops), others believe it is wrong to ordain women as priests. This is a particularly difficult subject for the PCC, especially when the vicar may hold one view, and the PCC (or some of its members) take a different view. (It took the Church hundreds of years to decide whether Jesus Christ was God, or man, or both!) Only time will prove whether or not it is the will of God to have women priests. Thus, the Church has declared that we are now in a 'period of discernment'. General Synod stated it is desirable that all concerned should try to ensure (1) 'that discernment in the wider Church of the rightness or otherwise of the decision to ordain women should be as open as possible. (2) The highest possible degree of communion should be maintained within each diocese. (3) The integrity of differing beliefs and positions should be mutually recognized and accepted.'

The Episcopal Ministry Act of Synod 1993 makes provision for the continuing differences of opinion in the Church of England. Every PCC is free to discuss and vote upon resolutions A, B and C, as follows:

Resolution A 'that this Parochial Church Council would not accept a woman as the minister who presides at or celebrates the Holy Communion or pronounces the Absolution in the parish.'

Resolution B 'that this Parochial Church Council would not accept a woman as the incumbent or priest in charge of the benefice or as a team vicar for the benefice.'

Procedure for discussing Resolution A and Resolution B
The wording of the Resolution must be exactly as written, in order to be valid.

Any PCC member may ask that resolution A, or Resolution B, or both Resolutions, be placed on the Agenda for the PCC. There is no time limit about when they may be discussed, nor about keeping them in force.

The PCC Secretary must give members at least four weeks' notice of the time and place of the meeting, together with the exact wording of the resolutions (as above). In a case where the chairman of the PCC refuses to call a meeting to discuss the resolutions (or neglects to do so) not less than one third of the members of the PCC may sign a request requiring him or her to call a meeting. If he or she still refuses to do so, then those members may call a meeting under Church Representation Rules (General Provisions relating to PCCs, Rule 15, para. 3, appendix 2).

The PCC meeting must be attended by at least half of the members of the PCC who are entitled to attend. Only a simple majority is needed to pass either resolution A or resolution B (i.e., more than half of the PCC members who are present and voting). All 'ex-officio' members of the PCC and co-opted members have full voting rights.

Resolution A cannot be discussed by the PCC if the incumbent, priest in charge, or any team vicar or assistant curate of the benefice is a woman priest. Resolution B can be considered where there is a woman priest.

A district church council cannot pass the Resolutions – only the official PCC can do that. However, the PCC should be sensitive to the views of the district church council. A conventional district is allowed to consider the resolutions under the terms of the Measure. Likewise, where there is a team or group ministry, or the churches are held 'in plurality', then only the official PCC can formally consider the resolutions.

When resolution A, or resolution B, or both resolutions, are passed, a copy of the resolution must be sent to the following by the PCC secretary:

(a) The diocesan bishop
(b) The rural dean
(c) The lay chairman of the deanery synod
(d) The 'designated officer' under the Patronage (Benefices) Measure 1986 (who is usually, but not always, the diocesan registrar)
(e) The registered patron of the living

Procedure for petitioning for episcopal duties under the Episcopal Ministry Act of Synod, 1993   When the PCC has passed either Resolution A or B, or both, the PCC can consider passing Resolution C, as follows:

Resolution C   'that this Parochial Church Council resolves to petition the diocesan bishop requesting that appropriate episcopal duties in the parish should be carried out in accordance with the Episcopal Ministry Act of Synod, 1993'.

Steps to be taken before considering resolution C
(a) Consult widely in the parish about the matter.
(b) Ask the advice of the appropriate Provincial Episcopal Visitor (PEV or 'flying bishop' for your area). His name and address, and phone number, can be obtained from the Church's Enquiry Centre – Tel: 020–7898 1445.
(c) The PCC secretary must give at least four weeks' notice about the time and place of the meeting. The meeting must be attended by at least one half of the members of the PCC.

(d) People may well hold different views, and feel strongly about the matter. PCC members need to be very sensitive when considering the matter.

(e) The diocesan bishop is not obliged to make arrangements for episcopal duties to be carried out in the parish under the terms of the Episcopal Ministry Act of Synod unless at least two-thirds of the PCC members present and voting are in favour of the resolution. When the PCC passes the resolution by a simple majority – but fails to achieve a two-thirds majority, or the incumbent or priest in charge is not in favour of the resolution, then the diocesan bishop may still make arrangements under the Act of Synod if he believes it is appropriate to do so.

(f) If resolution C is passed, (by a simple majority or a two-thirds one) the PCC Secretary should inform (i) the diocesan bishop, (ii) the rural dean (iii) the lay chairman of the deanery synod, (iv) the 'designated officer' under the Patronage (Benefices) Measure 1986 (who is usually but not always the diocesan registrar), and (v) the diocesan registrar.

Reviewing resolution C The PCC is required to review the working of the arrangements for Resolution C at least once in every five years.

WORK Daily work is not simply a way to earn a living. Many take a pride in their work and offer and dedicate it to God, whether it is in office, factory or home.

Christians sometimes keep quiet at work about their membership of the Church, in case they meet hostility or ridicule. Your place of work is a testing ground for your faith. It is also an opportunity for the outward penetration of the Church into the world by your words and example.

Questions for discussion

1. How can the PCC support members of the church who meet with hostility at work because of their Christian faith?
2. Can the PCC help in any way with the problem of unemployment in the area?
3. Could the PCC organize a pre-retirement or post-retirement course?

YOGA AND CHRISTIANS Some Christians may be suspicious of this ancient Hindu art of mental and bodily relaxation and control. However, the Christian Church has taken over many pagan things and 'Christianized' them. Many Christian monks and nuns practise yoga. The value of yoga for a Christian is that it teaches you how to relax, and sit still or kneel without fidgeting and wanting to move. That surely is very important in learning how to pray. Apart from individuals, a group of people may benefit from yoga, using Christian meditations. Some specifically Christian books on yoga include:

1. *Exploration into Contemplative Prayer* by Fr Herbert Slade (a Church of England monk of the Society of St John the Evangelist). It is published by Darton, Longman & Todd, and it goes quite deeply into the subject.
2. *Everyday Yoga for Christians* by the Revd Eric W. Hayden (a Baptist minister). Published by Arthur James Ltd, Evesham, it is a very practical book and easy to follow.
3. *Christian Yoga* by Fr Dechanet (a French Roman Catholic priest). Published by Search Press. This is for those who wish to take yoga beyond its basic stages.

YOUTH WORK AND THE PCC The children of church members do not automatically become regular worshippers as adults. Perhaps part of the reason for this is connected with the quality of the Christian life of their parents. The quality of the worship and the friendliness of the congregation also play a part. Certainly seeds sown in early years may bear fruit in years to come.

In former years the Church has done magnificent things in terms of youth work, but now there are many problems connected with it. There is strong competition for the time and allegiance of young people. The PCC should never give up on young people, even when there is no one under 40 years of age in the congregation. Every PCC needs to pray, and to think carefully about its responsibilities towards the young people of the area. Perhaps the Diocesan Youth Adviser, or Diocesan Education Team, could be invited to a PCC meeting devoted entirely to young people (without anything else on the agenda)?.

Leaders need selecting with great care. People sometimes volunteer to help with young people for the wrong reasons, and many problems may be caused. (*See* **PROTECTION OF CHILDREN FROM ABUSE** on page 160). Youth work can be demanding. Leaders need much understanding and insight, as they are the people who are out in front for others to follow. A leader needs to be able to exercise discipline, but at the same time to be friendly. Young people need someone who is stable, knows the principles on which he or she stands, and will not deviate from those standards. The ability to communicate with young people is important, especially when so many parents cannot or will not give the time for their children. Time is perhaps the most valuable thing a parent or youth leader can give to a child.

Information

1. Diocesan Youth Officer or Diocesan Children's Officer.
2. Church Pastoral Aid Society (Evangelical) are specialists in children's and youth ministry. Details: CPAS, Athena Drive, Tachbrook Park, Warwick, CV34 6NG. Tel: 01926 458458
3. 'Sheep-pen' (13 yrs and over) and 'Sheep-dip' (10–14 yrs) organize residential weekends and other events, celebrating the faith. (Anglican Catholic). Details: Faith House, 7 Tufton Street, London SW1P 3QN. Tel: 0207–976 0727.

Questions for discussion

1. What can the PCC do to encourage young members of the choir, the servers and the Sunday school?
2. Could the PCC involve young people through drama – an ad hoc children's orchestra – a walk in the countryside – bell ringing – Bible Reading Festival ?
3. Is the PCC aware of the resources available from the diocese?
4. Could the PCC organize a residential holiday – or holiday course at home – for young people?
5. Join a Pilgrimage for young people? (*See **Walsingham and Glastonbury** under* **PILGRIMAGES** *on page 156*).

ZEAL – 'Where is thy zeal and thy strength?' (Isaiah 63,15).

Christian Bookshops

ALTON	Redemptorist Bookshop, Alphonsus House, Chawton, Alton, Hants, GU34 3HQ. Tel. 01420–88222. Fax 01420–88805. Email: rp@redempt.org
BIRMINGHAM	SPCK, 12 Ethel Street, B2 4DG. Tel. 0121–643 2617. Fax 0121–633 3459. Email: birmingham@spck.org.uk
BRADFORD	SPCK, 14 North Parade, W. Yorks, BD1 3HY. Tel. 01274–728669. Fax 01274–759982 Email: bradford@spck.org.uk
BRISTOL	SPCK, 79 Park Street, BS1 5PF. Tel. 01179–273461. Fax 01179–293525 Email: bristol@spck.org.uk
CAMBRIDGE	SPCK, 15/16 Sussex Street, CB1 1PA. Tel. 01223–358452. Email: cambridge@spck.org.uk
CANTERBURY	SPCK, 7 St Peter's Street, Kent, CT1 2EF. Tel. 01227–462881. Fax 01227–456297 Email: canterbury@spck.org.uk
CARDIFF	SPCK, City Church, Windsor Place, CF10 3BZ. Tel. 02920–227736. Fax 02920–227515. Email: cardiff@spck.org.uk
CARLISLE	SPCK, The Lodge, Carlisle Cathedral, Cumbria, CA3 8TZ. Tel. 01228–543498. Fax 01228–402857. Email: carlisle@spck.org.uk

CHESTER SPCK, 7/11 Werburgh Street, Chester, Cheshire, CH1 2EJ. Tel. 01244–404010 Fax 01244–404019.
Email: chester@spck.org.uk

CHICHESTER SPCK, St Olave's Church, North Street, W. Sussex, PO19 1LQ.
Tel. 01243–782790.
Fax 01243–784604.
Email: chichester@spck.org.uk

DURHAM SPCK, The Great Kitchen, Durham Cathedral, DH1 3EQ. Tel. 0191–386 2972.
Fax 0191–384 2834.
Email: durham@spck.org.uk

EXETER SPCK, 1/2 Catherine Street, Cathedral Yard, Devon, EX1 1EX.
Tel. 01392–260270.
Fax 01392–260279.
Email: exeter@spck.org.uk

GUILDFORD SPCK, St Mary's Church, Quarry Street, Surrey, GU1 4AU. Tel. 01483–560316.
Fax 01483–457173.
Email: guildford@spck.org.uk

HEREFORD SPCK, Palace Yard, HR4 9BJ.
Tel. 01432–266785.
Fax 01432–279040.
Email: hereford@spck.org.uk

LEEDS SPCK, The Pilgrim Bookshop, First Floor, 20 New Market Street, LS1 6DG.
Tel. 0113–237 6480.
Fax 0113–237 6486.
Email: leeds@spck.org.uk

LEICESTER SPCK, Pilgrim House, 10 Bishop Street, LE1 6AF. Tel. 01162–854499.
Fax 01162–755948.
Email: leicester@spck.org.uk

LINCOLN SPCK, 36 Steep Hill, LN2 1LU.
Tel. 01522–527486.
Fax 01522–534484.
Email: lincoln@spck.org.uk

LIVERPOOL SPCK, Liverpool Cathedral, St James Mount, L1 7AZ. Tel. 0151–709 1897.
Fax: 0151–702 7294.
Email: liverpool@spck.org.uk

LONDON	SPCK, Holy Trinity Church, Marylebone Road, NW1 4DU. Tel. 020–7643 0398. Fax 020–7643 0391. Email: london@spck.org.uk FAITH HOUSE BOOKSHOP, 7 Tufton Street, SW1P 3QN. Tel. 020–7222 6952. Fax 020–7976 7180. Email: enquiries@faithhousebookshop.co.uk CHURCH HOUSE BOOKSHOP, 31 Great Smith Street, SW1P 3BN. Tel: 020–7898 1300. Fax 020–7898 1305. Email: bookshop@c-of-e.org.uk
NEWCASTLE-UPON-TYNE	SPCK, 8 Ridley Place, Tyne & Wear, NE1 8JW. Tel. 0191–232 3466. Fax 0191–230 2265. Email: newcastle@spck.org.uk
NORWICH	SPCK, 19 Pottergate, Norfolk, NR2 1DS. Tel. 01603–627332. Fax 01603–219309. Email: norwich@spck.org.uk
NOTTINGHAM	SPCK College Bookshop, St John's College, Chilwell Lane, Bramacote, NG9 3DS. Tel./Fax 0115–925 1839. Email: nottingham@spck.org.uk
SALISBURY	SPCK, 51 High Street, Wilts, SP1 2PE. Tel. 01722–334535. Fax 01722–414904. Email: salisbury@spck.org.uk
SHEFFIELD	SPCK, 8 East Parade, S.Yorks, S1 2ET. Tel. 0114–272 3454. Fax 0114–279 7751. Email: sheffield@spck.org.uk
TRURO	SPCK, 8 St Mary's Street, Cornwall, TR1 2AF. Tel. 01872–272771. Fax 01872–260491. Email: truro@spck.org.uk
WINCHESTER	SPCK, 24 The Square, Hants, SO23 9EX. Tel. 01962–866617. Fax 01962–890312. Email: winchester@spck.org.uk
WORCESTER	SPCK, 105 High Street, WR1 2HS. Tel./Fax 01905–24396. Email: worcester@spck.org.uk
YORK	SPCK, 28 Goodramgate, YO1 2LG. Tel. 01904–654176. Fax 01904–670931. Email: york@spck.org.uk

Useful Addresses and Telephone Numbers

Actors' Church Union The Senior Chaplain, St Paul's Church, Bedford Street, Covent Garden, London WC2E 9ED. Tel. 020–7240 0344.

Additional Curates Society The General Secretary, Gordon Browning House, 8 Spitfire Road, Birmingham B24 9PB. Tel. 0121–382 5533.

Anglican Evangelical Assembly PO Box 93, Heaton, Newcastle upon Tyne, NE6 5WL. Tel. & Fax: 0191–240 2084.

Anglican Society for the Welfare of Animals The Correspondence Secretary, PO Box 7193, Hook, Hants, RG27 8GT. Tel. 0118–932 6586.

Association for Promoting Retreats The Administrator, The Central Hall, 256 Bermondsey Street, London SE1 3UJ. Tel. 020–7357 7736.

Bible Society Chief Executive, Bible Society, Stonehill Green, Westlea, Swindon, Wilts, SN5 7DG. Tel. 01793–418100.

BRF – Bible Reading Fellowship Chief Executive, BRF, First Floor, Elsfield Hall, 15–17 Elsfield Way, Oxford OX2 8AP. Tel. 01865–319700.

Central Council of Church Bell Ringers Hon. Secretary, 50 Cramhurst Lane, Witley, Godalming, Surrey GU8 5QZ. Tel. & Fax: 01483–682790.

Children's Society Rudolph House, Margery Street, London WC1X 0JL. Tel. 020–7841 4436.

Christians Abroad The Director, Suite 233, Bon Marche Centre, 241–251 Ferndale Road, London SW9 8BJ. Tel. 020–7346 5956.

Christian Aid Inter Church House, 35–41 Lower Marsh, London SE1 7RL. Tel. 020–7620 4444.

Church Army Enquiries, Church Army Headquarters, Independence Road, Blackheath, London SE3 9LG. Tel. 020–8318 1226.

Church Missionary Society The General Secretary, CMS, Partnership House, 157 Waterloo Road, London SE1 8UU. Tel. 020–7928 8681.

Church Pastoral Aid Society CPAS, Athena Drive, Tachbrook Park, Warwick CV34 6NG. Tel. 01926–458458

Church Union 7 Tufton Street, London SW1P 3QN. Tel. 020–7222 6952.

Church Urban Fund Church Urban Fund Office, 1 Millbank, London SW1P 3JZ. Tel. 020–7898 1000. Fax: 020–7976 7180. Email: churchunion@core4free.net

Churches' Council for Health and Healing The Secretary, St Luke's Hospital, 14 Fitzroy Square, London W1P 6AH. Tel. & Fax: 020–7388 7903.

Ecclesiastical Insurance Office Beaufort House, Brunswick Road, Gloucester GL1 1JZ. Tel. 01452–384848.

Enquiry Centre Enquiries Officer, Mr Stephen Empson, Church House, Great Smith Street, London SW1P 3NZ. Tel. 020–7898 1445.

Ecumenical Society of the Blessed Virgin Mary The Secretary, ECBVM, 11 Belmont Road, Wallington, Surrey SM6 8TE. Tel: 020–8647 5992.

Evangelical Alliance UK Whitefield House, 186 Kennington Park Road, London SE11 4BT. Tel: 020 7207 2100.

Forward in Faith The Director, Mr Stephen Parkinson, Faith House, 7 Tufton Street, London SW1P 3QN. Tel. & Fax: 020–7976 0727.

Guild of St Barnabas for Nurses Organizing Secretary, Mrs Mary Morrow, 16 Copperwood, Ashford, Kent, TN24 8PZ. Tel. 01233–635334.

Historic Churches Preservation Trust The Secretary, Wing Cdr M Tippen, Fulham Palace, London SW6 6EA. Tel. 020–7736 3054.

Intercontinental Church Society Communications Manager, Mr David Healey, 1 Athena Drive, Tachbrook Park, Warwick CV34 6NL. Tel. 01926–430347.

Leprosy Mission The Director, Goldhay Way, Orton Goldhay, Peterborough PE2 5GZ. Tel. 01733–370505.

Missions to Seafarers The General Secretary, St Michael Paternoster Royal, College Hill, London EC4R 2RL. Tel. 020–7248 5202.

221

Mothers' Union   Mary Sumner House, 24 Tufton Street, Westminster, London SW1P 3RB. Tel. 020–7222 5533.

National Society for Promoting Religious Education   Church House, Great Smith Street, London SW1P 3NZ. Tel. 020–7898 1518.

Prayer Book Society   The Hon. Secretary, PBS Office, St James Garlickhythe, Garlick Hill, London EC4V 2AF. Tel. 01243–784832.

Reform   The Administrators, Mr & Mrs Lockwood, Reform, PO Box 1183, Sheffield S10 3YA. Tel. & Fax: 0114–230 9256.

Relate (formerly National Marriage Guidance)   Enquiries, Herbert Gray College, Little Church Street, Rugby, Warwickshire, CV21 3AP. Tel. 01788–573241.

Scripture Union   Chief Executive, Scripture Union, 207–209 Queensway, Bletchley, Milton Keynes, MK2 2EB. Tel. 01908–856000.

South American Missionary Society   General Secretary, Allen Gardiner House, 12 Fox Hill, Birmingham B29 4AG. Tel. 0121–472 2616.

United Society for the Propagation of the Gospel (USPG)   Partnership House,157 Waterloo Road, London SE1 8AX. Tel. 020–7928 8681.

Women's World Day of Prayer   Administrator Mrs L. Lynam, WWDP, Commercial Road, Tunbridge Wells, Kent, TN1 2RR. Tel. & Fax: 01892–541411.